26573

# Divided We Stand

# Divided We Stand

### EDITED BY
## Gary Geddes

## PETER MARTIN ASSOCIATES LIMITED

**Canadian Cataloguing in Publication Data**

Main entry under title:

Divided we stand

ISBN 9-88778-174-8 bd.                          ISBN 0-88778-175-6 pa.

1. Canada — Addresses, essays, lectures.
2. Nationalism — Canada — Addresses, essays, lectures.
I. Geddes, Gary, 1940-

FC98.D58                      971.06'4'4                      C77-001517-4
F1027.D58

Design: Diana McElroy

PETER MARTIN ASSOCIATES LIMITED
280 Bloor Street West, Toronto, Canada M5S 1W1

# Contents

# Introduction

In February I was sitting at a table in the expensive Tokyo Palace Hotel, eating a meal which cost more than my entire food bill for the previous two weeks in Hong Kong, when I overheard a fascinating conversation at the next table. A deep American male voice, resonant, assured, a voice to fill a warehouse full of pork-barrels, was addressing itself to four immaculately dressed and politely nodding Japanese men, seated two on each side of the table, their heads moving to and fro with the flow of words which emanated first from the American and then from the woman at the far end of the table who acted as interpreter. Occasionally one of the four would nod vigorously, utter a few phrases, then fall silent again, assuming a mask that to the untrained Western eye would have seemed expressionless, noncommittal or, at the most, faintly unbelieving.

I should explain that my presence at the Tokyo Palace Hotel was a coincidence. The CP Air flight which was to take me home to Edmonton had been delayed because of mechanical problems, so, as a consolation prize, I had been put up in the city's poshest accommodations. A far cry from the Tokyo YMCA at which I had stayed the previous night or from the dingy establishment on the Chinese mainland which I had shared with an exotic troupe of students, travelers, white female "escorts" and dabblers in various shades of the illicit.

I had just completed my research for a book about the Canadian soldiers who had been sent during World War II to defend the Hong Kong garrison against the possibility of a Japanese invasion, 1975 officers and men of the Winnipeg Grenadiers and the Royal Rifles of Canada, thrown in at the eleventh hour for political rather than military reasons. They had set sail from Vancouver on October 27, 1941, some without completing basic training, others without ever having fired live ammunition; and they sailed through the Straits of Juan de Fuca without the 212 transport vessels necessary for waging a modern war. The

Rifles and Grenadiers were in Hong Kong only three weeks before the first Japanese bombs fell on the colony. On December 25, 1941, after eighteen days of fighting, Canada's beleaguered forces, along with their Scots, Middlesex and Rajput comrades, celebrated the birth of Christ by surrendering to the Japanese. The whole affair, which the survivors were later to describe as a "farce", was whitewashed by the government which, at that time, was more concerned with rounding up Japanese-Canadians, confiscating their property and placing them in detention camps under the auspices of the first War Measures Act.

"There *was* no oil shortage," The Voice was saying at the next table, as he advised his Japanese labour associates concerning the strategy that would be necessary if they were to keep ahead of the communist-led unions. His words, though constantly interrupted for translation, were as carefully tailored as the garments of the other four men. All in all, they were fit to kill.

The gist of the Tokyo Palace conference was that the major oil companies were undergoing a facelift, changing their image to reflect a concern for energy rather than oil. They had created an artificial crisis in order to justify the price increases which were needed for revenue to finance the purchase of all the earth's coal reserves. Something about the gasification of coal as the next big phase in the Energy Game and Shell Oil already owning all the coal in Burma and Thailand—or was it Indonesia? The figure which I remember, representing the amount of the world's known coal reserves in the hands of the major companies, is 75 per cent.

More serious nodding of heads, but not a surprised look in the lot.

What struck me so forcibly about this Asian interlude, and my reason for dwelling upon it here at such length, was its incongruity. I wondered then, as I do now, who was busy purchasing those seams of coal on Vancouver Island, once so ruthlessly exploited by Lord Dunsmuir, or the enormous deposits in Alberta and other parts of the country, while we in Canada go through the motions of working out our destinies at the political level. The image which came to mind, as I eavesdropped on this making-of-history, was of nation after nation falling like tenpins before such colossal deals, of Canada, too, concerned with cultural and linguistic matters, with the state of its collective soul, at a time when such considerations may already be academic, no more than a cosmetic, an opiate, to give the sensitive and outspoken of the population the illusion of control over their futures. Could there be any point concerning ourselves about the national conscience, as seen in the Hong Kong farce and the War Measures legislation, or about regional distinctiveness, when there is already a 75 per cent chance that Canada (and this includes Quebec, within or without the federation) will not survive this century as a distinct cultural and political entity?

We are already perilously close in Canada to becoming another invisible people, or peoples, since we have so far failed to control not only our economy, but also our means of information dispersal: broadcasting, a lifeline for the body politic, is in the hands of about 100 private and corporate interests, whose concern is not political survival or the quality of life, but profit; and education, the jugular of a people, controlling the movement of blood and oxygen to the brain, is still being mercilessly squeezed by foreign interests. We suffer from hardening of the cultural arteries. Too often our bureaucrats and elected representatives, at both federal and provincial levels, lacking a vision and misguided by imported ideals and ideologies, have failed to provide the leadership necessary to educate and transform the society. Consequently, we remain unaware of our uniqueness, unconversant with our strengths and weaknesses, and lacking in the kind of attitudes and machinery of government required if we are to meet the inevitable changes and challenges in our domestic and foreign relations with assurance and grace, rather than with troops and Madison Avenue slogans.

The controversy surrounding Robert Scully's article, "What It Means to Be French in Canada", appearing on May 1, 1977 in the *Manchester Guardian* and reprinted in various Canadian newspapers, should concern us all. Scully was severely criticized in Quebec for his painful and moving description of his people as "a non-group, a country of cripples", "a small, forgotten, culturally deprived, hyperactive and insecure community", whose people are up against "an invisible glass wall. Like the dog in the pet shop window," living "nowhere" and "perpetually on the brink of extinction". And yet, in 1956, Pierre Trudeau had described French Canadians, from an historical point of view, as "a people vanquished, occupied, leaderless, kept aside from business life and away from the cities, gradually reduced to a minority role and deprived of influence in a country which, after all, it had discovered, explored, and settled". And André Laurendeau, explaining his involvement with *A Manifesto of the Younger Generation* during the Depression, uses terms identical to Scully's: "So the reaction was one of wounded pride. We felt humiliated, and we rebelled at the fact of our *non-existence*. It was a brand of nationalism that is at one and the same time very emotional and very formalist, therefore very profound, for what is at stake is the issue of personal dignity."

There is no longer any doubt in the minds of thinking Canadians that the French fact has suffered enormous setbacks in this country: the hanging of Louis Riel and the subsequent elimination of French as a language of instruction in Manitoba was by no means the first nail in the coffin of Confederation; and the iniquitous War Measures Act of October 1970, as humiliating and unwarranted as its predecessor in 1942, will probably not be the last. Laurendeau, who struggled so desperately to understand and articulate the contradictions of this country, confessed to feeling suffocated by the "bitter solitude" of his people in Quebec and to feeling that, at times, he lived in an occupied country. And yet he shared a hope that difficulties would gradually be solved, that the Canadian experiment could be made to work to the advantage of all citizens. Had he lived to see soldiers deployed in the streets of Montreal, citizens harassed and jailed, perhaps he would have rejected that dream and returned to the separatist enthusiasms of his youth.

As he wrote in *Le Magazine Maclean* in November 1961, "Either English Canada will see the light in time, in which case it will begin to work towards a fundamental transformation of the central state, a development I have never ceased to hope for, or . . . it is possible, after the experiment has gone on for years, that French Canadians may slowly become convinced that the house is not, in fact, habitable. Then, given the right international context, given *(and this is most important)* that independence has become a serious project and not just an adventure, given that we have successfully laid the foundations of our dwelling, why then the will to be completely free under our own roof will become irresistible."

Perhaps that will is already irresistible. By March 1962, Laurendeau had to admit that "the concept of Canada is becoming more fragile by the hour". That same year, in December, Lester Pearson, as leader of the opposition, said in parliament that Canada was going through another "national crisis". He lamented our increasing rather than decreasing cultural and economic dependence upon the U.S. and our inability to agree upon the symbols of national unity. He warned against complacency, indifference. However, after mentioning these serious matters and outlining Quebec's development from a condition of rural isolation to an aggressive and outward-looking industrial society with increasing demands for self-determination, all he had to offer as a remedy for the nation's ills was a modest dose of bilingualism.

The threat to Canadian unity is not Quebec, or the Parti Québécois, but the federal government, which has consistently soft-pedalled on the vital issues of cultural and economic nationalism. How can we expect such a government to come to the negotiating table in good faith, to work towards that "fundamental transformation of the central state" which Laurendeau hoped for, which Pearson implicitly acknowledged was necessary, and which Lévesque struggled to realize? Lévesque said on the Pierre Berton show in 1963, "Confederation to most French Canadians has no sentimental pull." "It was a bargain . . . and the bargain was not very good and if it's not changed in some deep and profound ways—well, it's like a couple; if you can't sleep together, you might as well have separate beds."

We have been misled by the so-called internationalists in our midst, who, perhaps out of the war experience and the rise of Nazism, came to identify national aspirations entirely with intolerance, totalitarianism. In academic and educational circles such people have been responsible for the failure to promote Canadian studies. Culturally, too, they have kept Canadian art out of the galleries and cinemas and theatres and textbooks. Pearson, as much as anyone else, perpetuated the myth of Canada as an international peacemaker. In the speech I mentioned, he spells out his position:

> Today, when the greatest need of free men and free nations is to come closer together, politically, economically and culturally, to accept and act on the compulsions and opportunities of interdependence; at this time of all times it would be a tragic thing for Canadians to have to admit their failure to unify their own country in any real and meaningful sense, which means unity without sacrificing special and separate values. No Canadian, surely, could contemplate with anything but bitter regret the weakening, let alone the failure, of Confederation, especially when Canada has grown so much in stature and achieved so much respect in the world.

The key word here is "interdependence", which stands as a deliberate alternative to "independence", and is a concept that most peoples and nations would endorse. Nations, like individuals, do not mature in isolation; besides which, political and economic alliances and agreements are an inescapable fact of modern times. The problem is that a healthy international situation, like a healthy marriage or relationship, can only exist when each of the participants has achieved a sense of dignity and worth, which comes from feeling comfortable with one's place, one's heritage. Lévesque himself held a view not unlike that of Pearson for a time: "I became so impressed about the important issues in the world that Quebec's problems seemed trivial. The war made me an internationalist, which is a very easy thing to be." George Grant has argued, rightly, I believe, that "if we skip the state of nationalism we become not internationals (there are no such animals), but Americans. It's as simple as that."

If the federal state is a microcosm of the international situation, all the more reason to restructure it in such a way that the regions be encouraged to develop their own unique characteristics. British Columbians should be concerned that Quebec's culture and language are protected within Confederation, because that is a way of ensuring their own rights; and Quebeckers, French-Canadians in particular, should be favourably disposed to continued participation in a federal system that has its interests constitutionally guaranteed, rather than take its chances on dealing directly with a superpower that may well play one bordering region off against another.

One of the problems which faces us, then, and it is a crucial matter, is to discover what measures must be taken not only to preserve Quebec's unique culture, but also to redress the neglect that has rendered bitter such regions as the Maritimes and such peoples as the Indians, Métis and northern Canadians. Lévesque spoke of the need for "deep and profound" changes; Laurendeau, of a "fundamental transformation of the central state". Pearson, though he would not, perhaps could not, write out the prescription, surely diagnosed the problem accurately when he asked if we were still prepared to pay the price of being Canadian, which is the price of cultural dualism, the price of not being American, and the price of a federal-provincial division of powers.

So far our politicians have refused to face up to the problem of cultural and economic takeover. Walter Gordon was one exception, and he was given his walking-papers by the federal Liberals. Some years ago English Canada was, to use Laurendeau's phrase, "a vast collective hesitation", so much so that Pierre Berton could say in *Maclean's* that "without Quebec we are nothing: without Quebec English Canada makes no sense as a nation; without Quebec we lose the one aspect of our society that makes us unique; without Quebec we are carbon-copy Americans, lacking only a vote in Congress". If English Canada has been slow to articulate its identity and aims, the regions have not; the muses have long been acclimatized in British Columbia, in the Prairies, and in the Maritimes. It is Ontario, perhaps more than any other region, that has had trouble defining itself, because it has not been able to make the distinction, which is so simple for Quebeckers and for the rest of us, between its own interests and the national interest. A federation is, by definition, somewhat hesitant, because it must act in accordance with the needs of its various regions; that is what keeps it civilized and responsible. In a restructured Canada, it may be advisable to make the provincial premiers into a genuine executive committee, so that some of the regional strength and vitality will also be felt at the federal, or national, level. Such a committee would be a genuine acknowledgment of the federal, not the central, nature of this country and would serve to initiate and police important legislation.

In order to bring about a transformation of the central state, we must first discover what it is that we mean when we use words such as "state", "nation", "confederation", "sovereignty", "independence". What, for example, can Laurendeau possibly mean when he speaks of being "completely free under our own roof"? Is the desire to be *maîtres chez nous* in Quebec, and in Canada, more than a romantic fantasy? We must understand why the Parti Québécois has shifted emphasis from a term with possible negative connotations, like "separation", to more positive terms such as "sovereignty" and "independence". We must also ask ourselves why Prime Minister Trudeau uses inflammatory rhetoric, such loaded, value-charged phrases as "separatist *con game*", "the *enemy* within" and "*crime* against humanity" in his discussion of the Parti Québécois and its aims, when that very group is generally agreed to have been elected on a platform of honest government.

Pearson acknowledged in 1962 that there had developed a misunderstanding, or a blurring, of the meaning of Confederation: "It is this difference in interpretation of Confederation itself which has created and is creating today confusion, frustration and indeed some conflict." Today we hear the word "marriage" used frequently as a metaphor to describe French-English relations in Canada. However, this metaphor is not very helpful because it is misleading and carries connotations and strong emotional overtones that serve only to distort the issues at hand. For one thing, while addressing itself to the cultural duality of Canada, it does not accommodate the political reality of a *ménage à douze,* of ten provinces and two territories. If Canada is a marriage, is it a love-match or an arranged affair, a *mariage de convenance*? These metaphors are crucial, because they influence the way we think about ourselves and can severely limit our sense of the nature of things and the possibilities for significant change. Canada is a marriage; Canada is a house that must be made habitable for all; Canada is a poem; Canada is a set of contradictions; Canada is a daily miracle; Canada is a bad bargain; Canada is a dream; Canada is a spider web of interconnectedness. Canada is . . . . Unless we come to terms with these problems, we will all be saying Canada was, Quebec was.

An anglophone writer in Quebec wrote an impassioned three-page letter to me speaking excitedly of the "birth" of a new nation in Quebec, during the course of which the same phenomenon was described in terms of "conception" and even "possible existence". The choice, finally, the writer concluded, might be between "a dynamic Quebec and a drag-ass Canada". When I wrote to ask if I could publish the letter, I received the following telegram:

> DO NOT PUBLISH LETTER. NATIONALISM IS BAD, QUEBECOIS OR CANADIAN. WHEN IT BECOMES EFFECTIVE, IT IS NEGATIVE AND DEFENSIVE. OPENNESS IS ALL. BLAKE SAYS ENERGY IS ETERNAL DELIGHT.

We do not want to say the word that will become flesh, that will become law. There is a desire to keep the discussions "in the air", figuratively and literally, in order to prevent a hardening of opinion, and in order to prevent the words from saying, as is their wont, less or more than we mean. And, most important, we do not want to lose the excitement, the sense of new possibilities, new horizons, that the present, perhaps one should say the continuing, crisis provides.

Patrick Watson wrote to say that there was nothing he could write now that he would not repudiate a month later, so quickly are things changing in the country. However, it is sometimes necessary to formulate the questions and perhaps venture a tentative answer, even if that answer raises three more equally difficult questions. Margaret Atwood once described our national disease as paranoid schizophrenia, insisting that because Canada is such an easy country to leave it takes a painful determination to stay here. The poems included here give imaginative expression to that and other attitudes we hold collectively; and yet they are also a personal refutation of those attitudes. Herschel Hardin, in his struggle to articulate the contradictions within our system, takes refuge in paradox:

> It is because Canadian civilization is so vulnerable, because every once in a while it seems to be coming apart at the seams under the pressure of centrifugal forces, that it has been so fruitful, and has slowly developed a subterannean strength. Nothing has added to that strength, and to that vulnerability, more than the separatist movement, and English Canada's facing up to the possibility it symbolizes, and the attempts of René Lévesque and others to explain to English Canadians the logic behind the possibility.

What we greatly need is a revolution of the word in Canada. As Paulo Friere has said: "To exist, humanly, is to name the world, to change it. Once named, the world in its turn reappears to the namers as a problem and requires of them a *new naming*." Canada has presented itself again as a problem, requiring a new naming. The Cree word for Canada, according to Harold Cardinal, is Ka-Kanata, "the land that is clean", "the clean land". The Cree's Canadianism consists in the knowledge that he is part of this "clean land", a son of its creator. Cardinal makes a comparison with Catholic baptism, after which a child is given a new name, a special name. The Cree term Nee-Yow means "I am born into that tribe which will look to this land as its patron, or as its guardian and guide through life." How to create a society that lives up to such a beautiful tribute . . . ? "There is no true word," Friere says, "that is not at the same time a praxis [a combination of reflection and action: to speak is to do]. Thus, to speak a true word is to transform the world."

That is what this book is all about.

Gary Geddes

# For an Independent Quebec

## René Lévesque

What does Quebec want? The question is an old cliché in Canadian political folklore. Again and again, during the more than thirty years since the end of World War II, it's been raised whenever Quebec's attitudes made it the odd man out in the permanent pull and tug of our federal-provincial relations. In fact, it's a question which could go back to the British conquest of an obscure French colony some fifteen years before American Independence, and then run right through the stubborn survival of those 70,000 settlers and their descendants during the following two centuries.

By now, there are some six million of them in Canada, not counting the progeny of the many thousands who were forced by poverty, especially around the turn of the century, to migrate to the United States and now constitute substantial "Franco" communities in practically all the New England states.

But Quebec remains the homeland. All along the valley of the St. Lawrence, from the Ottawa River down to the Gaspé Peninsula and the great Gulf, in the ancient settlements which grew into the big cities of Montreal and Quebec, in hundreds of smaller towns and villages from the American border to the mining centres and power projects in the north, there are now some 4.8 million Québécois. That's 81 per cent of the population of the largest and second most populous of Canada's ten provinces.

What does French Quebec want? Sometime during the next few years, the question may be answered. And there are growing possibilities that the answer could very well be—independence.

1

Launched in 1967-68, the Parti Québécois, whose platform is based on political sovereignty, now fills the role of Her Majesty's Loyal Opposition in the National Assembly—as we nostalgically designate our provincial legislature. In its first electoral test in 1970 it had already won 24 per cent of the votes. Then in 1973, a second general election saw it jump to 30 per cent and, although holding only six out of 110 seats, become what our British-type parliamentary system calls the Official Opposition, i.e., the government's main interlocutor and challenger.

The next election might come any time now; this year in the fall, just after the Montreal Olympics, or at the latest in the fall of 1977. Whenever it does, all available indicators, including an impressive series of public opinion polls, tell us that for the first time the outcome is totally uncertain. The present provincial government, a branch of that same Liberal Party which also holds power at the federal level under Pierre Elliott Trudeau, is obviously on the way out. It has been in power for six years, and ever since its second and Pyrrhic victory in 1973 (102 seats) it has been going steadily downhill. Apart from a host of social and economic troubles, some imported but many more of its own making, there is around it a pervasive smell of incompetence and corruption. The scandal-ridden atmosphere surrounding the Olympic construction sites and the incredible billion-dollar deficit which is now forecast are just the most visible aspects of a rather complete political and administrative disaster.

Looking for an alternative, the French voter is now leaning quite clearly toward the Parti Québécois. In that "national" majority, we are at least evenly matched with Premier Robert Bourassa's Liberals, and probably ahead. As for the anglophone minority of more than a million people, whose natural attachment to the status quo normally makes them the staunchest supporters of the reigning federalist party, they are confused as never before. Composed of a dwindling proportion of Anglo-Saxon descendants of eighteenth-century conquerors or American Loyalists, along with those of nineteenth-century Irish immigrants and a steadily growing "ethnic" mosaic (Jewish, Italian, Greek, etc.), in the crunch most of this minority will probably end up, as usual, supporting the Liberals. But not with the traditional unanimity. Caught between the Charybdis of dissatisfaction and the Scylla of secessionism, many are looking for some kind of "third force". Others, especially younger people, are ready to go along with the Parti Québécois whose minority vote should be a little less marginal next time than last.

So, all in all, there is quite a serious possibility that an "independentist" government will soon be elected in Quebec. At first sight, this looks like a dramatically rapid development, this burgeoning and flowering over a very few years of a political emancipation movement in a population which, until recently, was commonly referred to as quiet old Quebec. But in fact its success would mean, very simply, the normal, healthy end result of a long and laborious national evolution.

There was the definite outline of a nation in that small French colony which was taken over, in 1763, by the British Empire at its apogee. For over a century and a half, beginning just before the Pilgrim Fathers landed in the Boston area, that curious mixture of peasants and adventurers had been writing a proud history all over the continent. From Hudson Bay to the Gulf of Mexico and from Labrador to the Rockies, they had been the discoverers, the fur-traders, the fort-builders. Out of this far-ranging saga, historically brief though it was, and the tenacious roots which at the same time were being sunk into the St. Lawrence lowlands, there slowly developed an identity quite different from the original stock as well as from France of the *ancien régime*; just as different, in its way, as the American identity had become from its own British seeds. Thus, despite the traumatic shock of the conquest, it had enough staying power to survive, tightly knit around its Catholic clergy and country landowners.

Throughout the next hundred years, while English Canada was being built, slowly but surely, out of the leftovers of the American Revolution and as a rampart against America's recurrent attacks of Manifest Destiny, French Quebec managed to hang on—mostly because of its "revenge of the cradles". It was desperately poor, cut off from the decision-making centres both at home and in Great Britain, and deprived of any cultural nourishment from its former mother country. But its rural, frugal society remained incredibly prolific. So it grew impressively, at least in numbers. And it held on obstinately, according to its lights and as much as its humble means made it possible, to those two major ingredients of national identity—land and language. The hold on the land was at best tenuous and as in any colonial context confined to a multitude of small farm holdings. Everything else—from the growth of major cities to the setting-up of manufacturing industries and then the rush of resource development—was the exclusive and undisputed field of action of *"les Anglais"*, the growing minority of Anglo-Saxon and then assimilated immigrant groups who ran most of Quebec under the compact leadership of Montreal-based entrepreneurs, financiers and merchant kings.

As for the French élite, it remained mostly made up of doctors, lawyers, and priests—"essential services" for the bodies and souls of cheap labor, whose miraculous birthrate kept the supply continuously overabundant. And naturally, there were politicians, practically all of the typical colonial breed which is tolerated as long as it keeps natives happily excited about accessories and divided on essentials.

Needless to say, the educational system was made both to reflect this type of society and to keep it going nicely and quietly. There was a modest collection of church-run seminaries, where the main accent was on recruiting for the priesthood, and which for over a century led to just one underdeveloped university. For nine-tenths of the children there was nothing but grammar school, if that. Read and write barely enough to sign your name and then, without any time for "getting ideas", graduate to obedient respectful employment by any boss generous enough to offer a steady modest job.

Such was the culturally starved and economically inferior, but well-insulated and thus highly resistant, French Quebec which 109 years ago was led into that final mutation of British North America and its supreme defense against American expansionism: Confederation, a union of four eastern colonies as a beginning, but soon to run north of the border "from sea to sea". Into that impressive Dominion, originally as one of four and eventually one of ten provinces, Quebec was incorporated without trouble and generally without enthusiasm. From now on it was to be a minority forever, and with the help of a dynamic federal immigration policy a steadily diminishing one. In due time it would probably merge and disappear into the mainstream, or at the most remain as a relatively insignificant and yet convenient ghetto: *la différence.*

As the building of Canada accelerated during the late nineteenth and early twentieth centuries, a tradition was established that Quebec was to get its measured share of the work, any time there was enough to go around—and the same for rewards. And so, in a nutshell, it went until fairly recently. All told, it hasn't been such a bad deal, this status of "inner colony" in a country owned and managed by another national entity. Undoubtedly French Quebec was (as it remains to this day) the least ill-treated of all colonies in the world. Under a highly centralized federal system, which is much closer to a unitary regime than American federalism, it was allowed its full panoply of provincial institutions: cabinet, legislature, courts, along with the quasi-permanent fun of great squabbles, usually leading to exciting election campaigns, about the defense or extension of its "state rights"! On three occasions during the last eighty years, one of "its own" has even been called upon—at times when there was felt a particular need to keep the natives quiet—to fill the most flattering of all offices, that of federal prime minister. Last but not least of the three, Mr. Trudeau, of whose "Canadian nationalism" it is naturally part and parcel, did as splendidly as was humanly possible for most of the last ten years in this big-chief-of-Quebec dimension of the job. But the law of diminishing returns, along with the inevitable way of all (including political) flesh, has been catching up with his so-called French Power in Ottawa. And no replacement seems to be in sight.

But this is getting ahead of our story. To understand the rise of Quebec's own new nationalism and its unprecedented drive toward self-government, we must go back at least as far as World War II. Not that the dream had completely vanished during the two long centuries of survival which have just been described—from an admittedly partisan but, I honestly believe, not unfair viewpoint. In the 1830s, for instance, there was even an ill-advised and disastrous armed rebellion by a few hundred "Patriots", leading to bloody repression and lasting memories about what not to do. And it is rather significant, by the way, that it took until just now before the poor heroic victims of that abortive rebellion became truly rehabilitated in popular opinion.

Small and impotent though it was, and in spite of feeling that this condition would possibly last forever, French Quebec never quite forgot the potential nation it had once been, never quite gave up dreaming about some miracle which might bring back its chance in the future. In some distant, indescribable future. Now and then, there were stirrings: a writer here, a small political coterie there; a great upsurge of nationalist emotions, in the 1880s, around the Riel affair—the hanging by *les Anglais* of the French-speaking leader of the Prairie Métis; then in 1917, on the conscription issue, a bitter and frequently violent confrontation between the Empire-minded English and the "isolationist" French; faint stirrings again in the twenties; stronger ones in the thirties.

Then World War II, with a repeat in 1944 of the total disagreement on conscription. But mostly, here as elsewhere, this most terrible of all wars was also a midwife for revolutionary change. Thankfully in less disruptive a manner than in other parts of the world, it did start a revolution in Quebec. Wartime service, both overseas and on the industrial home front, dealt a mortal blow to the old order, gave an irresistible impetus to urbanization and started the breakup of the traditional rural-parish ideal, yanked women by the thousands into war-plant industry and as many men into battle-dress discovery of the great wide world. For a small cooped-up society, this was a more traumatic experience than for most others. And then when the postwar years brought the Roaring Fifties, unprecedented mobility and television along with a consumer society, the revolution had to become permanent.

The beginning of the 1960s saw it baptized officially: the Quiet Revolution, with the adjective implying that "quaint old Quebec" couldn't have changed all that much. But it had. Its old set of values literally shattered, it was feeling collectively naked, like a lobster during its shedding season, looking frantically about for a new armour with which to face the modern world. The first and most obvious move was toward education. After so prolonged and scandalous a neglect of this most basic instrument of development, it was quickly realized that here was the first urgent bootstrap operation that had to be launched. It was done with a vengeance: from one of the lowest in the Western world, Quebec per capita investment in education rapidly became, and remains, one of the very highest. Not always well spent (but who is to throw the first stone?), with many mistakes along the way, the job still far from complete (which it will never be anyway), but the essential results are there and multiplying: human resources that are at long last getting required development, along with a somewhat equal chance for all and a normal furious rise in general expectations. The same, naturally, is happening also in other fields, particularly in that of economics, the very first where such rising expectations were bound to strike against the wall of an entrenched colonial setup, with its now intolerable second-class status of the French majority and the stifling remote control of nearly all major decisions either from Ottawa or from alien corporate offices.

Inevitably, there had to be a spillover into politics. More than half of our public revenue and most of the decisions that count were and are in outside hands, in a federal establishment which was basically instituted not by or for us but by others and always first and foremost for their own purposes. With the highly centralized financial system that this establishment constitutionally lords over, this means, for example, that about 80 per cent of Quebec savings and potential investment capital ends up in banks and insurance companies whose operations are none of our business. It also means, just for example once again, that immigration is also practically none of our business; and this could have and is having murderous effects on a minority people with a birthrate, changed like everything else in less than a generation, down from its former prodigious level to close to zero population growth.

Throughout the 1960s, these and other problems were interminably argued about and batted back and forth between federal politicians and bureaucrats ("What we have we hold, until we get more") and a succession of insistent but orthodox, no more than rock-the-boat, nationalists in Quebec. But while this dialogue of the deaf was going on and on, the idea of political independence reappeared as it had to. Not as a dream this time but as a project, and very quickly as a serious one. This developed by leaps and bounds from easily ridiculed marginal groups to small semi-organized political factions, and finally to a full-fledged national party in 1967-68. These were the same two years during which, by pure coincidence, Mr. Trudeau was just as rapidly being elevated to the heights as a new federalist champion from Quebec.

But in spite of his best efforts and those of his party's branch-plant in provincial government, and through an unceasing barrage of money, vilification and rather repugnant fear-inducing propaganda, the voters have democratically brought the Parti Québécois ever closer to power. Which brings us right back to our starting-point. . . .

Let us suppose it does happen, and Quebec peacefully elects such a government. What then?

The way we see it, it would have to go somewhat like this. There is a new Quebec government which is totally dedicated to political independence. But this same Quebec, for the time being, is still very much a component of federal Canada, with its quite legitimate body of elected representatives in Ottawa. This calls, first of all, for at least a try at negotiation. But fruitful talk between two equally legitimate and diametrically opposed levels of government, without any further pressure from the population—that would be a real first in Canadian political history! Obviously, there would have to be the referendum which the Parti Québécois proposes in order to get the decisive yes-or-no answer to the tired question: What *does* Quebec want? (This was precisely the procedure by which the only new province to join Confederation during our recent democratic past, Newfoundland, was consulted in 1948-49 about whether or not to opt in. So why not about opting out?) If the answer should be no, then there's nothing to do but wait for the momentum of change to keep on working until we all find out whether or not there is finally to be a nation here. If the answer is yes, out, then the pressure is on Ottawa, along with a rather dramatic surge of outside attention, and we all get a privileged opportunity to study the recently inked Helsinki Declaration and other noble documents about self-determination for all peoples.

Fully confident of the basic integrity of Canadian democracy, and just as conscious that any silliness would be very costly for both sides, we firmly believe that the matter would then be brought to a negotiated settlement. Especially since the Parti Québécois, far from aiming at any kind of mutual hostility or absurd Berlin Wall, will then repeat its standing offer of a new kind of association, once it is agreed to get rid of our illusion of deep unshakable national unity when in fact two quite real and distinct entities exist in an obsolete and increasingly morbid majority/minority relationship. Our aim is simply full equality by the only means through which a smaller nation can reasonably expect to achieve it with a larger one: self-government. But we are definitely not unaware of the shock waves that such a break, after so long an illusion of eternity, is bound to send through the Canadian political fabric.

We do not accept the simplistic domino theory whereby Quebec's departure is presented as the beginning of fatal dislocation, with "separatism" spreading in all directions like a galloping disease until the balkanized bits and pieces are swallowed up by the huge maw next door. In spite of the somewhat unsure character of its national identity and its excessive satellization by the American economic and cultural empire, Canada-without-Quebec has enough *différence* left, sufficient traditions and institutional originality, to withstand the extraction of its "foreign body" and find a way to go on from there. It might even turn out to be a heaven-sent opportunity to revamp the overcentralized and ridiculously bureaucratized federal system, that century-old sacred cow which, for the moment, nobody dares to touch seriously for fear of encouraging Quebec's subversive leanings!

Be that as it may, we know there would be a traumatic moment and a delicate transition time during which things might go wrong between us for quite a while; or else, one would hope, start going right as never before. With this strange new-coloured Quebec on the map between Ontario and the Maritime provinces, Canada must be kept from feeling incurably "Pakistanized", so we must address ourselves without delay to the problem of keeping a land bridge open with as much free flow of people and goods as is humanly possible; as much and more as there is, I would imagine, between Alaska and the main body of the United States over the western land bridge.

Such a scenario would call, as a decisive first step, for a customs union, as full-fledged as both countries consider to be mutually advantageous. We have, in fact, been proposing that ever since the Parti Québécois was founded, and naturally meeting with the most resonant silence in all orthodox federalist circles. But in the midst of that silence, not a single responsible politician, nor for that matter a single important businessman, has been heard to declare that it wouldn't happen if and when the time comes. For indisputably such a partnership, carefully negotiated on the basis of equality, is bound to be in the cards. Nothing prevents one envisaging it, for instance, going immediately, or at least very quickly, as far as the kind of monetary union which the European Common Market with its original six and now nine members has been fitfully aiming at for so many years. And building on this foundation, it would lead this new "northern tier" to a future immeasurably richer and more stimulating than the 109-year-old bind in which two nations more often than not feel and act like Churchill's two scorpions in the same bottle.

What of Quebec's own national future, both internal and international, in this context of sovereignty-cum-interdependence?

The answers here, for obvious reasons, must be brief, even sketchy and essentially tentative. The perspective of nationhood, for people who haven't been there yet, is bound to have an uncertain horizon. The more so in a period of history like ours, when so much is changing so fast one gets the feeling that change itself is perhaps becoming the only sure law. Who can pretend to know exactly what or where his country will be twenty-five or even ten years from now?

One thing sure is that Quebec will not end up, either soon or in any foreseeable future, as the anarchic caricature of a revolutionary banana republic which adverse propaganda has been having great sinister fun depicting in advance. Either-Ottawa-or is very simply inspired by prejudice, the origin of this nonsense mostly to be found in the tragic events of October 1970 and the great "crisis" which our political establishments, under the astutely calculating Mr. Trudeau, managed to make out of a couple of dozen young terrorists whose ideology was a hopeless hodgepodge of anarcho-nationalism and kindergarten Marxism with no chance of having any kind of serious impact. What they *did* accomplish was two kidnappings and, most cynically welcome of all, one murder—highly unfortunate but then also particularly par for the course in the international climate at the time. What was not par at all, however, was the incredible abuse of power for which those events, relatively minor per se, were used as a pretext: the careful buildup of public hysteria, army trucks rolling in during the night, and then, for months on end, the application in Quebec, and solely in Quebec, of a federal War Measures Act for which no peacetime precedent exists in any democratic country. A great spectacle produced in order to terrorize the Québécois forever back into unquestioning submissiveness, and, outside, to feed the mill of scary propaganda about how dangerous this tame animal could nevertheless be!

In actual fact, French Quebec, with its normal share of troubles, disquiet and now the same kind of social turmoil and search for new values that are rampant all over the Western world, remains at bottom a very solid, well-knit and nonviolent society. Even its new and demanding nationalism has about it something less strident and essentially more self-confident than its current pan-Canadian counterpart. For Quebec has an assurance of identity, along with a relative lack of aggressiveness, which are the result of that one major factor of national durability lacking in the rest of Canada: a different language and the cultural fabric that goes with it.

Now how does the Parti Québécois see this society begin to find its way as an independent nation? What is the general outline of the political, social and economic structure we hope to bring forth? Serious observers have been calling our programme basically social-democratic, rather comparable to the Scandinavian models although certainly not a carbon copy since all people, through their own experiences, have to invent their own "mix".

The way we have been trying to rough it out democratically through half a dozen national party conventions, ours would call for a presidential regime, as much of an equal-opportunity social system as we could afford, and a decent measure, as quickly as possible but as carefully as indicated, of economic "repatriation". This last would begin to happen immediately, and normally without any great perturbation, through the very fact of sovereignty: with the gathering in of all of our public revenues and the full legislative control which any self-respecting national state has to implement over its main financial institutions, banks, insurance companies and the like. In the latter case, this would allow us to break the stranglehold in which the old British-inspired banking system of just a handful of "majors" has always kept the people's money and financial initiative. The dominant position in our repatriated financial circuit would be handed over to Quebec's co-operative institutions, which happen to be particularly well developed in that very field and, being strongly organized on a regional basis, would afford our population a decent chance for better-balanced, responsible, democratic development. And that, by the way, is just one fundamental aspect of the kind of evolution toward a new economic democracy, from the lowest rung in the marketplace up to boardroom levels, that all advanced societies not already doing so had better start thinking about in the very near future.

As to non-resident enterprise, apart from the universal minimums concerning incorporations and due respect for Quebec taxes, language and other classic national requirements, what we have been fashioning over the last few years is an outline of a policy which we think is both logical and promising. It would take the form of an "investment code", giving a clear-cut picture, by sectors, of what parts of our economic life we would insist on keeping under home ownership (e.g., culturally oriented activities, basic steel and forest resources), what other parts we would like to see under mixed control (a very few selected but strategic cases) and finally, the multitude of fields (tied to markets and to technological and/or capital necessities) where foreign interests would be allowed to stay or to enter provided they do not tend to own us along with their businesses.

In brief, Quebec's most privileged links, aside from its most essential relationship with the Canadian partner, would be first with the United States—where there is no imaginable reason to frown on such a tardy but natural and healthy development (especially during a Bicentennial year). Then Quebec would look to other francophone or "Latin" countries as cultural respondents, and to France herself—who would certainly not be indifferent to the fact that this new nation would constitute the second most important French-speaking country in the world. In brief, such is the peaceful and, we confidently hope, fruitfully progressive state which may very well appear on the map of North America before the end of the decade.

# Canada is a Poem

## Robert Kroetsch

We are Canadians. We know we dreamt, but we cannot remember what.

One of the functions of revolution is this: to renew time. It enables us to begin again. As Canadians, we fear that we are a people without a beginning. Canadians as old as those in Quebec prepare, now, again, to give themselves a beginning. Like the new people on the prairies, they dream a next-year country against all the crop failures of the past.

The Quebec poet, Gatien Lapointe, in "The Snow-Knight I":

> We come back in couples from the beginning of the world
> Our hands support the dawn being born
> My country is this fire burning under the snow
> My country is this word in the hand of a child
>
> This is where we'll plant the original dream

We cannot find our beginning. There is no Declaration of Independence, no Magna Carta, no Bastille Day. We live with a terrible unease at not having begun. Canada is a poem. We dreamt a poem, and now we must try to write it down. We have a gift of languages, and now we must make the poem.

Arrivals are not enough. The arrival of John Cabot at the eastern coast
is not enough. The arrival of Jacques Cartier at the entering place is not
enough. The arrival of Samuel de Champlain at the interior is not
enough. The arrival of Alexander Mackenzie at the western coast is not
enough. We want a beginning.

The Quebec poet, Jacques Brault, in his "Suite For My Brother":

> It has no name this country that I affirm and repudiate as
> long as I live
> my country scalped of its youth
> My country born in the orphanage of the snow

Not the past, but the future. We are Canadians. We are tempted to
escape the nightmare of history. General Wolfe, General Middleton:
they are only the bungling aliens who won, the gunmen of reality. I
grew up thinking Wolfe a sort of sneaky bastard, climbing that cliff-side
in the dark. For Middleton I was only embarrassed, a man of such
ill-consequence, allowed to ride a horse.

The Plains of Abraham, Batoche: now they are the sacred names of
some mysterious loss. The old orders had their victories. But in winning
they taught us to hear our need. "My country is this word in the hand
of a child." We listen for the voice of the visionary, the poet. Against
the mere facts, we listen to the men who might have dared to dream.
Riel. Aberhart. Douglas. Diefenbaker. Lévesque. . . . Not the past, but
the future.

We are Canadians. We believe in the history of rivers. I was born on the
prairies, and yet the story of the St. Lawrence is my story. The voya-
geurs who came from the St. Lawrence, to the Saskatchewan system, to
Batoche, to the Battle River of my childhood—they brought a story I
could act out, in a pig trough on a slough, dodging my way through

willows. They gave me a story I could repeat, in my own time, on a riverboat on the Mackenzie.

That web of rivers, of people: it gave to the Prairies the poem of Gabriel Dumont and Louis Riel. Those two men, in their uprising that was not an uprising at all—in their necessary revolution of the perceiving self—they showed us that we are a new people in a new landscape. They are the poets of place, telling us to see. The conquerors are not our heroes. We, the slow listeners, like the Prairie writer Rudy Wiebe, share the temptations of Big Bear. When the language fails—then we hear the language. Then we begin the poem.

Utopia and revolution: two branches, one river. We are Canadians. We feel both superior and deprived because we have not tested the dream with cobblestones and iron. Thus we are not Europeans. Thus we are not Americans. Without the terrible occasion of freedom, we doubt that we are free. Without the bonding of the occasion we feel, first, our aloneness.

Joe Lepage, for many years, was the station agent in Heisler, Alberta, the small prairie town near which I was a boy. When, many years later, I wrote down the hero, Hazard Lepage, the loner French-Canadian who dreams a new breed of horse in *The Studhorse Man,* the metaphor was real. Lepage was not only my own aloneness, he was his own. Kroetsch. Lepage. We are Canadians.

We are not so much existentialists in our individual lives as in our version of nationhood. Canada invents itself daily. Perhaps the newspaper is our poem, our weather the poem's subject.

We are the northern edge of the New World. We are the weather of ourselves. The search for the Northwest Passage is always part of our dream, and of our nightmare too. We look for a route through the weather. It reveals itself in our architecture. In our clothing. In our sports. "My country is this fire burning under the snow."

Margaret Laurence, dreaming the necessary death, the birth of the new, dreams Jules Tonnerre. A prairie writer, she dreams a French name. She dreams thunder. A prairie writer, she dreams a river.

Arrivals are not enough. Gatien Lapointe, in "Ode au Saint-Laurent":

Je balise le premier jour de l'homme

Nous sommes Canadiens. We play hockey like a people who cannot tell a dream from a nightmare. Perhaps the hockey game is our poem, our idea of community the poem's subject. Perhaps it is the body, first, that feels the place, the country. Now, we break our silence. At last, we are here.

# In Praise of Imprecision

## Naim Kattan

*Translated by William J. Guthrie*

In the course of my travels, it has always been a source of amusement for me to turn over the pages of telephone directories in the cities I visit. One is struck by the variety of names, the diversity of their origin, in Paris, London or Brussels. But at any distance from the great metropolises, foreign names appear more and more exotic. In Canada, in whatever city one happens to be, large or small, names which seem foreign to us are rare. It is obvious that names with a French or English ring everywhere constitute the majority, but names from the four corners of the earth find a place in our directories, and that seems to us not only commonplace but natural.

Hybrid origins and multiform authenticity are not limited to names, by any means. A city's profile and its aspect do not embody set forms but offer an uncertain and ambiguous expression of a country, and it is not at all simply a matter of the architecture of houses, or even cookery (qualified as Chinese or Italian), furniture, toys and entertainments. In the lives of peoples and groups there is a constant aspiration toward clarity and precision. Demarcating a territory, drawing up a frontier, provide security and safeguard against the threat of the outer world. But the outer world is made up of neighbours, altogether as athirst for security and altogether as apprehensive of an invader's attack.

In order to fulfil this boundless need for security and in order to conquer fear, one becomes a conqueror, an assailant, an invader. The need for clarity and precision has often been a synonym for conflict, war, conflagration. Groups and peoples may seek unity in order to assert their presence and repel their neighbour's influence. Yet cohesion founded on a power relation leads to confrontation over power sharing and asserting authority. There are other forms of relation: exchange, mutual enrichment, an openness to influence.

For me, the noblest race is the Métis race.

And the only groups whose identity is clear and precise are dead groups. The others survive by transformation, metamorphosis, by multiple bonds and constant exchanges. The history of Canada is made up not of the demarcation by each group of its own territory, but of compromise, of influences endured or accepted, of bonds one welcomes or to which one becomes resigned. Compromise is less heroic than conquest and confrontation, just as life has less precision and less clarity than death. The virtue of a living group is in lasting.

Threatened cultures seek protection in clarity and precision. They invent dogma which breaks their dynamic spirit instead of liberating it. They impose precepts and set models for their members. What ought to have been free exchange is transformed into authoritarianism and what claims to be protection of life becomes oppressive totalitarianism. It is fortunate that Canada's founding cultures and her constituent cultures have never been defined with clarity and precision. They metamorphose and each definition of them gives the lie to the one preceding, for life in imposing movement reduces any definition to ephemera.

We chose not to cut ourselves off from Europe but rather to retain its contribution and its richness without feeling that America was a land of exile for all that. Ambiguity of that kind resists precision. Rejection of defiance and rebellion were the foundations of an uncertain freedom by which we live and which is the great heritage that nourishes us. Those individuals who disembarked on the coast, east or west, those groups who settled on the plains or the shores of the ocean, did not have identity bestowed upon them immediately on arrival. Identity was and still is a long process, a quest. Some groups followed parallel paths in their search, torn between memory and prospect, allegiance and the promise of the present, the unquiet and joyous anticipation of the future.

I am happy that no identity was determined before I arrived, before my birth. I experienced that freedom which allows the possibility of action. The individual humbly marks his passage; a scratch on the surface of the earth. In a society of free exchange where one may voyage among regions, languages and cultures, the individual is not suffocated by group exigencies. The group is there to liberate in him the particular, the original, the specific. A society without dogma, such as ours, does not offer easy ideological and emotional security, which always ends in suffocation. Our society sets us on the path of creating freedom, an uncertain freedom, a fragile freedom, a sense of which must be kept alive so it will not die out. In this society, the faithful and the heretic, the person entirely absorbed into the collectivity and the traitor, do not exist.

Although they are sources of insecurity for power, the imprecision of groups, the uncertainty of borders separating collectivities, are also guaranties of freedom for the individual. I learned in Canada that collective freedom has meaning only if it protects individual freedom, only if it allows the individual to utilize his resources fully and without constraint. I know that the domain of freedom is shrinking and that excuses and ideological or political explanations are being sought to justify its fading away, all the more so because free men rarely know they are free until they are deprived of freedom. It is troublesome and occasionally embarrassing not being able to define oneself at all as a Canadian. We are scarcely beginning to develop exterior symbols of our own, to differentiate ourselves. I prefer that imprecision and that ambiguity to dogma, to totalitarianism and to oppressive authority. Defining identity is a long road and fortunately in Canada identity is not imposed by a superior authority; no one here can claim to be mandated to fulfil the role of defining conscience and identity. In a free society, each citizen, all citizens, are definers of identity. And in the matter of defining myself and explaining my identity, I prefer to be embarrassed than to have to lament my lost freedom.

# Listen. Just Listen

Margaret Laurence

On a raw and windy day in March 1977, with the sky a speckless prairie blue and the snow now unseasonably scant on the black Saskatchewan soil, I made a pilgrimage. I had wanted to make it for many years. I walked over the rough ground where the battle of Batoche took place in the spring of 1885, the last battle when the regiments and cannons of the Canadian government forces took three days to overcome the hungry, ill-equipped forces of the Métis people under the leadership of Louis Riel and the heroic Gabriel Dumont. The pleas of the Métis for rights to their ancestral lands had been persistently ignored by Sir John A. Macdonald and his government, and it was only out of desperation that the Métis finally resorted to battle. Middleton's cannon and the well-armed although poorly trained boys from Upper Canada fought the Métis buffalo hunters, who, running out of ammunition, used the last of their powder to fire nails and stones from their rifles. After that defeat, the voices of the Métis fell into silence for years, only to rise again with the present-day descendents of those courageous men and women.

But the old voices are here yet, and anyone who comes here must surely hear them. They are everywhere in the wind. The Métis people who live here now hear those voices and respect them. Only fairly recently was the area declared officially an historic site, but it has always been cared for by the local people. Around the battle area there are fences made in the old way, poplar poles bound with willow strips. No crops are ever planted in that place. It is a sacred ground, in a sense.

The small white-painted timber church, built in 1884, is still here. Riel and Gabriel must have prayed here, and Gabriel, when he returned home out of exile, must have spent many hours here, remembering.

In the Métis graveyard at Batoche a rough wooden cross stands blunt and huge against the sky. The tombstone of Gabriel Dumont is a slab of red-gray fieldstone, put up a few years ago by the government of the province. The people hereabouts, I am told, preferred the old grave marker, a small plain wooden cross. The big fieldstone, they say, is suitable enough as a gravestone, but it obscures Gabriel's favourite view of his river, the slow-moving broad South Saskatchewan, where he ran a ferry during some of the years when he served as leader of the South Saskatchewan Métis.

Standing there in the wind, in the prairie spring, in my own land, I said Gabriel's prayer, for myself and as homage to him, and probably for my people and my land as well. Gabriel composed this prayer on his way back from Montana to Saskatchewan with Louis Riel in 1884, and he thereafter said it every day of his life.

Lord, strengthen my courage, my faith and my honour, that I may profit in my life from the blessing I have received in Thy Holy Name.

I thought of a previous pilgrimage I had made, to the grave of Louis Riel, just outside of St. Boniface Cathedral in Manitoba, my home province. Riel's body was brought back to his home, to the province which he more than anyone else brought into Confederation, despite the fact that as an elected member of the House of Commons he was turned out and refused entry, given over into the years of exile in Montana until he returned in 1884, at his people's request, to Saskatchewan. The stone in St. Boniface cemetery is inscribed:

**RIEL**
16 novembre
1885

No first names, no birth date, no epitaph. This is enough. No more need be said. Those who know of him know how much is said here. The date is the date of his death in Regina, on the scaffold, when he very consciously gave his death to his people and his soul into the keeping of his God.

Why should I feel so strongly about these men, about their people? They were Métis, French-Cree. My people were Celts, Scots and Irish, who had no reason to love imperialism, either. But there are more and deeper things between myself and Riel, myself and Dumont. We are prairie.

That day at Batoche, I thought of another form of the name Gabriel. Gabrielle. Like myself a writer, a woman, a person prairie born and raised. Gabrielle Roy, who has now lived for many years in Quebec. I have not met her, but we have corresponded and read each other's writing. I am honoured to call her my friend.

We are, all of us, it seems to me, bound up in one another's history. I am prairie. I am by ancestry Scots-Irish. I am Canadian.

I first learned my view of the world in my place of birth. I honour my ancestors and I also feel that there is a profound sense in which the ancestors ultimately become all our ancestors. We in spirit, being linked to the land, are also linked to the ancestral voices which arise out of many sources.

When I think of my own birth area of this land, I think of prairie writers. In this one area alone, our names are Cree, French, Scots, Irish, Métis, English, Jewish, Ukrainian, Hungarian, Mennonite, Icelandic, German, and more. Such diversity is found everywhere in anglophone Canada.

I find myself desperately wanting to explain to the people of Quebec my sense of my own people's reality. "English Canada" is, of course, a misnomer. We are a mixed people who use the English language as a language of communication. For a great many of us, the English language may not be that of our ancestors, but it is our birth language or one of our birth languages, and we love it. It is for us no longer the language of England, nor does it have the connotations of colonialism, for we have changed it and made it our own. I am linked in many ways with the language and literature of Britain, just like every other person who writes in this language. But in a profound sense what I speak and write is Canadian, a form of the language which emanated from England, a form of it which makes use of our own idiom, our own frames of reference, our own perceptions of the life around us.

We, in anglophone Canada, are a nation, just as the Québécois are a nation. I pray that this country will continue to be one, from Vancouver Island to Newfoundland. But if Quebec does ultimately decide to separate, I want to proclaim my belief that the rest of Canada would continue to remain together. Despite all our differences, and despite all the legitimate grievances of the west, say, or the Atlantic Provinces, we have a·common cause. We are a very varied family, but we are a family. We will not, I think, **permit** this land of ours to go by default to our powerful neighbour and cousin to the south of us. Our identity? To me it is as rich and many-faceted as the names of our people. There has never been any doubt about that identity in my mind. Further, I feel no more need of defining it than I do of defining God. I simply know it is there. I can see it and feel it and relate to it in the works of our writers. Wole Soyinka, the Nigerian writer, once said in reference to "négritude", "Does a tiger have to define its tigritude?" If this identity, this sense of belonging, were not there, why else would I feel such a sense of connection with my tribal sisters and brothers, the writers all across this land who are writing in my language? Because we are all writers? True, but I have known writers in England and have felt a common bond of writing with them, and yet not the same deep bond as I do with those of my own people. I would like to feel this bond with the writers of Quebec as well, and I *do* feel it through those of their works which I have read. I would like to see many many more translations, going both ways, for surely the reading of our two nations' writing is one of the best means of getting to feel one another's deepest reality.

I find myself wanting to say to the people of Quebec—*Listen. Just listen.* Please. We are the people of anglophone Canada, and our real views aren't being communicated to you by governments, either about your situation or our own. We are teachers and fishermen, farmers and writers, housewives and storekeepers. We care about this land. Our ancestors came from all over the world. Within our diversity lies our strength. It is not a strength which desires to control or devour other lands. It is a growing strength which wishes to free ourselves and our own land from control by other powers. It is a rising strength which wants to reclaim those parts of our land and our resources which have been subject to the neo-colonialism of American governments and corporations, and this in no way affects our feeling of cousinhood with the American people themselves. Cannot yourselves and ourselves, our two nations in Canada, join as we never yet have? My barometer, my gauge of the spiritual and emotional weather, is the writing of my contemporaries in both languages, Canadian and Canadien. We are different. Differences are to be honoured, recognized and understood on both sides. I cannot, quite honestly, visualize a course in the literature of this country in which the writings of either of our two nations could be excluded.

Yet how dare I presume to try to speak to the Québécois, and how dare I ask them to listen to the reality of my people, of all my people in our incredible variety? I dare to do so because I would like to proclaim that we are real, too, and that we are not unacquainted with suffering. I want to speak of the prairie farmers who weathered somehow, or who did not weather, the drought and the Depression of the 1930s, of the bone-poor Newfoundland outporters who lost their men to the sea and their children to the murderous cities, of the West Coast Japanese Canadians who totally without justice or reason (under the iniquitous War Measures Act) in the Second World War were in their thousands wrenched from their homes and put into detention camps and who to this day have never received compensation for their property which was seized from them, and—more than anything—in the beginning of this country as a "country", the taking away of the land from the native peoples by colonialists who believed men could actually *own* the land, whereas the original inhabitants believed that the land belonged to God, the Great Spirit, and was for mankind's shared use.

The oppression—and God knows it has gone on long—of the Québécois, is part of an entire system of colonialism and oppression and I think it must be seen as such.

Despite all these aspects of our common history, I would not presume to try to speak to the Québécois if I were not, first and foremost, wanting to address myself to myself and to my own people.

How shall we speak what is in our hearts? How shall we find ways in which to communicate, really communicate, our deepest feelings to the other nation in this land? Will they listen? Will they believe that a very great many of us do care, do sympathize and agree with their feelings of nationhood? We must go on speaking, reaching out and hoping.

But we must first listen to them. My hope is that someday we will not have to say "Us" and "Them", but that the people of this country may be able to live in equality and diversity.

*Listen. Just Listen.*

In anglophone Canada, we have not listened well in the past. That is indisputable. The grievances and the true anger of the people of Quebec, those who have ancestral roots there, have been a long time smouldering. The dried leaves of their discontent have now burst into flames. Why should anyone be surprised? It is time, and more than time, that such a thing happened.

Is there still time? I must believe that there is always time, for everything. And also that there is not much time at all.

If we are to listen truly to what they are saying, we must take into ourselves views which are passionate, though passionately different from our own, views which extend beyond our experience but which also encompass our history.

And yet I still pray that this country, from Vancouver Island to Newfoundland, may remain one. Not in its present constitutional form, for the grievances of the Québécois, and also those of the prairies and the Atlantic Provinces and the west coast, are real and go deep.

We are faced with a turning point sharper than any in our history. If we can communicate well and truly, if we can listen to and hear one another, at the grassroots, then the present situation could become our greatest opportunity yet, to right old wrongs and to learn about one another. I believe this is possible. I do not place my faith in governments, and yet I think that we must influence governments, or replace them.

Just before I went to Batoche, I was talking with Rudy Wiebe. He is prairie, Mennonite, and one of our finest writers. His novel, *The Temptations Of Big Bear,* is the best work I know which deals with the Indians' uprising of 1885, and his new novel about Riel and Dumont, called *The Scorched-Wood People,* will soon be published. He knows Batoche well.

"When you get there," he said, "listen. Just listen."

The voices in the wind at the Métis cemetery that day spoke of courage and of faith and of injustice. They spoke of our intertwined history, of our ancestors, of our children.

*Listen. Just Listen.*

# Batoche. May 12, 1885

Rudy Wiebe

(Narrator: a Métis voice)

The charge of the Royal Grenadiers and the Midland Regiment drove our men from the trenches, as it would have had it been made that first Saturday, but now they had less ammunition with which to defend themselves. Betwen the first and second line of rifle pits were killed Michel Trottier, André Batoche, Calixte Tourond and his brother Elzéar, two Sioux warriors, all by bayonet, Jose Vandal who had both arms broken first and then was finished off by bayonet, Donald Ross and Isidore Boyer, both over seventy-five and killed by bayonet, John Swan, and also Demase Carrière, shooting until his rifle was empty and then clubbing the red soldiers bellowing over him as his leg was shattered by a ball and finally a cavalryman threw a rope around his neck and dragged him at a gallop through ravines and brush and stones up the slope again and into the zareba before he tried to control his foaming horse. By that time most of the men had been driven back to the trees before Batoche and four houses including the Council House were on fire.

Gabriel Dumont was on high ground in the second line; with Patrice Tourond and Napoleon Nault and Old Ouellette he stopped the centre of the Royal Grenadiers for a time. There was, as Gabriel laughed, no shortage of targets: it was just a problem of selection. The inevitable red crept gradually closer as behind them the flanking troops already thundered, cheered in the woods and finally he sent Patrice back, then Napoleon to rally our men across the river, reluctantly but he went

26

when Gabriel swung *Le Petit* around at him in threat, and then there was only Old Ouellette to convince; three times, but he refused.

"Father," Gabriel shouted in his ear again, "we have to retreat! Come now!"

The old man was pouring powder into his muzzle-loader with the same steady deliberation he had for four days; a bullet splintered the top of the log, the earth sprayed at them; the bullets singing lower and lower did not so much as quiver his bony hand.

"Wait a minute," he said, "I won't get another chance." He was already taking aim over the logs. "I want to kill one more English."

He was ninety-three, ten years older than Gabriel's father. He had fought in every battle of the Scorched-Wood People: Seven Oaks, 1816, Missouri Coteau, 1852, Fort Garry, 1869; he could not be carried back, even if that had been possible in the barrage.

"All right," Gabriel levered *Le Petit* again, "we can die here."

There was a movement in the near brush, right, and he waited. Behind him Ouellette's rifle fired; waited while a Snider protruded there and gradually a shape and then until he was certain, and he fired; that Snider jerked into the brush, crashed, gotcha bastard, and he was laughing, turning, but there was the old man hurled against the wall of the pit and he remembered the "thud!" familiar enough; he had recognized it, somewhere, just as he pulled the trigger. He crept forward, cursing himself for that split second of certainty, the trap so baited, and the old man grinned at him.

"I got that English," he grimaced momentarily. "I think, anyway. But there's too many more . . . now you go."

"I can carry you to—"

"No. In two minutes I'll be dead, so, they need . . . "

There was red burping at the corner of his lip; something sloshing red as it seemed through his slow words.

"I've lived long enough . . . longer than our nation."

Gabriel was firing with one hand, low, ahead into the unstoppable Canadians, his left hand on Ouellette's hair, it was so fine it felt like a child's, praying that prayer he had spoken so often and so thankful for this old man's courage, faith and honour, he longed suddenly to kiss him. And he did that, with fierce commitment, that shrunken dirty face already glazed in death. Then he was running, crouched down and running as he had never run through rain that slashed against him with the blessing of the Indian Thunderbird to hide him from his enemies and he ran erect, heaving *Le Petit* up into the driving rain and bellowing in fury as something tore in him he had not known was there, was ripped apart as he ran roaring through the thunder and rain towards his men firing gravel at the Canadians already bayoneting their way into the trees.

He screamed the men under the trees into turning around; when Moïse Ouellette suggested they retreat Gabriel smashed him to the ground with his fist. "We stop them here! Anybody runs I'll kill him myself!" So they held the Canadians at the edge of the trees for half an hour. Charles Tourond ran barefoot through a fusilade to the Council House and returned with an unopened barrel of powder. They fired bent nails, gravel, even chewed metal buttons at the Canadians with it. Gabriel still had a dozen Winchester bullets and when a Canadian captain peered around the Council House corner, Gabriel shot him; a soldier dashed toward the body and he killed him too. But then the ammunition was finished and they retreated to the ferry where Gabriel had hidden two boxes of bullets; Riel was there shouting orders as the women and children jostled, crammed onto the ferry. It was strangely quiet there as the drenched, dirty men dashed out of the trees; the women screamed in terror momentarily but fell silent as the men sur-rounded them, tried to heave the ferry, almost awash, out into the river which still flowed imperturbably on.

"What are we going to do?" Riel shouted at Gabriel. "They have broken through, we are beaten!" He was lifting his arms to heaven and Gabriel knocked him aside, heaved up a stone beside the cable support.

"We die, that's what we do!" He was clawing at the mud, finding one then another box of bullets. "I told you, once you start shooting you have to take whatever they shoot back. Well, let them kill us."

Patrice Tourond staggered out of the muddy river, keeping his balance on the cable, his open face running blood, "We need a miracle, now, Brother Louis!"

"Gabriel—Gabriel!" Riel was clawing at his shoulder, his face contorted but not with fear, even in his fury Gabriel recognized that, only pain. He pushed Patrice away, grabbed Riel's hand, crushed it.

"Shut up and get all the women away, across the river. I've got forty bullets left, I'll do the killing."

"Gabriel, don't expose yourself so much, don't—"

"You'll need blankets, I'll send some back from the houses, just get them all away, over!"

"If you get killed what—"

"No Canadian'll kill me, and never no Englishman!"

His pockets were stuffed tight with bullets, *Le Petit* slammed full and he ran up the trail, smashed two soldiers down as they came out of a rifled tent and threw out the blankets there. He was breathing thunderously; he charged out, ripped the bullet-belts off the still-twitching soldiers—Goddamn it, Winchesters!—and sprinted up through the trees where red troops were running from house to house trailing blankets, dropping dishes, furs and sacred pictures—

"Gabriel!"

It was his wife, God in heaven! He seized her, she was sobbing against his chest and he thrust her away, not seeing her, his eyes leaping here and there as he spoke, almost shouting, "There's blankets in that tent, there, take them to the ferry, Louis's getting the women over, they'll need blankets; you get over, it's too hot here—"

"Gabriel!" Madeleine cried into his face, "Gabriel!"

But he had already knocked her hands aside, was running towards the edge of the woods where rifles still sputtered, the heavy thump of bullets so good in his pockets, by Jesus he'd kill them, they'd all be crawling for holes, God help him!

And for two days he flickered through the valley of Batoche a killer haunt in tattered shirt and pants. He shot at and perhaps killed more men than he knew: a sentry he whistled into terror first, a teamster feeding horses; a looter looking carefully out of a house, his arms full; an officer on a stroll kicking idly through the ash of a burned house. He saw the soldiers carry armfuls of paper out of the Council House, still only partially burned but the Flag of Our Lord gone from the mast, and he picked off two of them, Louis's papers exploding over dust and mud holes like goose feathers before they drove him off, deeper into the woods. The second night he found a camp of women and children still on the east side of the river, Madeleine among them, and Eli too. His brother had killed a cow to feed them around their tiny fire hidden in a hole and the children were lying under damp hay Eli had cut, burrowed down like animals, their naked feet blue in the night air. As he wolfed some beef he cut the rawhide into pieces, tied it to the children's feet with strips of leather.

"Please stop, Gabriel," Madeleine begged him. "It's over, over."

"Where's Riel?"

"It's over, ride to the States, they'll—"

"Where's Riel?" he glared at her. "With him I can still kill them all! All summer some here, some there, and we'll go to the Indians, I'll kill every white myself."

"Gabriel!" Madeleine wailed.

"Shut up then," he was already going, "tell me nothing. At least if you see him, I'll be at my father's place tomorrow night. Just shut up." She could not recognize him now, he who so gently, momentarily, had cut bootlets for children and had always loved her, she knew it, but he was in some savagery beyond her worst experience of any man. "If the soldiers find you, you haven't seen me. Understand?" He wheeled on her as if he would tear her apart. "No shit police can handle me and neither can you. Just shut up!"

He found a herd of horses and jumped a wild pinto and stampeded the herd through the Canadian zareba, riding the pinto like a devil in the intermittent moonlight and laughing, the very wolves stopped howling under the cold stars.

# Thoughts that Try to Go Somewhere, but Stop Short: Canadian Style

Leonard Peterson

Dumb luck. Half a continent for Canadians. A handful of heroes did their bit and we end up so rich we can make monumental mistakes, individually and collectively, again and again, and not suffer for them. Yet.

One of my boyhood heroes was a demigod by the name of Dionne. He was the best Goddamn softball pitcher I ever saw. We played softball on the Prairies in the Dirty Thirties because nobody could afford a glove. Dionne used a snakelike whiplash delivery, not the straightarm swing of today's fastballers. Dionne could hit too. He was what Babe Ruth would've been if nobody'd bought the Babe a glove. Dionne was also rich. He owned a bicycle and had a job. He was a telegram delivery boy. On a bike nobody could beat Dionne. Sometimes he let me borrow his bike to ride underbar. And he taught me to do back flips from a two-handed lift. There's never been a greater guy than Dionne. Not in my world. I guess he was French. I never thought of him as anything but Dionne. Since he never spoke French or got excited, was he almost English? Who cares? He was Dionne.

Dear Dr. Sam Johnson: Patriotism the last refuge of a scoundrel, you say? Maybe in your country, Doc. In mine it's race. It used to be religion.

If my parents had been True Believers, I would never have been born. In 1905 Norway separated from Sweden, peacefully. Shortly after separation my father, Nils, a Norwegian, fell in love with my mother, Marion, a Swede, they married and had children, including me. Having been a near non-baby, unimagined, unconceived, has not made me a passionate separatist, though when I view it from the point of view of my affronted and fed-up Gallic friends I sometimes see merit in it. A true Canadian: without convictions.

I feel I am living in a country conquered and occupied. (It is a feeling I share with many, and it is in no way unique to the French.) But such a strange conquest and occupation, this. It affects all that I do and am. We, the conquered, admire, envy and ape our conquerors. We offer no resistance. We offer the conquerors more than they demand (in the name of freedom and profitable trade, theirs, not ours). Most strangely, even the conquerors here eventually feel conquered, conquered by our emptiness of soul and head, conquered by our impossible fancies and foolish fears.

Parallel developments: same time; contrasting patterns.

New France. A tight little colony administratively. No Huguenots, no dissenters. Everything well ordered. Needs and problems referred back to France. Decisions by the Home Office, the King and his ministers. No printing press till after the Fall (British Rule).

New England. Colonies established by dissenters. Printing presses brought with them. Within a few years Harvard established with its library. Their charters allowed them to set up head offices and conduct annual meetings this side of the Atlantic. Decide matters for themselves. No waiting for a year or years or forever for decisions.

Canadians: folk whose spirits reside elsewhere, outside the borders of their country. That describes them, but sure as hell doesn't explain them. How did we get this kinky? No sense of self, no sense of community.

Just a decade and a half after the Canadiens had their bureaucracy restructured by an unpleasant conference on the Plains of Abraham, the Continental Congresses invited the Canadiens to shuck the British colonial system of administration for the New World republican system that was set on keeping taxation swag and concomitant power this side of the waters. But a deal (the Quebec Act) struck between the Canadiens and the Home Office allowed the Canadiens continuing popery. The New Englanders, unfortunately, had condemned the Quebec Act for its tolerance. The Canadiens feared for their religion and language if they teamed up with the dissenting colonists. They opted to stay "conquered". Conquered, of course, they escaped the French Revolution and Faith-Reason turmoil and the likelihood of being sold by Napoleon along with Louisiana to the Americans when he was short of petty cash.

Clipped from the classifieds:

> FOR SALE. Former province, used, badly, now [in] a state. American buyer preferred. No English-Canadian need apply. Write: Quebec, Quebec.

If there is virtue in Quebec separating from the rest of Canada, might there not be virtue in the Indians and Eskimos of Quebec separating from sovereign Quebec to become masters in their own house? I can imagine a time as well when the Gaspé will not be comfortable with Montreal or Montreal with Quebec City. No end of possibilities.

Ah, and the fracturing of the rest of Canada! Gonna be nice. Hallelujah.

Hello out there! So little of the Canadian fact in our theatres, movie houses, magazine racks, record albums, radio, television, school books. A land of zombies? If we weren't occupied would we exist at all?

Loyalists flooded into our Maritimes and Upper Canada from the revolutionary British colonies to the south and naturally expected to be rewarded for their passionate loyalty to the mother country. But there were bigger fish for the mother country to fry than loyalty: enterprise and profits. And the disloyal colonies had 'em wholesale. That's where Britain invested her pounds and people after the Revolution. Whenever she had to side in favour of the Loyal or Disloyal, she sided with the Disloyal. A good example: the Oswald-Franklin negotiations that gave the Ohio Valley country to the Rebels. Canada: a drag, a bore, an expense, an embarrassment, a land of uninteresting delusions.

The past became the proccupation of both the English and the French in Loyal North America. To remember became a fine art. To be was okay so long as you kept glancing back. France goes ahead, England goes ahead, Canada remembers.

I was born at the eye of the storm, the racist storm, at Pile o' Bones. It was a nothin' spot on the western prairies beside a small creek till the railway pushed through. Then it became a slightly noticeable spot 'cause of buffalo bones gathered and stacked beside the tracks for shipment east to be made into soap, buttons and porcelain. Pile o' Bones: a short-lived monument to the rape of the nor'west prairie wilderness. When the impetuous Imperialists made Pile o' Bones the capital of the Northwest Territories, they thunked up a grander name for that nothin' spot: Regina, Queen City of the Plains. There on the outskirts of town, three years later, they hanged Louis Riel, the Métis leader, who would not kowtow to the obtuse, arrogant English. But the justices eternally present in the clouds that drift over this country saw to it that the hanging rope caught John A's federal party in its noose as well as Riel. The prairies till then had been as much French and Indian as English. The hanging was a loud, clear message to the French. Go back or stay back in Quebec. Or if you come out here, forget you're French. Take up English like any other immigrants! You say you opened up our northwest lands? So what? The grim message was backed up by grim legislation. In 1877 Manitoba had made English and French the languages of the law, courts and Legislature. But in 1890 French got the boot. A year later the Northwest Territories legislated— only English spoke here. And Saskatchewan and Manitoba, when they came into being in 1905, stuck with the no-French nonsense. In 1913 Ontario, with Regulation 17, stopped education in their own language for the French. Even in the country's capital, Ottawa, mother-tongue education for the French was cut to a snippet. Quebec stayed the only open province with French and English the official languages. Recently the country generally has re-recognized bilingualism, not through any grassroots swell of sentiment and conviction, but through government fiat. And Quebec, after a century of suffering quietly these indignities to its French citizenry, hits back. To hell with the English! To hell with their Goddamn language!

How do we differ from the Americans? They feel their destiny lies within their own hands. What do we feel?

Why Canada? Does it exist only to preserve the French fact in North America?

All those French moving from Quebec to the States, are they still a French fact? Or Americans? Or both? All OK, no? Does it matter to anybody but pigeonholers and zealots?

"A Norwegian is a Swede with his brains knocked out." "A Swede is a Norwegian with his brains knocked out." The great downputters I got hurled at me when I was a kid. But they didn't sting. Somehow I sensed I almost "passed". I was not a member of the ruling élite, the Imperialists, bestowing British freedom and justice on the lesser breeds, but I was not enemy, I was not hunky, one of the brutes brought on to the Prairies in carloads by Ottawa and Sifton and the CPR to make the Prairies profitable. No word hurled into the wind stung like that word. Hunky! Jesusjesus, all the tight bodies and stone faces that word made. Kike was another stinger. Catlicker was half in fun. More than anything it was the sting in the word hunky that made me question the glory, idealism, kindness, achievements and hopes of British Imperialism on the Prairies, indeed anywhere. My heroes in Canadian history were mostly French. Champlain, Frontenac, Riel. I thought Simcoe great too for outlawing slavery so early. And the Baldwins and Gourlay were okay guys. But many other British-Canadians, whose accomplishments I admired, were hard to take because of all the royalty, loyalty, mother country, empire festooning they did. Their high-blown talk made everything here less than everything there, made me and my friends inferior. We existed only for the monarch, for Britain and the Empire. I was grateful though to the Imperialists for the grand Parliament Building they caused to rise from the empty prairie to overawe the Indians, Métis and unwashed hordes from Europe. The building had wide, deep steps with short risers at the main entrance: ideal for practicing walking up and down stairs on my hands. I used the steps a lot, but never entered the building, except to climb to the dome and gawk out over the wheat fields and dusty streets of the Queen City. Inconceivable: anything going on inside that building that would be of any good to me . . . I was as Indian as an Indian that way. As hunky as a hunky. As halfbreed as a Métis.

English literature. A dumb name for what we study in school? In real life there's world literature, literature in one's mother tongue(s) and one's indigenous literature. Ignore any of the three and you end up a funny-looking animal.

My old man was never much of a tribal man. His attitude: you get along with whoever you gotta get along with. If English is the big language at forty below on the Prairies you speak English. Not many to speak Norwegian to about your freezing whatevers. That attitude: probably the attitude of the Vikings a thousand years ago. They moved into Britain, France, Ireland, Italy, Russia, Germany, Canada, and became Englishmen, Scotsmen, Frenchmen, Irishmen, Italians, Russians, Germans, Indians and Eskimos. Nobody seemed insuperably foreign to my old man. The ways of his Viking ancestors being what they were, who mightn't be a distant cousin, legitimate or illegitimate? So hello, nice day, except for the weather.

For a while in the army I was ordered about by NCOs who could only speak French joual. No problem though for the anglophone soldiers, since what we were up to in the army was so simple-minded that growls, grunts and shrugs conveyed all necessary info. Talk when we boozed and caroused together though called for more than that, so we cooked up a Prairie-Ontarian-Québec-quois joual of obscenities and blasphemies and disaffections. Okay for wartime playtime, but none of us thought we was makin' a new language for literature or scholarly dissertations.

Differences, tensions, conflicts: they have their good sides too. The Greek tragic poets discovered that long ago. One voice, one view, has its limitations. A second voice questions, challenges. Two or more voices make discoveries impossible to a lone voice. Many voices in Canada: but who listens? The English voice is more interesting when challenged by the French. But there are all those other voices too, ethnic, Indian and Eskimo, that have on their tonguetips stories, views, memories, discoveries, experiences, wonderings to challenge and expand our founding races' outlook of superiority and exclusivity.

The CBC (like the railways and the Flag and the Queen and the NHL) is a great unifying force in this country. First it was through radio, then through television as well, this bringing Canadians together all in the family. A good example: the first Canadian coast-to-coast CBC-TV network show (July 1, 1958): written by this native ethnic and hosted by René Lévesque and Joyce Davidson. Davidson now resides in the States, Lévesque is the leader and prophet of the Break-Up-Canada Movement and the CBC is uncomfortable with my scribblings these days since I am not American enough to qualify as Canadian content.

Imperialism and colonialism: matters of profit to Britain, matters of soul to Canadians.

The Empire goes, the colonies go, and Canada's left hanging on to apron strings with no "muthuh" at the other end of them. Our politicians, scholars and artists boohoo. "Muthuh! where are you?"

Psssst! she's shacked up in New York-Washington, the transplanted capital of the Anglo-Saxon world.

Ahhhh! what a relief. Dumb ducklings, unable to distinguish a lion from an eagle, we cuddle up to our new Imperial City, we cling. As long as it's big it's "muthuh". We got no other game, no other life. French or English. Tory or Grit. Federalist of separatist.

Ouch! "Literature pursued as an end, for its own sake, not for the truths of which it may be the vehicle, is a worthless affair." Scribbled by a New Yorker, name of George Strong, middle of the last century, but it comes too close to describing what is called Canlit today.

Everything's up for grabs. A nice time. A reaching-out time. Dangerous but promising. That's how it was in the early 1600s in Canada. And in the late 1700s. And in the mid-1800s. Good times. When spirits were tested.

I remember better days when the artists of the two solitudes were not alienated. (Actually there are more than two dumb solitudes in Canada, but the superior and exclusive only recognize the two.) But now one of my writing friends of Montreal says to me: "Go away, leave us alone, we want to be alone! Go away!" He says it ex cathedra, like a bishop, like a cardinal. I laugh. "Who's we?" I ask. "Us! French! Go away, you English!" My grip on reality goes totally, when I'm pushed into having to cope with those handles: English, French. So into reality I go with my friend, Marcel. We wrangle with his reality. The English to my friend includes the Scots, the Irish, the Jews, the Americans, the Eskimos, the Italians, the Germans, the Japanese, the Ukrainians, the Swiss, the Belgians, even the barbaric Scandihoovians. Yes! and the French (the lost French) outside the Province of Quebec. The French, to my friend, are the Québécois descendents of the happy 10,000 who came from France before the Fall. I quip ineptly, "Not as sexist but as exclusive as the DAR." He concedes that the Québécois, when votes are needed, might include the English, Italians, Jews, et cetera. I try to get a bench mark on whom we English, besides dividing into upper and lower classes, include and exclude. English is British but British is more than English and brothers unto death (except when they're enemies) with the Scots, Welsh, some Irish, Caribbeans, Africans, India Indians, Canadiens, and so on. And being British is a privilege and not a right. Or the other way around. Or maybe only if you're English. "Bugger your rights and privileges!" my friend says, when I manage by some verbal legerdemain to make him English and British and all that's wonderful. "Go away! We want to be alone." He is passionate now. "Québécois businessmen and workers," I ask, "they want to be locked up in your small world? They don't need maneuverability? Portability?" "We'll make arrangements with the English after we separate." "Marcel, their bad consciences keep them quiet. But if you ever move toward any likelihood of separation, and the details, they will be different beasts." "Go away!" "Marcel, come join us mongrels. We got the whole world in us! Bust out of this exclusivity-superiority bind. Too simplistic for anybody but journalists, politicians and song writers! Send word back to Pile o'Bones, Edmonton, Winnipeg, Toronto. Tell them you're coming out. The whole country's yours. Much as anybody's!" "Come out and disappear? Forget I'm French?" "I've not disappeared." "No? What's a Scandihoovian in Canada? Read the papers for a whole year. Any mention of them?" I put on my imaginary horned helmet. "Scandihoovians? Vikings? First ones here, after the Indians and Eskimos." "But no clout." "What's a clout? You can't win that game. On a continent with a quarter of a billion mongrels you think are English?" "Go away!" Marcel says. I go. Trim my flapping sail, set my warped rudder, and rejoin the mongrels. I don't scare them. They don't scare me. I think of Champlain, coming out of the Renaissance to Canada. Shakespeare is alive, Cervantes is alive, Galileo is alive. I think of him a lot, Champlain, outward bound so many ways.

Solving racism with racism? Like treating a child, howling with an earache, by beating it to death. Sure, you cure the earache.

# Canada as a Series of Contradictions

## Herschel Hardin

To get at the Canadian circumstance, and through it, to identity, and to escape from riddles with no answers, is above all to see the country in terms of its contradictions—the contending forces that underlie the character of the people. The same methodology of contradictions can also provide luminous insight into certain societies with strong common symbolism, like China and the United States, or into historical characteristics shared by a group of countries (western Europe, and so on) that lend themselves to such an approach.

The central contradiction of Chinese civilization, for example, is the one between the educated élite and the masses of the people—a contradiction rooted in the ancient circumstances of the Chinese people.

From the earliest days of settlement of the Yellow River Valley, the Han people realized that only a strong, central authority could maintain and synchronize the necessary diking and canal systems over long stretches of the river. This centralized control, in turn, was impossible without an administrative class. Chinese civilization, the unique Chinese mentality, the codes of behaviour (Confucianism, Maoism) which are characteristic of the Chinese, are the products of the contradiction between this class (mandarins, Communist Party cadres), without whose consent no dynasty could govern, and the peasantry—the mass of society—without whose consent no dynasty could survive.

One could almost say that only in terms of that fundamental age-old contradiction does Maoism in its antibureaucratic thrust, the Cultural Revolution, the particular route by which China has become a modernized mass democracy—only in those terms does any of it become

From *A Nation Unaware: The Canadian Economic Culture* (J.J. Douglas, 1974).

intelligible, do the Chinese become visible as Chinese rather than as inscrutable Europeans with yellow skins.

In the same way, not the only or the most useful, but the richest appreciation of American character comes not from celebrating or deploring Americans' legendary materialism and violence, or from observing them worshipping their myths and demonstrating their patriotism, but from exploring the contradictory phenomenon of an American irrationally, intolerantly absorbed in the myth of rational, liberal freedom.

This is the contradiction which Louis Hartz illuminated with such gusto in *The Liberal Tradition in America.* "Here is a doctrine [liberalism]," wrote Hartz, "which everywhere in the West has been a glorious symbol of individual liberty, yet in America its compulsive power has been so great that it has posed a threat to liberty itself." The mark of Hartz's originality was that he gave this "compulsive power" such bold and suggestive names that they encapsulate in a few words the particular psychic, parochial dilemma which is America—names like "colossal liberal absolutism", "the national irrational liberalism", "the grip of Locke", and the "Americanistic mechanism" of terrifying dissenters. But part and parcel of the American contradiction, with its Red scares and its absolutist intolerance in the name of freedom, is a quality of individual freedom and creative energy unknown to the rest of history, but again, an individualism and a creativity of a special kind—the American kind.

Contradictions also inform the industrial European experience—the contradictions of class. Merely to mention them is to write a footnote to Marx, to all of the European Marxists, to all the European anti-Marxists, and to all the non-Marxist, non-anti-Marxist appreciations of European class differences. Whatever the strength of class contradictions in Europe now, modern European society has evolved by the elaboration of those contradictions, and I doubt if there is any European who does not have fragments of that elaboration embedded in his psyche.

What are the basic contradictions of the Canadian experience? There are three of them: (1) French Canada as against English Canada; (2) the regions as against the federal centre; and (3) Canada as against the United States. The second one incorporates much of the first, Quebec being both the thrust of French Canada and the most centrifugal, psychically, of the regions. It is across these contradictions that Canada has defined itself.

That these three contradictions are at the centre of the Canadian experience, that they have been the forcing ground of our identity, is obvious. But Canadians have exquisite ways of missing the point.

One poignant case sticks in my mind, because it illustrates the leading Canadian contradiction at work on a man whose identity as a Canadian was still in the process of formation. It was during the St. Léonard controversy over whether there should be English-language instruction available as well. An ethnic spokesman caught in the cross-fire protested with quiet emotion to CBC Radio that his group was an innocent victim of an inexplicable quarrel, all the more innocent because they had had no ingrained hostility against the French Canadians. We're not against the French Canadians, he said. And we're not against the English Canadians. We just want to be Canadian.

It never occurred to him that having to explore this linguistic conflict, having to get behind it in order to understand it and cope with it, and in intensely passionate, practical circumstances, would give him more insight into what it meant to be a Canadian than most Canadians would gather from a lifetime. Even while he was protesting, he probably had already realized there was no total escape from the contradiction other than by leaving the country. Wasn't that why he was protesting in the first place? And after going through that experience, would he ever agree that being a Canadian and an American involved more or less the same thing?

Here is where the Canadian character is working itself out in passion, and even in blood. By contrast, the dispatch of available search parties on exotic missions into the tundra and muskeg and the land of stunted conifers, where few Canadians actually live or have visited, in search of identity, is escapist fantasy.

Canadian identity is in the guts of the physical and psychological settlement, not on the periphery of the hinterland.

On top of that familiar Canadian syndrome of "identification with the subhuman"—the northern subhuman now—and tied into it, we now perceive, also, the self-demeaning habit by which a once confident people has been conditioned to look at itself through the narrowing eyes of other peoples infected with other contradictions—to search after other peoples' kinds of mythology—which habit is the colonial mentality.

In other words, if you ask an American, or a European, or a Chinese question, you won't get a Canadian answer.

"There is no great national hero who cut down a maple tree, threw a silver dollar across the St. Lawrence and then proceeded to lead a revolution and govern the victorious nation wisely and judiciously," we are told. Nor are there any "great Canadian charters of freedom or independence expressing the collective will of the people", which we can put behind glass in our post offices or tack onto the walls of our offices and workshops, we are told. Then, when we are told that "Canadians have both thought and acted like contemporary nationalists" by throwing up tariffs and building the CPR, we still wonder why John A. Macdonald couldn't have thrown a silver dollar instead of giving away twenty-five million paper ones. The assiduously researched fact that Macdonald was an alcoholic is good stuff, but as we know in our bones, it's a poor substitute for George Washington's encounter with a cherry tree. It would never survive, if it weren't for the tariff on history.

But any Canadian substitutes for the War of Independence and the other objects in the American museum will be poor myth because they will be weak in Canadian contradictions. They will be the symbolic outcroppings and residue of nothing at all. The languishing after a common symbolism, in the way that the national mythology of Britain or China or France or the U.S.A. is common to the citizenry, is a sorrowful wild goose chase—a Canada Goose chase. It is the uncommonly Canadian, uncommon symbolism we should be trying to uncover, and it is here, because we are.

The colonial wives' tale that, being a country of immigrants, Canada is "a land with little common civilization" also misses the point—misses several points—and in the same way. It begs the question: What kind of immigrants and in what historical context? It ignores the powerful effect which indigenous influences and circumstances can have on immigrants, if the new country is politically and economically free. A spirit of independence abroad in the land is crucial if the indigenous circumstances are to have an impact.

The United States is also a country of immigrants. Yet was there any doubt, even from the earlier days of settlement before the War of

Independence, that life in America was different in kind from life in Europe, that it functioned by a different ethic and in a different spirit, quite apart from the novel economic demands of the frontier? An immigrant, from out of the class contradictions of Europe, came to America, a land of immigrants—and nothing else except the beleaguered Indians—and he was a new man almost overnight. And this new dimension which America brought out in him, and which he shared in common with other immigrants, had little to do with his own past loyalties or with shared historical experience in Europe. The American way of life was in the air of the new society, and having to breathe, he breathed it in, and breathed it in freely, without a European sack over his head—that was important to the exercise.

Nevertheless, there were scholars and commentators from "civilized" Europe who continued to see the United States as a country of immigrants with little common civilization other than economic techniques and the legal and parliamentary traditions and other cultural hand-me-downs inherited from Great Britain. James M. Minifie reminds us that in the early days of the Republic, Englishmen, when they wanted to be friendly, often expressed the view that between the two peoples there wasn't much difference—that Americans were just "trans-atlantic John Bulls"—and that they were amazed at the apoplectic reception they received. Tocqueville knew better. (In the same way, a correspondent of the *Washington Post* wrote recently that we are "undeniably similar", although "nothing annoys some Canadians more than to be told [as much] by well-meaning Americans".)

The "Canadian way of life", as seen in terms of its own contradictions rather than other peoples', is similarly different in kind from American civilization, and is roughly just as old, dating back at least to the Conquest, when French Canadians began to realize that their only chance of survival was inside a state dominated by English-speaking power and later English-speaking numbers, and when English-speaking Canadians began to realize that the French Canadians existed in a body and might even endure. Then, and ever since, that contradiction has infected everything.

Now, if you consider common civilizations in their European sense only, and look to them for national identities, you are forced to conclude that immigrants become Canadians by joining one of the two sides. But that way, in fact, they just become English Canadians or

French Canadians. It is only when they are caught up in the elaboration of the primal Canadian contradiction between the two groups that the inescapable, dense, bewildering sense of what it means to be a Canadian rather than a transplanted European, or American, hits home, as many an immigrant parent in Montreal can testify. Newcomers become transformed into natives almost overnight, and without common histories, in Canada too.

Two hundred years and more of the elaboration of a constant set of defining contradictions is not a long time as some civilizations go. But it is not a short time either. It parallels, for example, the entire duration of the industrial age, with its antecedents in the mercantile glories of England and France.

Canada is not a young country. Canada is not "a land without real history . . . rootless, cut off, out of touch, and therefore barren". Canada is not "collectively youthful". Canada is not "culturally immature". Canada is a country of immigrants only incidentally. The notion that "the Canadian reaction to life is a strictly contemporary one", that we can "escape history", not having had a continuous history which has formed our characters, holds true only outside the Canadian contradictions, which means that it doesn't hold true at all. There is a thick continuity in us, as a collectivity, which has been deeply felt when Canadians have been in an independent mood.

The more independent the mood, the greater the self-definition. In that most independent of Canadian times, the 1830s, when Canada was actually and obviously young, there were nevertheless binding psychological roots put down in the country, in Lower Canada among the French Canadians, but in English Canada as well. Since then—since the failure of the rebellions in 1837—we have been conscientious colonials. Over the years, little by little, our identity has gone begging.

But look back to the 1830s.

When Lord Durham, Canada's Tocqueville, came to the country from the outside to look at the anatomy of the anti-imperialist rebellions, he noticed immediately the "two nations warring inside the bosom of a single state". This was so peculiar, and so unlike the American experiment, that Durham's solution was to assimilate the one side—a solution which had no practical application. Being liberal and perspicacious, he was able to analyze the social forces giving definition to

Canada. But being an outsider, he was not able to identify with more than an incomplete part of them, and then only from a psychological distance.

Compare this to the appreciation of an equally articulate liberal, but one infected with the indigenous spirit—William Lyon Mackenzie. Mackenzie, as a journalist and politician living in the colony, was too closely tied to the particular circumstances of the country to mistake it for another one. His sensitivity to the reality that is Canada was so uncanny that, passionately put down on paper in the 1820s, long before even Confederation, it still, save for the details, speaks for the native soul. . . .

> If there is, *and I begin to imagine that you have some shadow of cause for saying so* (for the Canadians have been very ill used and feel it), a French Canadian party who would wish to obtain the ascendancy in Canada, for the purpose of visiting on the heads of the population of your origin and mine the sins of the old tyrannical governments of unreformed England, believe me, for I say it most sincerely, I am the last Scotsman in Upper Canada who would be their tool or their slave—but in as far as it is sought by the House of Assembly of Lower Canada to educate all and give all equal rights, why should there be two opinions?
>
> As to the friendship of Canadians of French origin towards the English, Scotch and Irish—perhaps it is less warm than I had supposed—but, be this as it may, it is us who are to blame. England conquered their country—turned their *colleges into a barrack*—kept their people in ignorance—insulted their leading men—neglected their best interests—forgot to conciliate and trust in them—preferred strangers to their language, manners and customs—*appeared to* give them popular institutions forty years ago, and now declared them virtually unfit to enjoy them!
>
> United to the States, the vast revenue raised at our seaports would go to swell the funds of congress; their southern and northern generals would be ours; their slave questions and immense territory might not add to our happiness; . . .
>
> Greatly therefore, although I admire them as a people, and I do admire their course as a nation, and glory in their success, as affording a proof of the practical utility of the representative system of government, yet do I believe that these colonies might be fully as happy separated from them; but if better measures are not taken, and a more statesmanlike policy pursued by us (by the colonists) disunion among ourselves will end only in making us conquered states, sneered at though received into the Union.

Everything is there to be wondered at—English as against French, region binding region, Canada versus the United States.

Instead of disunion among the colonies, Mackenzie recommended a "federal system" or a "federative union"—also uncannily farsighted.

Even with the cumulative insights provided by a century of federalism, nothing still has quite that lyrical sensitivity to French-Canadian grievances and, at the same time, to the dangers of unstatesmanlike disunity between the regions as against the thrust of the United States, as do the above passages. Mackenzie, though fiercely partisan in the debate between privilege and democracy, was one of the few able to perceive, and to sympathize with, both sides of the leading Canadian contradiction.

Settlement of Upper Canada west of Kingston had only really begun at the turn of the century. Mackenzie didn't arrive until 1820. The immigrant, pluralistic character of the peoples in the colony was self-evident, and celebrated often by Mackenzie. His rhapsodical account of the diversity of peoples at an election meeting in Niagara in 1824 is as delightful a description of man's variety as one could find anywhere. But taking in Canada directly, in travels, reportage and political activity, Mackenzie saw them above all as Canadians—a community with a bond, linked essentially to the other Canadians, including the French-speaking majority in Lower Canada, different from the Americans, different from the British, and as deserving of independence, as a people, as the Irish and the Poles whom he often cited as examples. Also, without *arrière-pensées,* and identifying spontaneously the way a Frenchman might identify with Joan of Arc, Mackenzie made mighty appeals to the Canadians' sense of history, although there were only twenty or thirty years of it, and although a good part of the people who responded to the appeals hadn't even been around that long, as Mackenzie hadn't either.

The argument, in Mackenzie's case, is that because he was an egalitarian liberal, and a passionate democratic rabble-rouser, he was really an American in disguise, and that the definitive Canadian character exhibited itself in the élitism and conservatism which followed the failure of the rebellions. William Kilbourn, in his biography of Mackenzie, feels obliged to give him only a discontinued tangential line on the "main graph of Canadian history".

In fact, the conservative social structure is only a skin which has bound Canada in, the way it has restricted countless other countries. When it is shed, Canada will be as different from the United States as it always has been, and will see the difference more. Similarly, the egalitarianism, the work ethic, the economic dynamism of the Republic, no longer are distinctive to the United States, and were not considered as such by Mackenzie in his own time. Had the populist, democratic impulse triumphed in Canada in the early 1830s, before disunity was upon British North American, it is just as likely as not that a Canada would be in existence today.

The proof of Mackenzie's identity is in himself. He was closely attached, intellectually and emotionally, to the British liberal reform movement and to the ideals of British justice. But when he visited Great Britain in 1832, only twelve years after he had emigrated to Canada, he was already the outsider, noticing more and more the great distance between his community and Europe. Exile in the United States, for all Mackenzie's admiration of the American yeoman, was also disillusioning.

Louis Hartz, to make a point about the absolute distinctiveness of the newly effulgent liberal America in the nineteenth century, imagines Andrew Jackson across the Atlantic, and the point is made. "Where would he have stood?" asks Hartz. "Would he have stood with Disraeli and the land, or with Cobbett and the workers, or with the petty enterprisers who scarcely had an independent leadership? The fact is, he would not have known where to stand. He would have wandered homelessly over the face of Europe, a lost giant from another world, finding parts of his personality in various places but the whole of it nowhere. Victorious in the liberal society of America, he would have been, precisely for that reason, a massive misfit in the old society of Europe."

Mackenzie was a massive misfit both in the old society and in the new, American one—and in the colonial Canada as well! Mackenzie was not an American in the wrong country. He was a Canadian at the wrong time.

English Canadians like to talk about Canada's age of innocence, meaning the whole of Canadian history, and how it was shattered by the events of October 1970. Mackenzie may have been utopian, but he never had any illusions about the innocence of his country. Creating a simulacrum of innocence is only a way colonials have of avoiding their condition.

If Canadians had an identity, then Riel and Mackenzie would be heroes, writes the poet, the idea not entering his head that they *are* heroes and that Canada does have identity, but that the colonial habit will not admit it. "America is all around us," proclaims an American immigrant, in his backward fondness for the Canadian difference, "and a psychic cartographer for this continent would place Canada somewhere around Kansas-Nebraska." Spoken like a true colonial, domiciled in post-rebellion, colonial Toronto. Mackenzie and Papineau would have scolded him into the Gulf of Mexico.

When the rebellions failed, all that indigenous self-perception—and it was just beginning—came to an end. Not the granting of self-government, nor the National Economic Policy, nor Laurier's pan-Canadianism, nor Mackenzie King's weaning of Canada from the wrinkled British imperial mother, nor French-Canadian attempts to encourage in other Canadians an equal commitment to a native outlook, nor all of the exegeses of scholars and speeches of politicians . . . none of it has freed the Canadian identity (as distinct from the French-Canadian identity alone) from its borrowed, frustrating, wrong-headed perspectives.


To explore contradictions further . . .

Contradictions, as an analytical tool, lend themselves to a dialectical appreciation of social forces, and are rich in suggestion and capable of considerable subtlety. Most important for our purposes: when contradictions are internal to a single community, they express themselves best in paradoxes, and these paradoxes are often so unique in their absurdity that if we understand how they are absurd, we understand everything.

What could be more absurd, for example, than for Americans to form super-patriotic agencies to protect liberties, but whose sole function was to suppress them? The committee to investigate unamerican activities was the most unamerican turn of all. Senator Joseph McCarthy was, at one and the same time, the least American and the most typically American of public figures. To be "born equal", as Tocqueville remarked of America, and yet to be unequally imprisoned by a "tyranny of opinion" is a paradox on the face of it.

The ordinary Chinese Communist Party cadre, not being an American (which is the best way of putting it), would probably not be able to make head nor tail of that, just as the ordinary American libertarian

activist would be altogether perplexed if confronted in his daily experience with a perfectly understandable, to the Chinese, Maoist imperative
to show initiative and flexibility—to use one's own imagination and be
responsive to the people—and yet, at the same time, to give unswerving
obedience to the correct party line. What makes such a paradoxical
lesson understandable to the Chinese, whereas liberal orthodoxy has
judged it pernicious and mind-boggling, is indigenous experience. The
contradiction is informed not just by Chairman Mao's elucidation of
the paradox, in his theoretical work on internal (non-antagonistic) contradictions, but also by practical examples and public debate at all
levels which, cumulatively, go to make up the native perspective.

Even with years, or centuries, of precedent, and intensive training,
however, the practical application of a paradox can be excruciating.
Young Communist Party cadres in China, in the late 1950s, were re-
ported to have suffered an unusual incidence of nervous breakdowns,
faced with the performance demands of the Great Leap Forward but
without either themselves or the participants in the commune system
having sufficient ideological preparation. The cadres did not have
enough sensitivity to the paradoxical requirements expected of them.

The United States, based on individual liberty but restricting that
liberty with an excessive ideological conformism, also suffers from a
malaise of paradox, which has broken out in violent, brutal pathological
symptoms, aside from the scandal of racism which is a chronic betrayal
of that liberty.

And so is Canada continually bewildered by its own paradoxical
character.

Salvador de Madariaga observed in *Spain: A Modern History* that
Catalonia, being the most separatist (and in that sense, the most disloyal) of provinces, was also the most characteristically Spanish (and in
that sense, the most loyal) of the provinces, by so being. So he saw
nothing untoward about a strong central power in Madrid keeping
Catalonia in check, and nothing regressive, either, about Catalonia
checking that central power with its own autonomous thrust whenever
it could. Madariaga's paradoxical definition of Catalan "nationalism" is
totally absurd, and, to a Canadian, perfectly reasonable.

Madariaga, in turn, would have likely recognized as familiar Daniel
Johnson's contention that the only way to save Canada was to give the
Quebec government control over all decisions affecting the social,

economic and cultural life of the people; in other words, the only way to save Canada was effectively to eliminate it. Jean-Jacques Bertrand, when he was prime minister of Quebec, doggedly advocated the same kind of autonomy. Also, he had "separatists" (at least, ultra-nationalists) in his cabinet, and he exclaimed at a particularly sensitive moment in federal-provincial relations that Canada was "the happiest land in the world".

W.A.C. Bennett, at the end of an era of rapid aggrandizement of provincial power—late 1969—argued, as premier of British Columbia, that the federal government was too strong relative to the regions, and that was why Canada was weak. The implication was that if the regions were given more power, there would be less regional alienation and hence more national loyalty. Weaken the weak centre so that the excessively strong centre will hold! Madariaga would have understood.

Although the *raison d'être* of the Parti Québécois is *indépendance*—at least that—Bennett, at the time, told western Canadians that René Lévesque was not a separatist, but a nationalist, like all Québécois, and that the federal government, which at that period was trying to bring itself closer to Quebeckers, was destroying Confederation, and therefore itself, by doing so. Two inferences can be drawn from Bennett's perceptions: one, that Lévesque, the separatist, was playing the Canadian game and was one of the few, along with Bennett, playing it fairly; and two, that the federal government is more representative when it represents less.

W.A.C. Bennett considers himself a Canadian patriot, and while an Englishman or a Peruvian or a parochial misfit in Toronto might find that astounding, what citizen informed by the Canadian paradox can deny it?

The contradiction is such that Lévesque is in fact a Canadian benefactor without intending to be one. Many French Canadians complain bitterly that the French fact in Canada was hardly recognized until the movement for more provincial autonomy, and then Quebec separatism, grew—which is finally, belatedly, to realize that history is the product of broad social forces rather than of abstract judgements about what is fair and what isn't. That, in any case, is how the Canadian dialectic works.

By the strange laws of Canadian federalism, a man campaigning among French Canadians in Quebec may end up having an equal in-

fluence on English Canadians outside Quebec, and by forcing an opening up of the federation to French Canadians—a policy which he considers a trap—may in the long run undercut his own movement.

Every political move taken by René Lévesque has within it the
possibility that it will have an equal and opposite reaction. On the other
hand, and from the opposite direction, the federal government, attempting to head off separatism, allocates large sums of money for
regional development programs in eastern Quebec, and strengthens the
textile quota to protect the province's textile industry, and builds an
airport, and hands out subsidies, even for the Montreal region, to help
reinforce Quebec's economy, which, if fully successful, will give
Quebec the economic infrastructure and entrepreneurial cadres necessary to make independence work in practice.

The two forces in the contradiction reinforce their opposites while
reinforcing themselves. Canadian politics is the art of suffering gladly a
horrible ambiguity in one's own actions. There is no way to overcome
this and to get a grip on affairs by establishing a lineal cause and effect,
because contradictions are irrational. They are fast in the blindness of
history. Eventually the man of action just gets tired of trying to sort
things out—of trying to straddle the contradiction from both sides,
which would paralyze him—and inserts himself into the contradiction in
a certain direction, dictated by his own past, and keeps on going.

Perhaps this is why so many Canadians—federalists and separatists—
find Claude Ryan's stance in *Le Devoir* so maddening and ambiguous,
and why it *is* so maddening and ambiguous. Ryan's role, as an analyst
of the Canadian contradiction, is to make rational sense out of the
irrational meeting of historical forces, which is impossible, and which
leads his analysis to go on and on, growing increasingly tortuous and
refined, in a vain attempt to tie the contradiction down. But Ryan's
contribution is absolutely essential. Only through direct analysis does
a reader's appreciation of the contradiction, by indirection, grow in
sensitivity.

Following the Quebec election in 1970, a commentator on CBC
English-language radio wondered how Ryan, an avowed "federalist" as
he described him, and as he was then, could write so passionately of the
political virtues of René Lévesque, and of the blow to Quebec of Lévesque's failure to win a seat. That was absurd, said the commentator.
If you're a federalist, surely you want a man like Lévesque to lose. Why
doesn't Ryan make up his mind?

The observation that Ryan's position was absurd was correct but irrelevant. Should French Canadians "concentrate on the territory of Quebec" or should they "take Canada in its entirety?" asked Pierre Elliott Trudeau. And the collectivity in Quebec, by producing a Trudeau and a Lévesque in the same generation, answered yes to both questions, and is satisfied by neither answer. Quebec, like Catalonia in Spain, has the whole of the contradiction within itself.

As if that weren't enough, chance arranged it so that Trudeau, the champion of federalism, was formed inside the Quebec political hothouse, and fought the battle against Duplessis and centralism with autonomous instruments like *Cité Libre*, whereas Lévesque, the saint of separatism, came to be a public figure through Radio-Canada which, as one of the most distinctive and creative products of federalism, enabled him to animate French-Canadian society and broaden its viewpoint, at a time when the provincial government had drawn down the blinds.

The Canadian contradiction suggests another paradox: that the greatest Canadian nationalists are also the greatest internationalists. The more nationalist one is, the more one becomes involved in the phenomenon of cultural dualism, and, in turn, the greater the check on chauvinism and ethnocentric arrogance.

This paradox knows no bounds. The most militant Canadian nationalists, for the most part English-speaking, are sensitive to the ethnocentric blindness of the United States because, among other things, they have been taught to be sensitive by French Canada's defiance of a similar sort of arrogance in their English-speaking community. And they are so sensitive to French Canada's defiance that, militant nationalists and all, a good number of them cannot bring themselves to critically oppose the separatist movement, which subverts their nationalism. They are called chauvinists for their troubles.

Similarly, when an English Canadian in an English-speaking city wishes his French-Canadian colleagues a happy Saint Jean-Baptiste June 24, but absent-mindedly, out of habit, goes through July 1 like any other day off, he is acting out a covert nationalist ritual. Canadians do not assert their nationalism by looking for it, as the historian claims. They assert it by not finding it.

These contradictions across which a society defines itself are not solved, and are resolved only in some unimaginable utopia. The tension and conflict arising out of Canadian dualism, or out of Canadian regionalism, will not be settled, no matter how ingenious new constitutional formulas might be. If they were, Canada would no longer exist. It would be robbed of its dynamic.

Contradictions are not resolved, they are only elaborated on. And when the elaboration occurs on a large scale, or involves important social forces, it constitutes civilization.

In China, under the Empire, the civilization was codified as Confucianism. Now the code is Maoism. In both cases, a dense and complex social fabric has been maintained, involving a unique combination of interpersonal relationships, with an unmistakable character in the government and the arts of the people. The same can be said, and is said, of "American civilization" or the "American way of life", and of "European civilization" and "French civilization" and so on. Still, to the ear, "Canadian civilization" sounds a bit strange. Does the Canadian experience deserve it?

The question can be put another way: Does Canadian civilization represent a significantly instructive experiment in social relationships, as Maoism and American liberalism certainly do in their different ways, although Americans are blind to the first and the Chinese to the second?

On that scale, the coming together in one state of at least two ethnically contrary "nations", and maybe others if the native peoples assert themselves, and the simultaneous overlapping and coming together of powerful regionalisms, *has* been the making of a civilization in the commonly understood sense of the word.

It is because Canadian civilization is so vulnerable, because every once in a while it seems to be coming apart at the seams under the pressure of centrifugal forces, that it has been so fruitful, and has slowly developed a subterranean strength. Nothing has added to that strength, and to that vulnerability, more than the separatist movement, and English Canada's facing up to the possibility it symbolizes, and the attempts of René Lévesque and others to explain to English Canadians the logic behind the possibility.

Our historic rebellions, and our terrorism, and our bizarre, passionate regional movements taken into account, the greatest argument against describing the Canadian system as "dull, grey federalism" is Lévesque himself. If Quebec were a North American Switzerland, or a Norway—a small nation of common values, in the words of a citation in *Option Québec*—there would be no René Lévesque with his sharp relentless insights into the contradictions between peoples, only a slightly eccentric, chain-smoking ambassador amusing his routinized counterparts with his misplaced enthusiasm.

The more one opens one's eyes, the more "the relatively stable, satisfied societies of squares"—an outsider's recent description of federal peoples—fits Swiss federalism, and West German federalism, and even Australian federalism, but the less it fits exasperating Canada, where the contradictions stretch over geographic and cultural chasms. And, after all, hasn't Lévesque himself called Canadian federalism a madhouse?

(Of course, if you have a civilization, you also have to have barbarians. To the ancient Chinese, anybody who did not belong to the Empire was a barbarian, no matter how knowledgeable and gentle he was, whereas presumably somebody, no matter how cruel, who wanted to reform or simply take over the Empire—nobody thought of changing it—was civilized. To the Americans, unamericans are beyond the pale, and, in George Kennan's words, because of [Americans'] "inveterate tendency to judge others by the extent to which they contrive to be like ourselves", Americans have turned up just about as many barbarians in the world as the Chinese. As with the Chinese, the alien becomes identified with the unintelligible. To the archetypal Canadian, schooled by his country's dualism to beware of ethnocentric arrogance, the lack of similar sensitivity by the Americans or Chinese or anybody else, including his own countrymen, is barbarian, and is seen to have barbarous consequences, witness the rampage of the "absolute moral ethos" of Americanism in Vietnam. Grown men and women who wander around the Arctic looking for a national identity are barbarians. And Canadians who categorize other people as barbarians may well be barbarians.)

That is the political dimension. Canadian civilization, like the Chinese and the American, as I am going to argue, has also produced by the force of its contradictions a distinctive economic culture and a distinctive artistic culture—a singular Canadian way of life—which has been only imperfectly perceived, or hardly noticed at all, and has often as not been scorned by Canadians themselves, because of their heretofore dogged colonial mentality.

The colonial mentality aside, there is the inescapable feeling that Canada is an artificial creature. If the United States did not exist, neither would Canada, because there would be no external threat to keep the diverse regions, particularly Quebec, inside Confederation. Canada is a marriage of convenience rather than of love. Manifest Destiny was the external threat which bound the parties into Confederation in the first place, and made loyal British subjects out of the French-Canadian élite even before that, and it is still invoked by English-Canadian and French-Canadian federalists alike when they want to underscore the perils of Quebec independence.

Unlike the United States, which was "born equal"—freely born into its own world without a constricting legacy—Canadian civilization, like the Chinese Empire in its formative days, is a civilization of neccessity. The exigencies of the Yellow River forced on the Chinese the central administration of early Empire, from which everything else followed. The United States is our Yellow River.

Now, there are two ways of reflecting on that characteristic. Habitually, we have been negative. Canada is a defensive reaction against the United States, simply "the losing side of the American revolution" and nothing else, the "counter-revolution" school has told us; Canada is cursed with a hopeless, narrow-minded longing for an unamerican identity. Most Canadians have probably sometime in their lives confessed as much to themselves. Or, as the separatists maintain, Canada is an unnatural alliance; English Canadians have everything in common with Americans and very little in common with French Canadians; Canada is an impossibility, a common market against nature. Again, not just among French Canadians, but among all of us, the urge to escape our maddening contradictions, to be reborn free, is always just under our skin. The mythical, spontaneous, dynamic, liberating phenomenon of the United States remains in sight, on the other side of the 49th parallel, throwing into the soul of Canadians a chronic anguish.

But civilizations born without restraints—and there may be only one, the United States—have their own terrible flaw. Without the experience of accommodating antagonistic classes and cultural assumptions, they never rise above shallowness. They never "come of age". They suffer fatally, as Louis Hartz put it, from "atrophy of the philosophic impulse". White Americans are hopeless romantics. When their romanticism has been challenged by realists at home and abroad, like the American blacks, or the native peoples, or the Vietnamese, they have turned on them with a violent, absolutist vengeance, which is the underside of romanticism.

That is the other way of looking at it. There is a certain profundity of feeling and experience in the Canadian personality which is absent in America. The reflective citizen whose identity, in the collectivity, has been stretched to the breaking point by the play of contradictions, may come out of that uncertainty in an angry despair and start planting bombs in mailboxes or shouting at public meetings, "No French spoken here!"; but he also may come out of it powerfully liberated by an understanding denied to his American brother. Civilizations of necessity can also be great and liberating civilizations.

Either way, there's no guarantee that any particular civilization will endure. Canadian civilization can bog down in its own machinery just as surely as Imperial China fell over into anarchy, with only a slight European push, because of the encrusted, corrupt, absolutist rigidities of an aging Confucianism; or as America may well destroy itself by the compulsive, dogmatic pursuit of profit and property.

Canadians, in fact, almost always feel bogged down, as a matter of course. It's part of our civilized climate. It's the onerous burden of civilization upon us. Most of the weight is made up of discarded position papers from federal-provincial conferences, where the close, grating, bureaucratic, polite segment of elaboration usually takes place and, if agreement is reached, is codified. Protest and despair are common. A lead article in *Saturday Night* in 1970 angrily asked, "Can we go on arguing interminably about Dominion-provincial relationships and the constitution affecting them while cities become polluted, housing decays, trade opportunities are lost and the brain drain to the United States continues?" Their conclusion was that we can not. To Jacques Parizeau, Canadian federalism is so loaded down with federal-provincial committees (150 of them), with duplicated services (billions of dollars worth), and with tangled lines of responsibility, that the whole system will sink of its own weight, taking us down with it. "A sterile and tiresome game", is how Claude Ryan describes it. "An outdated, creaky, inefficient remnant of a nineteenth century colonial experiment . . . one of the most obsolete [systems] in the whole civilized world," says René Lévesque. And the fact is that civilizations have been known to sink into a morass of their own rules.

Canadian civilization may not only bog down in the centre, it may also unravel at the edges. Forced by regional pressures, particularly the pressure of separatism in Quebec, to create jobs and eliminate disparities, Ottawa has subsidized the intrusion of the American economy, which itself is undermining the civilization. Canada takes one contradiction in its teeth but has its tail bitten off by another. After the tail comes the body.

Or a civilization can simply lose its ideological steam, can simply have run its course; and unable to overcome a profound malaise in a vital part, it deteriorates, often with much bloodshed.

The key may be to let the elaboration of contradictions go on with the maximum of political freedom even if it means that the contradictions may be pulled apart.

Despite the War Measures Act, and not discounting less obvious curbs on free expression and politics, Canadian civilization does afford about as open an elaboration of contradictions as one could hope to find anywhere in history, not because Canadians are particularly generous or farsighted, but because of their unique historical circumstances. Michel Brunet is right when he says that the English in Canada should be credited only with realism, not with generosity, because they didn't attempt to suppress the French, although what he doesn't say is that realism in itself is a great virtue. The federalism which René Lévesque attacks is also the federalism which enables him to attack it with such potency, by leaving him a special geographical area to build his appeal on and by allowing, or encouraging, in that area an economic achievement like Hydro-Québec—advantages which are denied dissenters in the United States, or parties of class in Europe like the communist parties of France and Italy. And again, it is not because of English-Canadian generosity, but because of the inevitable way Canada was put together.

Still, there are incidents whose realism and humanity are so acute that the adjective "civilized" applies to them in its universal sense. And the fact that nobody wonders at them, that nobody cries out "Isn't that remarkable!" suggests that, although such incidents may be exceptional, Canadian civilization is an historical marvel.

To pick only one example among many: early in 1968, more than two years before the Parti Québécois's electoral inroads, the *Star Weekly* published a special section called "The View from Quebec", including an article by René Lévesque, "Why I believe a free Quebec is the best thing for you, too", and one about the young separatist élite, "We are fighting . . . fighting for a free Quebec!" The idea, according to the preface, was to present "the aims and aspirations of the people of

French Canada . . . set down in their own words". The total effect was an eloquent argument for separatism. But the *Toronto Star* organization has been outspokenly committed to federalism and national unity.

What it comes down to is that a group of people committed to a collectivity—and love of country is no lighthearted whim—allows another group passionately committed to destroying that collectivity to present that commitment in the best possible light. *Le Devoir* is another example of such openness, from the direction of French-Canadian nationalism. Here the paradox ceases to be mundane. It becomes wondrous.

A stranger coming to Canada, without any previous clues as to what kind of civilization it is, would likely be perplexed at finding citizens with a profound love of country who, at the same time, showed a natural sympathy for the man and the party who were intent on destroying that country. He would be even more puzzled that the apparent inconsistency of such contradictory feelings goes almost unnoticed by Canadians themselves. Trying somehow to make sense out of it all, he might also perceive, indirectly, that if Quebec decided to separate from Canada, *and if the rest of the country let it go peacefully,* it would be the greatest moment in the history of Canadian civilization. It would be. And, of course, also the most tragic.

# The Sweet Gift of Governing Oneself, or True Versus False Federalism

George Woodcock

It is vital for the future of Canada, if we wish it to have a future, to make a practical reality of the distinction between unity and uniformity, between unity and centralization. Canada is an unbroken geographical mass; it is united by a history based on a community of interests that goes back to 1812 and perhaps to earlier times. But it has never been uniform and never can be, for the regional variation which place and tradition both foster are by no means restricted to differences between those who speak English and those who speak French. And any centralized government of such a country will fail inevitably to overcome the problems—which are also the advantages—of distance and difference.

Most of our present political troubles, I am convinced, spring from a failure on the part of recent federal governments to recognize these simple but dominant facts. "Federal" has mistakenly been regarded as synonymous with "central". The attempt has been made to turn Canada into a nation-state, and a vast apparatus of over-government has been buttressed by the flimsy scaffolding of symbolic politics.

To quote the most agonizing example of symbolic politics, the Liberals imagined that if they decreed the use of two languages in the civil service and on the labels of soup tins, by some magic Québécois grievances would vanish away. In fact, the bilingualism programme has been an expensive failure, partly because of resistance by those individuals on whom it was forced as a condition of employment or promotion, but mainly because on the one hand the francophones saw through the transparent tokenism of the scheme, and on the other hand the anglophones, particularly in the west, were angered at the total irrelevance of the programme to their own problems.

Nobody paused, before this costly exercise in futility was put into operation, to consider that Switzerland has managed for centuries without the French-speaking or Italian-speaking cantons, or even the Romansch-speaking communes, being forced into any greater use of German than their inhabitants voluntarily desired; yet Swiss unity was not endangered. Nobody paused either to consider what actual utility might lie, for example, in a French-speaking television station in Vancouver, where only a minute fraction of the population, a fraction smaller than the German-speakers, or the Chinese-speakers, or the Dutch-speakers, has French for a first language. The establishment of the station was in fact an entirely symbolic gesture, and a false one, since it was based on the untenable assumption that only English-speakers and French-speakers had contributed to creating the Canada we know. Even in politics, that art of hollow men, symbols that have no relation to locally apprehensible realities are false and perilous.

I say all this as a functionally but voluntarily bilingual person, good enough as a translator from the French to pass without criticism if without great praise. I believe it is good for people to speak two languages, and preferably more, so that they can escape from the constricting duality (inherited from the days of the Norman conquest of England) of French-English; but I do not believe such learning should or can be forced upon them. I do, on the other hand, believe that there has never been any lack of willingness in either of the linguistic regions of Canada to learn about each other. Only the facilities have not been available, and I am sure that the government might have achieved far more towards mutual understanding if it had spent the money wasted in the moribund bilingualism programme on more effective teaching of second and third languages in the schools, on subsidizing large-scale translation of Quebec books into English and vice versa, and on encouraging exchanges of material between anglophone and francophone newspapers and periodicals. Such means would have brought far more positive results than can be gained from being able to buy a stamp in English in Montreal or to talk to a French-speaking receptionist in a Vancouver government office. The image of the poor monolingual Québécois stranded in Prince Rupert, with which the defenders of the bilingualism programme have tried to wring our hearts, is an insult to francophone and anglophone intelligences alike. Most people who travel are on the lookout for diversion which is also diversity, and a little linguistic difficulty gains added piquancy if it happens to be in one's own country. (Why go to China when you can be misunderstood in Rivière du Loup or in Biggar, Saskatchewan?) If people are not prepared for this kind of small-scale adventure, then they are pretty obviously stay-at-homes by nature.

The crucial difference between *encouragement* and *insistence* that emerges from an examination of the collapsing bilingualism programme parallels the difference between decentralized and participatory administration and centralized authority. Centralized authority is by its very nature insensitive to local needs, to local desires, to local prejudices. (And do not let us entirely condemn prejudice; it can sometimes denote a necessary intensity of passion and loyalty as it did in great social critics like William Cobbett and Pierre-Joseph Proudhon.) Politicians, especially when they isolate themselves from the realities of the regions of Canada (even the regions that elect them) in the isolation of an artificial capital like Ottawa, become addicted to abstract plans that are only loosely related to actuality, and that tend to eliminate the local and the regional, which in any case are regarded as inconvenient by the bureaucrats with their passion for the uniform, numbered, docketed and faceless man.

A conflict between local and central forms of government is almost inevitable given the political form which Canada has acquired as a result of the British North America Act. Canada was created a confederation, but the fact that residual areas of authority were left in the hands of the federal government has meant that, with the development of new facets of governmental concern in a technologically burgeoning society, Ottawa has acquired by default powers which were never contemplated by the Fathers of Confederation. When the government has fallen into the hands of Gallicist politicians, passionately devoted to the Jacobin concept of the nation-state, like Trudeau and his associates, these recently acquired powers have been used to create an imposed unity which is quite different from the natural and voluntary unity of a true confederation.

It is this attempt at increased centralization, this imposition of artificial unities, this effort to create a nation-state where no nation-state was ever intended, that is a major cause of the disintegrative tendencies so evident in Canada today. A centrifugal impulse is the inevitable reaction to excessive centralization, and the larger the country geographically, and the more diverse its cultures, the greater that impulse will be. We have been suffering in Canada for a decade or more from an excess of central government. Only recently a Canadian journalist who had been working in Europe remarked to me how much overgoverned, even in comparison with European countries, he found Canada on returning after several years. Many of us, perhaps most of us, have been unaware in a conscious way of the steady and cumulative growth of the central power in Canada, but we have nevertheless been aware of it on the levels where frustration builds, and there is no doubt at all in my mind that the Quebec election, and the consequent manifestations of separatist feeling in the west, were signs that the Canadian political structure had become so heavy and rigid that an explosion of some kind was inevitable. But if anyone must be held responsible for the victory of the Parti Québécois and for the disaffection of the west, it is not René Lévesque or his petty imitators who are creating secessionist groups in Alberta and British Columbia; it is Pierre Trudeau and his ministers, who have made such reactions inevitable by their attempts to transform the federalism they so demonstratively embrace into its opposite, a deadeningly monolithic society. If any real plot against Canadian federalism is on foot, we must seek out the conspirators at the cabinet table.

If such a policy of centralizing power prevails in Ottawa, we can give up any hope of reasserting true Canadian unity. The departure of Quebec will move out of possibility into inevitability, and the remainder of Canada will be riven by the attempt of Ontario to retain its ascendancy in the rump of a land. By the end of the century the fragments of Canada, even if they remain nominally independent, will probably have negotiated customs unions with the United States which will mean that we shall become *de facto* Americans without the privileges that accrue from citizenship. Manifest Destiny will have triumphed after all, and the early years of the third millenium will see the political absorption of Canada. The ghosts of Brock and de Salsberry and Tecumseh will turn away from us in shame and in reproach.

That is the scenario of probable events if the attempt continues to weld Canada into a tightly knit nation-state. But such an attempt is in fact a denial of the very basis on which Confederation was achieved, and it is a denial also of the whole concept of a confederal country which Canadian history sanctifies and which Canadian geography demands. Canadians did not come together in an imposed unity, except in so far as they recognized that unity was necessary to counter the growing threat from south of the border. They came together voluntarily as a group of autonomous political entities, the responsibly governed colonies of British North America. Implicit in this original contract was the assumption that those who came together of their own free will could part of their own free will, so that there is no moral or historical justification for preventing the Québécois from leaving Canada if they wish to do so. (All we can do is persuade them that Canada is too good to leave.) The agreement worked out with Riel's Provisional Government for the accession of the Red River colony, and the terms under which British Columbia entered Confederation in 1871 clearly showed that in these cases also the peoples concerned were joining a federal system and not submitting their liberties to the dictates of a nation-state; they were entering a confederation of free and equal units, and contained in this fact was the implication that they were free to depart; British Columbia indeed came very near to seceding during the 1870s.

True confederations are not really held together by constitutions, even if such exist, but by the common interest that makes participation in them more attractive to the constituent groups than independent existence as mini-nations. In this way, confederations are the most promising political form for the modern world. The nation-state, which developed in eighteenth- and nineteenth-century Europe, has been rendered obsolete by changes in military technology, and it was never in any case workable in countries as large as Canada, as is demonstrated by the perpetual failure of Russia as a Tsarist and later as a Bolshevik nation-state to achieve either social harmony or economic viability. Nowadays even the nation-states that to some degree succeeded in the past, like France and Britain, are riven by regional strife and are being forced along the way to some kind of confederation.

Here perhaps a little re-establishment of right definitions is needed. Trudeau and his associates have completely and deliberately misused the word "federalism" until it has become a synonym for *centralism;* their talk of a *strong* federal government is a contradiction in terms, for a true federal system is one in which strength lies in the regions (as it lies in the cantons of Switzerland) and is *delegated* from the regions to the centre, whose function is that of co-ordinating common interests and administering those very few categories that cannot be handled locally, such as foreign relations, Canada-wide transport and communications, national resources that are of general Canadian importance, and currency. (I am assuming that a truly federal country would abandon the nation-state's obsession with the tokens of military glory and declare neutrality a central principle.)

Now it is here, it seems to me, that Canada has not only the means of solving her own ills, but also the means for creating an exemplary model of the world's political future, if the world, like Canada, hopes to survive. It is obvious that Quebec can be retained only if the Canadian constitution is radically reconstructed in such a way that it becomes a confederation in fact if not in name. In such an event the principle of association of which the francophone separatists talk would be applied not merely between Quebec and English-speaking Canada, but between all the Canadian regions, between all Canadian provinces, between all Canadian municipalities. The strengthening of unity would demand far greater direct participation of citizens in the administration of their lives, and consequently the municipality would have (like the Swiss commune) to take over everything of merely local concern, with ward councils and even block committees looking after matters of very limited interest. From the municipalities the leap might be to area boards, and then to the provincial administrations. But even here there is the possibility of mini-confederations, like the Atlantic Provinces grouped together or the three Prairie Provinces, representing clearly defined geographical regions and perhaps intervening as another level of responsibility before one reaches the central government, which would become little more than an elaborate co-ordinating committee of the regions and provinces, and which would decide on matters of general Canadian concern with as much modesty as the federal governing council of the Swiss Confederation, the name of whose president is almost unknown in his own country, mainly because the power he wields, and the prestige he exacts as a consequence, is very slight.

For such a system, a model for the future, Canada is peculiarly suited not only historically, having been created as a confederation (the "Dominion" was a titular afterthought), but also geographically, since such a large area can only be effectively administered when the greater share of administration and therefore of authority is left in the regions. Finally, it is really the only hope of retaining our unity, since the strong central government which the Liberals have so industriously sought to impose upon us can do nothing but alienate not only the Québécois, but also the people of every Canadian periphery, from British Columbia to Newfoundland and north to the Arctic Sea. The best and the sweetest thing in life is to govern oneself to the utmost degree of possibility. Make Canadians that gift, relieve them of the burden of excessive external government they are forced to bear today, loosen up the centre, and they will no longer think of living apart, but will settle down to enjoy their diversity and in the process to create a working confederation that could be the model of the world's future.

# The French Fact in Alberta

Louis Desrochers

Let me attempt to correct an impression held by many about Alberta and the French-English issue. It is often alleged that this province is the stronghold of anti-French feeling in Canada. I do not agree and I propose to tell you why.

I admit that there *is* anti-French feeling in this province, but in my view it is not any more intense or pervasive than in other parts of English-speaking Canada—or some of the English-speaking sections of the island of Montreal for that matter.

Indeed, there has developed here, as in other parts of Canada, a growing acceptance of the French fact. It has not grown with spontaneous enthusiasm. It has grown soberly out of the realization that assimilation has not, does not and will not solve the French-English problems. Canada does not appear to want a Belgian-type solution of hermetically-sealed cultural regions which would require me, for example, to move to Quebec in order to remain what I am. Accordingly, English-speaking Canada has allowed an accommodation to take place gradually over the past two to three decades. This phenomenon has taken place in this province also.

This growing accommodation has been facilitated by three factors. In the first place, the religious overtones which coloured the French-English issue of yesteryear have been virtually eliminated. In the second place, the decline of the melting pot theory in the U.S. coupled with the rise of multiculturalism in this country has rendered more acceptable a heterogeneous society in our midst. In the third place, the younger elements in our Alberta society appear to be more sympathetic to the French language.

As a result of this climate, we have witnessed some significant developments in the field of education in French in Alberta schools during the past two decades. Not long ago, education in French was virtually outlawed and to get it, one had to attend unsubsidized private schools which offered programmes adapted from Quebec or Ontario—of all places! There was an atmosphere of tension between French-speaking parents and educational authorities. Parents whose maternal tongue was not French, such as our distinguished speaker of the Legislative Assembly, had to conduct heroic campaigns in order to enroll their children in the bilingual programme then available.

That atmosphere no longer exists. The School Act has been amended. The Department of Education has commenced the work of establishing special programmes and, I am sure, will continue its work diligently. Where possible, students enrolled in what we call the bilingual programme are grouped more than in the past. In Edmonton there are, in addition to bilingual classes in both separate and public schools, two elementary schools and one secondary school reserved exclusively for those programmes and in which many English-speaking families enroll their children. Steps are being taken to increase and improve the French components of this curriculum all the time.

At the post-secondary level, The University of Alberta has its special bilingual programme of undergraduate studies in arts, science and education at the Collège Universitaire St. Jean. When I was on that campus nearly thirty years ago, parents and teachers paid for our education and there were only about a dozen students enrolled at the post-secondary level. Now, there are approximately 175 students in the counterpart programme (I am confident that this number will soon increase significantly) and they enjoy all the benefits of governmental support for studies in higher education. The institution is fully funded.

School board officials, teachers, university professors and administrators, officials of the Department of Education, the Department of Advanced Education, the Department of Culture as well as members of the two political parties which have conducted the affairs of this province during the past two decades have all played significant roles in the changes I have outlined. The French-speaking community may have prodded here and there but the changes were effected for its benefit and for the benefit of all those who wanted more French by English-speaking Albertans. All is not perfect by any means, but I am confident that improvements will continue to take place in an atmosphere of understanding and even magnanimity.

My perception of Alberta's reaction to the Official Languages Act of Canada is briefly this. Albertans, more than others, bemoan the fact that Ottawa officialdom does not appear to understand them and yet they speak the language predominately used by Ottawa officialdom. Albertans can and do understand that a government whose officials cannot effectively speak to or understand millions of its citizens in their language is a government with very questionable legitimacy. Accordingly, Albertans by and large accept the principle of that legislation and want to see the federal civil service able to serve the two language groups effectively.

On the other hand, implementation of some of the bilingualism programmes has given rise to adverse reaction. Too little preparatory work was done here and "national" formulas were introduced without respect for certain regional idiosyncrasies. My favourite example of unnecessary provocation is the official sign at the entrance of Jasper National Park. It used to read: "Jasper National Park". It now reads: "Parc National de Jasper National Park". While this form may be linguistically correct and cheaper because the name "Jasper" serves both languages, it has the great disadvantage of appearing to place the French language in a supreme or first position on a sign which is in a predominantly English-speaking area. It seems to me that the same national objective could have been achieved by the use of a sign which would have featured both languages but which would not *appear* to put French in the first place. It is a succession of these instances which has given rise to the reaction of some who say that "they don't want French to be rammed down their throats".

In addition, some public figures, pundits and syndicated columnists featured in English Canada's print media have vented their negative reactions with considerable effectiveness. Yet, despite that provocation, popular reaction has been subdued. Most of our political leaders at all levels have played a very responsible role and have helped their fellow citizens adapt to what has been in this area a very significant departure from the old accepted image of Canada.

As a French-speaking Canadian, I feel very much at home in the climate I have briefly sketched. The complex mentality of many French Canadians and conditions which with urbanization caused such alarming losses in French groups outside of Quebec during the last three decades have given way to an acceptance of the French fact and to conditions which should arrest these losses. We are quite rapidly developing the programmes which will allow those of us who wish to remain and those of us who wish to become French-speaking to do so more effectively. Many old hang-ups about the province of Quebec have been dispelled and this significant development has stimulated greater cultural exchanges across the country. The electronic media help to expose us to some of French Canada's prolific cultural output and, at times, contribute to it. In short, I feel we now have the elements with which to expose our children to the French language and French-Canadian culture in this area as never before.

This is how I see the French-English issue in Alberta, in a province that is alleged—wrongly—to be a stronghold of anti-French feeling in Canada.

# O Canada!

## Robin Skelton

In England I was a Yorkshireman; in Canada I am a Victorian. I visit the
country east of the Rockies as once I visited that south of the Humber,
an amiable cousin, eager to please and be pleased, but firmly assured of
the superiority of his own place. Others, I discover, share this attitude.
Canadians are passionate provincials devoted to local mythologies. The
grass in one's neighbour's garden is never so green as one's own, and,
though his apple tree may be larger and stronger and more fruitful, it is,
by being elsewhere, so much less an apple tree. The federal government
is everywhere suspect. It is composed of placeless people, people who
have never heard of the day the moose broke into the grocery, and who
are unaware that the only way to balance the national economy is to
have a good long talk with Joe.

This I relish, as I also relish the determined and perpetually frus-
trated attempts of Canadians to think or feel otherwise. I delight in the
frenzied and inchoate discussions in the newspapers and on the CBC
about where "Canada" is going, and what "Canada" is, and why "Confederation" must be preserved, and the importance of "Canadian Art"
and "Canadian Poetry" and even "The Canadian Way of Life". A country so seriously, and so comically, devoted to the discovery of its own
identity is my kind of country. I find myself mentally leaping into the
TV screen and shouting, "We are a speculation, a hope, a myth, a
figment, a riddle, a glory!" I rejoice in the muddled, informal, even
amateurish elements of Canadian life. The most elegant Receptions, the
most Official Occasions, have, like English cricket matches, an invari-
able concomitant of the approximate and impromptu. I rejoice in the

absurdity of the liquor laws, in the parish-pump deviousness of provincial politics, and in the serious way in which the clown Diefenbaker and the harlequin Trudeau cavort, self-mockingly, on the platform of our inattention. I like the boosters. I like the debunkers of the boosters. Pierre Berton is as preposterous a recreation of H.L. Mencken as are the Toronto Littérateurs of Mrs. Leo Hunter. I love books about being Canadian. I love the sound of "O Canada". I love that flag—my God, how I love that flag! I am a village boy, and a poet, and I feed upon the local, the absurd and the endearing. There is something magnificent about it all, something which Stephen Leacock knew and which Don Messer's Jubilee, for all the critics may say, dimly reflects. We may adopt rigorous intellectual standards; we may point, with every kind of justification, to the achievements of the National Film Board and the astonishing breadth of vision of the Canada Council; we may even announce the presence in Toronto or Vancouver of a cultural avant-garde, but always, finally, *entre nous,* we indulge in self-deflation and admit that we are natural citizens of Mariposa. Our satirical attacks upon the follies of our society are as clever and as delightedly malicious as one may find anywhere on the globe, for we thrive upon comedy, passion and dissent, yet, watching those television satirists and reading those excoriating columns in the papers, do I not detect a touch of self-mockery? Our critics are always happy to be a little absurd; our condemnations are invariably tinged with admiration for the rogues. We rage at corruption and skulduggery, but we rejoice in the cunning of our villains and respect those who display panache in flouting the law. And yet our folk heroes are not of the breed of Jesse James or Marshal Dillon; they are Turveys and John A. Macdonalds: we take the skrim-shankers and the eccentrics to our hearts. This is a country in which poets can rest easy.

It is a country for poets in other ways too. When first I arrived in Victoria I was taken to a house on Ten-Mile Point, and I wept at the sheer beauty of the country to which I had come. Happiness flooded me like a wave. Travelling through the Rockies, and even riding that long straight road from Calgary to Edmonton, I am awed and dazed at the grandeur of that imagination which is Canada. I have found space here, the freedom to move and, moving, breathe deep. The mountains preserve their solitude. The rivers are copious with life, the shores generous with oysters, mussels, clams and the sinewy symbolism of driftwood. From my house I watch the yachts like winged apotheoses establishing the rightness of Plato. Here there are intimations. Here poems find me. I am awed by the ability of Canadians to live in Canada without falling upon their knees.

I, too, however, am a Canadian, and sometimes I sit in a beer parlour with the Hungarians, the Czechs, the Danes, the Poles, the East Indians, the Ukrainians, the French, the Irish, the Austrians and the Scots and reflect upon the conglomeration which is my country. My cleaning woman is Russian. The baby calls her Babushka. My closest friend is German. We shop at a Chinese store. This is marvellous to me. I am in the very middle of the human family. I am in a nation of internationals. I am in a gathering place of humankind.

Yet not all Canadians are gathered so harmoniously together. I am angered at reports from my friends in the north of the conditions under which so many of the Métis live. I am infuriated by the red tape and bureaucratic small-mindedness that permits the Indian reserves to remain so squalid. I am appalled at the human wastage caused by the lack of adequate mental-health facilities and by the unimaginative rigidity and sheer incompetence of the majority of our schools and orphanages. Even while I grow enraged, however, I find myself recognizing that all across Canada my rage is shared. We are a people hunting for imaginative justice, for the humane society, and for our identities. I have a dream that my children's children may be in at the death of Squeers, Gradgrind, Pecksniff and Babbit.

No man can live without the necessity for a vision. Where there is no need of hope the spirit dies. As both poet and Canadian I am impelled to seek a vision, and in the face of this magnificence and absurdity which is Canada, this muddle and glory which is our country, I write harder and better, I make more collages, I involve myself more in the community, I battle bureaucracy more willingly than ever before. I am a younger man than I was five years ago, and a man more certain of his direction. Canada has given me both a home and a cause. It is a country in which every gesture counts. It is a country of welcomes. It is a country of possibilities. There is more potential greatness in Canada, I am sure, than anywhere else on earth, but our greatness will not, I believe (for I must believe), be in the mere accumulation of material power. Nor will it be in the creation of a vast totally unified country with a strong central government. It will be a greatness of the imagination that will permit us all to retain our absurdities, our muddle-headedness, our local mythologies and our earnest comedies, and it will create for our great-grandchildren a place where they can be freely and most completely themselves. That at least is my dream, for I am a poet, and that is one of the things that poetry is about.

*Postscript*

I wrote those words more than eight years ago, and I don't wish to alter them. I do find myself envying the optimism of that younger self, however. In the last eight years while the battle against injustice and narrow-mindedness has brought, on the whole, more victories than defeats, the federal government appears to have become even more centralist in its thinking than before, and the Ottawa bureaucracy has swollen into a monster. It seems as if our current government believes that Confederation can only be made to work in terms of an overwhelmingly strong central authority. It seems as if those who control our so-called national magazines, who organize our national exhibitions of art, and who run our national broadcasting company, believe that anything which happens outside the golden horseshoe is irrelevant or at the most of merely minor interest. It is this centralism, cultural and political, which poses the real threat to Confederation, for all across our country there is at present an enormous upsurge of creative energy and of regional pride, and an increasing feeling that Quebec, in its efforts to preserve its own cultural traditions and its independence of spirit, may have indicated one way to force the centralists into accepting true federalism. It may even be that federalism will only be saved if strong separatist movements in the east and in the west, as well as in Quebec, oblige the cultural and political oligarchy of Toronto and Ottawa to realize that this is a country composed of many richly various regions and peoples, all of whom are equally "Canadian", and each of which must be given the opportunity to develop individually and idiosyncratically in order to enhance the quality of life of the nation as a whole and fulfil the enormous potential of that great assembly which is Canada.

# The West

## Ken Mitchell

I was born in Moose Jaw in 1940, the first of the post-Depression generation. I was fortunate to have missed the Depression. But like everyone else in the west, I cannot escape history.

I grew up on the edge of the town, midway between urban and rural, a stone's throw from the buffalo compound of the Wild Animal Park. Inside the seven-foot-high page wire, a few buffalo roamed, along with some elk and a pair of spaced-out Tibetan yaks.

Around fourteen, I began climbing inside the fence and—inspired by Ernest Thompson Seton and the Boy Scouts—took to exploring the prairie wilderness along the coulees of the Moose Jaw Creek. In a grove of chokecherry and ash, I built lean-to shelters, laid traps, cooked bannock, "hunted" buffalo and slept under the stars.

History had its revenge around six o'clock one summer morning when the buffalo came crashing through this prairie Walden, flattening the lean-tos and driving me into a week-long state of shock. A valuable history lesson, no doubt.

About that time, I was learning fragments from Canadian history at school—something about Laura Secord, and Durham, who lied. No one ever told me then that I had been camping at the edge of the Willowbunch Trail. Or that Sitting Bull and his thousand Sioux warriors had pitched their tents at the same place, after annihilating Custer in 1876 and escaping to Canada—yet another of the long and honourable line of refugees from republican America.

It was only at university, years later, that I learned why "the Dirty

Thirties" had left such deep scars on my relatives. I also became informed about the period of frontier settlement: Riel, Dewdney, Peter Verigin, and Sitting Bull. Finally I began exploring "pre-history", that is, the millenia before the coming of the CPR. And I began to perceive why the west is uniquely different from the rest of Canada.

One begins with landscape, and its enormous influence on history and culture.

If Canada is a country of extremes, the west is a region of violent extremes—a massive contradiction of fire and ice, jagged mountains and endless plains.

This landscape has tempered a strange beed of Canadian, a kind of Super Canuck who strides from tooth-rattling February blizzards into the solar blast of 100-degree July. We watch vast expanses of gray boredom burst in dazzling displays of beauty as the sun cracks through the clouds to vitalize a hundred townships in the space of a single second.

What other region could contain such contrasting cities as Victoria, with its mock-Sussex gentility, and Edmonton, a massive brawl of Slavic dynamism?

I can see how outsiders fail to understand western politics. The same roots that nurtured the die-hard socialism of the Regina Manifesto also fed Social Credit's Bible-pounding free enterprise. Somehow the arrogant capitalism of oil-bank Alberta co-exists with Winnipeg's North-End Communism.

Provincial governments lurch from left to right like drunken lumberjacks: NDP to Social Credit (in B.C.); Conservative to NDP (in Manitoba). The safe middle of the road is nowhere in sight. Yet on national economics and taxes, these premiers act with more unity than the national Progressive Conservative party.

Our history is full of such contradictions. We are the product of two cultures. Not French and English, perhaps, so much as European and "native" peoples, that is migrants originally from Asia. The "civilizing" of the Indians by Europeans did more than destroy tribal culture: it produced a new nation, the Métis of the northwest.

On the plains, two mass migrations—one from the Pacific and one from the Atlantic—met and mixed. But their ascendancy was almost immediately shattered by Upper Canadian ignorance, with the help of the British army. Métis culture has since gone the way of the buffalo, but Louis David Riel is now seen as the Father of the West, in a way John A. Macdonald never could be. It was Riel and Gabriel Dumont who established the now-honourable tradition of battling the arrogant power-brokers of central Canada. This is "Western Alienation", one of those rare mass-media contributions to the Canadian lexicon.

One French phrase that westerners have mastered is, "Plus ça change, plus c'est la même chose." And no one more than the natives, who are still pressing for their original land claim settlements, challenging the drive for increasing resource "development". The emotions and basic principles have not changed in a hundred years.

Western alienation may be a negative force but like so many other Canadian forces, it is one which binds us together—despite class, political and racial differences. Our regional identity springs from a defiance of both the landscape and imperial central Canada. From the days of La Vérendrye and Henday, this has been the hinterland, supplying raw materials and cheap labour to industrial Ontario. With no manufacturing, little resource processing, and consumer goods made more expensive by Ontario tariffs, we have grown accustomed to, if not fond of, a boom-bust cycle as unpredictable as an August hail storm.

So it is not unexpected that this region would produce so much populist ferment, so much militant radicalism, so much sheer Stampede-style hell-raising. As our efforts to change the old Confederation economics failed—for the most part—the alienation intensified. Like ice and fire and Ontario-Quebec squabbling, it is a fact of life.

Yet certain positive results have stemmed from this frustration, such as the only significant parliamentary opposition to the eternal Liberal oligarchy. Without it, there would have been no farmers' movements, socialized health services, or modern Canadian literature. Occasionally, a short-lived national champion like John Diefenbaker appears—only to become symbolic as another Riel: gifted but full of arrogant defiance to the point of self-destruction. Out-pointed, but never licked, Dief will always be a chief in the west.

Like Diefenbaker and heroes such as J.S. Woodsworth and Nellie McClung, we all carry barn-sized chips around on our shoulders. Only toughened by the frontier and Depression experiences, a westerner will fight any challenge to his sense of moral superiority.

This does not help us much in our consideration of the "national unity crisis" we are being asked to help solve. If there is anything a westerner hates, it is special status for anyone, and the Liberal bilingualism programme has had farmers seeing red since tractor parts began showing up in French.

Now we have the PQ and the threat of regional separatism—apparently over the issue of language—and it has us all confused. Trudeau is from Quebec, isn't he? So where is French considered a put-down? Why does it seem that Quebeckers want to turn back the clock? Here, in a region of rich multi-ethnic culture and multi-ethnic pride, it is hard to see language being important enough to form a new country, or destroy an old one. But perhaps bilingualism is a false issue.

To us the parallels in the two regions seem obvious, and the rising tide of Quebec nationalism has been fascinating to watch—rather like a homely adolescent girl suddenly blooming into spectacular maturity. It is a surge of identity I think we all envy.

The creative effervescence in Quebec arts and social life and politics for the past fifteen years made the election of the PQ inevitable—though as a political solution, it is probably as illusory and as ill-fated as the rise of the Progressives in the west fifty years ago.

There is a very similar ferment going on between Thunder Bay and Long Beach. Never has there been so much regional music, literature and art as there is right now. Ten years ago, George Melnyk could never have started the *NeWest Review*, an Edmonton-based magazine of politics and culture, very much a voice of this new, post-Depression west. Our brightest apprentices no longer head east to make their mark: Myrna Kostash, The Dumptrucks, Rudy Wiebe, are all committed to doing their work well, and doing it here. Peter Lougheed would rather be Alberta premier than leader of Her Majesty's Loyal Opposition.

The new confidence is based on an important self-discovery that we, too, have our own history and our own voice. We have located an audience apparently eager to share our observations and lyrics about this very unusual land, an audience jaded by the chrome-plated violence of Hollywood-Toronto imports.

And we discovered something about the rest of North America: that it wasn't "ahead" of us, at all. All the luxurious "things" and flashy hedonism that dazzled for a while are now weighed in the balance with their attendant paranoia and aggression and envy. We've seen New York and Paris. Now we're staying at home and, on the whole, digging it.

Despite the history of grievance, there is no real western separatist movement. The future may indicate great wealth in wheat, oil, potash, and coal, but regional independence in the face of modern U.S. economic imperialism is an illusion—just as we believe it is for the Quebec separatists. If Quebec does evolve into an "economic association", the west would almost certainly demand a complete and total regional separation—and fall immediately into U.S. dominion. Trudeau may know something when he says, "It ain't gonna happen."

We have learned to tolerate Toronto-Ottawa-Montreal domination and stupidity for three generations now, and would sorely miss our stance of defiance toward "easterners". If we had to bombard our grievances at each other, the west—like Quebec—would disintegrate into a hundred bickering mini-separatists.

One cannot help thinking, however, that if Quebec and the west ignored the false language issue and formed the natural alliance they share (as do the Maritimes and the north) against the central power structure, a new and more realistic confederation would emerge. A civil war would not be necessary, as it was in the U.S., to redefine and unify the country.

Whatever the political makeup of the future, western Canada will continue to bubble and roar with excitement. The new frontiers stretching northward are not that different from the old. The contradictions of wealth and poverty, beauty and ugliness, toleration and neglect, will remain as we once again attack the tar sands, the coal seams, the land.

But it will be a future without stability, without boredom. They are not possible in this community of anarchists, prophets and madmen.

# Who Will Tell the Québécois about Canada?

## Richard Rohmer

In Claude Wagner's mind—and he is typical Québécois—there are in Canada "two communities" and "two cultures", French and English, and the "two languages".

I say that he and all Québécois are wrong. There are the two languages, yes. But only one is a language of both culture and communication—French. The other—the English language—is simply a language of communication between a whole series of cultures in Canada.

There are not just two cultures in Canada. There is the Québécois culture and outside Quebec there is a patchwork quilt—French, English, Scottish, Polish, German, Italian, Ukrainian, Jewish, Dutch, Norwegian, Swedish, Chinese, Pakistani and a host of others.

And there are not just two communities in Canada, the French and the English. To be sure there is the French community in Quebec and across Canada. That community is strong and vital and cohesive. Canada outside Quebec is not one but a series of communities defined by cultural, ethnic and regional differences but with a common communications mode—the English language and, as well, the British system of law and government.

Let us compare the Québécois society to the Canadian society in the rest of Canada.

1. The Québécois have one common language. It is a language which came directly from their ancestors, some 60,000 being present at the time of the conquest by the true English. The Canadians in the rest of Canada have either English as their mother tongue or as a second lan-

guage of communication, or they learn it when they arrive as immigrants. It does not have a genesis in any direct descendency from a single group, as with the Québécois, but rather a development as the language of communication between a multitude of cultures, races and languages which have been brought into the rest of Canada.

English in Canada is not the language of the culture, it is the language of communication. French is both the language upon which the Québécois culture rests and the means of communication.

Because of their own cultural perception of the French language, the Québécois erroneously see Canada as an English culture, all of whose people are directly descended from the Plains of Abraham.

And the tragedy is that we keep telling them we're "English"!

2. The Québécois have a common religion—Roman Catholicism—and it has had an enormously powerful impact on the development of the culture of the Québécois, an impact which has only lessened in the last decade or so. In the rest of Canada we have many Christian denominations as well as Jewish. Moslem and other forms are now emerging with the immigrants who are coming to Canada from all over the world. There is little commonality except through those churches, which are fundamentally Christian, and none of these churches has ever exerted the kind of influence on the culture of the people that the Roman Catholic Church has had on the culture of the Québécois.

The last census, 1971, showed that of a population of 21.5 million approximately only five million Canadians were of English ethnic origin. There were 1.3 million Germans, 730,000 Italians, 300,000 Jews and a similar number of Poles, 600,000 Ukrainians and about two million each of Scottish and Irish plus twenty-three other races which were listed.

These statistics show clearly that those of English stock in Canada are in a low minority position.

I think we should be telling our Quebec friends and anybody who calls us Canadians "English" to "get off our backs. Canada is not dominated by English. We are not English, we resent being called English."

Frankly, I resent and I believe countless Canadians resent being called English by the politicians and the media and the Québécois. I resent the fact that Canada outside Quebec is called "English" Canada. And I reject the misleading description of our society as "English".

Our society is not one society and it is not English. Even our Québécois cabinet ministers refer to us Canadians as English. Who is going to tell them we are not? That the only tie we have with the English is through their language and through the fiction of the Crown and the factual fiction that the British North America Act can only be patriated or amended at this time through an act of the British parliament, an anachronism which is another weapon in the vast arsenal of emotional, cultural and linguistic nationalism built up by the Parti Québécois.

Who is going to tell the Québécois that we are not what they perceive us to be, or indeed they may want to perceive us to be? Who is going to tell the Québécois that Canadians, in all their multitude of racial and ethnic origins, want Quebec and the Québécois to stay with us, and that we are prepared to see to changes in the constitution, to support across-the-board changes in the relationship between the federal government and the provinces: to work for a much-needed decentralization of power from Ottawa and a reduction in the emasculating power and inexorable growth of the civil service.

Ottawa is the scene of a centralization and removal from reality of a system of what once was a democratic form of government, responsive to and under the control of the elected representatives of the people. Today that government is almost totally controlled by the bureaucracy.

It is a level of government which is in constant competition against the provinces instead of working *with* them in order to further the interests of all the people of Canada. Who in Canada is going to tell the Québécois that the Ottawa bureaucracy—not its politicians—is *against all* of the provinces not just Quebec?

What will make or break Confederation is how the Québécois see themselves in relation to Canadians outside Quebec at the moment they put their ballots in the referendum boxes. If they can be brought to understand that we, in the rest of the country, consider ourselves no better and no worse than they; if they can be brought to understand that, except for a minority, we in Canada are not of English descent; and that we want them to have all of the freedoms and the cultural and linguistic security to which they are rightfully entitled; and that we can and must live in harmony, then there need be no fear of the results of a referendum. If there is fear it will exist only in Canada, not in Quebec.

Who will speak for Canada to the Québécois? That is of great concern to me as an individual Canadian and I do not mean a man to take the place of the prime minister, who is perfectly entitled to take whatever posture and position that he thinks appropriate as prime minister and a more capable Québécois on the issue of separation would be impossible to find.

The question is who and where is the Canadian who will speak for Canada in our dealings, now urgent, with the Québécois and Quebec?

# A Perspective on Canadian Federalism
## after the Quebec Election of 1976

John E. Trent

For more than a century, the English-Canadian majority has been unable to provide satisfactory structures for French-Canadian security and development in Canada. In the November 15, 1976 Quebec election a large number of French Canadians responded by voting for a separatist party. This is the essential lesson of the Parti Québécois victory. The score in the Canadian federal ball game is now one-all. Question: Can Canadians discover a new game where neither group loses face or fortune?

The game analogy may not be very appropriate. The situation in Canada is a little too desperate. All Canadians are in a situation in which their livelihood, their way of life, and possibly their lives are in jeopardy. This is no alarmist statement. All the history of state-making and breaking, and of ethnic rivalry confirm it. The answer to the question of the new game, the new federal equilibrium, depends on how clearly and realistically Canadians analyze their situation and the options open to them. Why is it worth preserving the Canadian federation? Why is it of value? How did Canada arrive at the current impasse? What can be expected to happen in the near future? What can Canadians hope and work for in the long run?

Before responding to these questions, it is wise to note the most significant result of the recent Quebec election. The independentist Parti Québécois now represents more francophones than any other party in Quebec and probably an absolute majority of them. These voters preferred the potential and even the risk of a party they knew to be separatist to a government they perceived to be bad. While there may be some logic to this electoral choice, it also raises questions about the strength of the federalist hold on these voters.

It is true that only 18 per cent of Quebeckers polled before the election and only 11 per cent polled after the election preferred separatism. It is also true the PQ only won approximately 40 per cent of the vote. And it is said the new PQ government only has a mandate for good government and not for independence. But the essential point is that a strong PQ won in ten of fourteen regions and was second in the other four; it collects more money on a per capita basis from its sympathizers than any other party in Canada. The strength of the PQ should not be doubted. The PQ, dedicated to separating Quebec from Canada, has power in Quebec for the next four years. And it has the tentative support of a majority of francophone Quebeckers. We must understand this not as a fluke but as the continuing progress of a seventeen-year-old nationalist movement with dedicated, competent leaders and thousands of hard-working activists. It will not be changed by temporary expedients.

The thesis in this article, is that because of the election of the Parti Québécois, Canada faces considerable dangers in the short term, that is, until a referendum or a new election clarifies the situation. If these dangers and ensuing instability can be minimized in the immediate future, the presence of the PQ may force the country into a highly beneficial reconsideration of its political and economic structures.

### The Advantages of Canadian Federalism

Canada is beset not only by the Quebec independence movement but by Alberta and B.C. separatism, the English-speaking backlash against a minimal bilingualism programme, the attitude of "to hell with them, let them go" and a certain apathy. Once again, those who believe in the superiority of the federal system must do moral and political battle with the doubters. What are the advantages of federalism? The following summary refers to the potential benefits of Canada's federal system without claiming these benefits are maximized all the time. The advantages of federalism are not inherent or inalienable. Simply saying there is a federal system does not wave a magic wand. The system may be less or more beneficial for various groups at various times. The system requires constant fine-tuning by the political technicians. Also, one may only contend that federalism is a contributing factor, not that it alone is responsible for all these advantages.

Canadians are noted for their tolerance and openness, their peacefulness and their stability. There has been an incredibly low level of political strife. Federalism helps at the institutional level by providing a balance of powers. This balance limits the tendency of governments to become all-powerful and provides a better chance for some good government most of the time.

At the individual level, when one lives in a system with two main cultures, ten provinces, five economic regions and a multitude of ethnic groups, one cannot help contending with others who have different ideas and interests. You learn that solutions come from positive compromises in which no one completely wins or loses. You share.

While it is difficult to estimate the direct impact of federalism on this result, we should never underestimate the fact that rarely have societies lived for so long in such peace and freedom. This situation is to be cherished. To a degree, Canada has become a world model and symbol for working out problems on an amicable basis.

Federalism has helped support democracy and a lower level of administrative and bureaucratic power, relative to most other countries. Our levels of government set up contending power structures which, because of their knowledge and interests, tend to inhibit each other from becoming too dominating or corrupt. They offer individual citizens somewhere else to turn when they try to struggle with the tentacles of government.

A system with different levels of government also offers a better decision-making system for large communities. While it is sufficiently centralized to get important decisions made and obeyed, it has its own built-in mechanism of decentralization, the benefits of which Canadians all too often ignore. When citizens around the world are bemoaning decisions made by far-off governments, Canadians are indeed fortunate to have provinces and municipalities with real powers, competence and resources. Many in the European Economic Community would like it to move toward a type of system with similar features.

Two cultures have worked together in one political unit in relative peace for more than 100 years. Having the French and English cohabiting in our federal structure offers, to those Canadians who wish it, the opportunity to know and appreciate two great, worldwide cultures. At a practical level, it is potentially easier to take part in trade and economic co-operation in most parts of the globe—a potential increasingly realized in the past decade. Also, because many Canadians have internalized in a very fundamental manner an understanding of the needs and aspirations of *different* cultures, it permits them to play a more perceptive role in international politics. One may mention the Canadian role in the Commonwealth, the francophone community, the United Nations in general and in peacekeeping, Law of the Sea and North-South Conferences in particular. After all, the world looks more like a mosaic than a mirror.

Finally, the federation has always inhibited Canada from being absorbed by the United States. Or, to put it more positively, Canadian unity has helped it maintain its independence from world powers and permitted it to play a role it could never fulfil if fragmented.

To this point, not a word has been said about economic advantages. This strategy has not been utilized by Ottawa and Premier Bourassa. All too often they have tried to sell the economic benefits of "profitable federalism". Not only does this not have much influence on men's feelings or loyalties, it is also a flimsy argument. In the short run, a local power might always claim it is more "profitable" for a unit to keep its own resources to itself and to manage things entirely at the local level. On the other hand, it is also possible to argue that a large unitary, rather than federal, state can better direct an economy. Nevertheless, within the bounds of these two arguments, federalism offers great economic advantages.

The simple fact is we are now better off than most people in the world (as are many modern federations such as Switzerland, West Germany, United States, Australia). There are two basic reasons.

The units of the federation share with each other. They share resources, capital manpower, and know-how. They are each other's markets and suppliers. Canada shares different sorts of energy, food products, forestry and mineral resources, manufacturing and service industry competence—all of which seems to take on a heightened importance for a limited time (such as Alberta's oil and gas right now). In addition, a federation shares an economical transportation and communications infrastructure and limits political interferences such as tariffs, customs and immigration. The whole has a better economic viability and wealth, in the long run, than each of the parts.

The units of a federation also protect each other. The mixture of different resources and products helps to minimize the damage of wild swings in world-wide production and markets, just as a diversified corporation is more protected against sectorial instability. Equalization payments also promote stability. Governmental transfers of wealth from rich to poor regions have helped provide a minimum standard of income for the vast majority of Canadians. In part, this has been achieved by transfers between provinces and in part by the federal-provincial social service programmes which, for example, are much more developed than those of the United States. In a sense, each province and region is a sort of built-in insurance programme for the others, in times of difficulty.

Finally, but not least, our federal system has helped all Canadians share a greater proportion of our surplus with poorer citizens of the world than would be possible in a fragmented or a militarized Canada. We have one of the few aid programmes in the whole international system which has continued to grow in recent years.

Canadian federalism, then, offers a balance of political, cultural, social and economic advantages. The task of politicians is to maintain an equilibrium between economic and cultural demands. There are a number of fundamental conditions. There needs to be a reasonable division of power between the various levels of government. The two cultures need to feel they can develop in security. Most important of all, people must believe that mutual sharing and protection are preferable to autarchy and isolation. This is the principle of the federal will. It demands an open mind and a willingness to understand others. These traits are difficult to find at the best of times. They need constant reinforcement in the face of ethnocentrism, localism, and the desire for clear, simple solutions to complex problems.

The conditions and equilibrium of federalism are extremely difficult to keep fine tuned in the face of rapid technological and economic change. There is reason to believe the Canadian system has not responded rapidly enough to changes in French-Canadian society, to the phenomenon of governmental centralization, to demands for equality and participation, and to debilitating foreign economic takeover. The division of powers, responsibilities and revenues in our federation were made in one historical period but the system must be flexible enough to adapt to changes through time. Canada has not been learning and innovating sufficiently as a political and economic system.

## Why the Current Impasse with Quebec?

Do not look for easy, short-term answers. It is not just what Premier Robert Bourassa and his Liberal government did or did not do. Rather, the impasse between Ottawa and Quebec and between French and English Canada comes from very fundamental changes in French-Canadian society to which Canada still has to adjust. French Canadians have both a new self-confidence and new fears about their collective identity and individual advancement. These are a result of extraordinary cultural and demographic changes.

The Quiet Revolution of the early 1960s in Quebec completely modified traditional French-Canadian education, as well as religious, family, employment and communications habits and patterns. The chief result, from the point of view of the current situation, was that more and more francophones were receiving complete, modern education in fields traditionally only of interest to anglophones. This gave them new interests and ambitions, and a new perspective on their position in Canada and the world. The consequence was more competition, contact and rivalry between French and English in Canada. The French Canadians, with a new sense of their power and competence, wanted to compete on an equal footing, both individually and collectively, with English Canadians—now. The Canadian political and economic systems have not been able to react quickly enough.

At the same time, French-Canadian birth rates dropped dramatically while immigrants to Quebec adhered more and more to the English culture. Outside Quebec, the rate of assimilation of the French to the English culture was alarming. Everywhere, the massive penetration of English language media was, and is, eroding the French culture.

The combination of these four factors stimulates fear that the French culture is no longer protected in Canada and is therefore doomed to extinction. In other words, the Canadian federal system, as described above, is no longer performing one of its major functions. Recent evidence of the low levels of success of the federal bilingualism programme coupled with an English-Canadian backlash (especially the debate over the use of French in the airways) have stimulated French-Canadian anxieties and frustrations. Hence, the general turn inward to Quebec as the only refuge of the French culture.

All those conditions affect first and foremost the French-Canadian élites and especially the intelligentsia. Those who have higher education and positions are more influenced by the general state of their society. And it is these people especially (but not entirely) who have long supported the nationalism of the Parti Québécois, once they perceived that French Canadians are at the bottom of the Canadian economic totem pole, that they have difficulty in competing for positions both in and outside Quebec, and that their power and even survival as a cultural group in Canada are threatened.

The disaffection of much of the Quebec intelligentsia is doubly damaging to the Canadian federation. First, it means that Canada no longer claims the allegiance and affection of many of those who run Quebec's most important institutions. Secondly, these people—educators, professionals, artists, bureaucrats, journalists, politicians, many unionists, and even businessmen—are largely responsible for forming the ideas of the Quebec people and particularly the young. It is, for instance, becoming increasingly difficult to find committed federalists among the Quebec university population. There has been a socialization away from Canada toward Quebec.

What the Quebec nationalists want is to protect their cultural identity and assure it a secure and flourishing future. While separatists do not include anything like a majority of Québécois, their ideas do represent the profound discontents and aspirations of many French Canadians. As the Parti Québécois explains it, their goals are pro-French, not anti-English. They believe only a maximization of control over their own state will permit them to make the basic decisions concerning their cultural, economic and social development. They also want to be more equal in a world of sovereign "nation-states". However, many, especially the leaders, are aware of the economic constraints on the ideal of maximized autonomy. Thus, in a nutshell, the Parti Québécois wants the greatest amount of political autonomy consonant with maintaining beneficial economic relations with the rest of Canada.

Put this way, and to the degree the idea of total independence can be set aside, these aims are not wholly excluded from the federalist framework. There is room for debate and negotiation and perhaps for the creation of innovative federal structures. But only if English Canada and Ottawa show some understanding of the basic Québécois fears and aspirations mentioned above.

### The Short Term Dilemma

A strong shock to the body can often kill. Canada received such a shock in the Quebec election of November 15. Most people were stunned that a party dedicated to the division of Canada could come to power with such a majority. But the real shock has still to be felt. If history and the example of other countries is a guide, the blow will be not just to Canadian sensitivities but to its entire polity and economy. What Canadians should expect in the short term is a spiraling cycle of economic difficulties and political recriminations leading to individual and collective distrust and ethnic antagonism. While this is not a prediction of what must happen, it is a likely scenario of what may happen based on past cases and the logic of the situation.

One could expect that initially there will be a net-disinvestment in Quebec and to a lesser degree in Canada, and this despite the rather mild and quizzical first reactions to the PQ win. Already there have been some doubts by major investors about the value of investments in Canada. They claim Canadian productivity is low and salaries and strike levels high. They say provincial-federal jurisdiction conflict leads to higher taxes and instability. Now, with the real threat of separatism, there is complete uncertainty until a referendum or another election is held.

Uncertainty is the key word. Traditionally, major investors flee it like the plague. In the present situation, uncertainty is likely to come from a number of sources. No one can predict what the future Quebec economy will look like or how it will be managed. No one knows, not even the Parti Québécois, which forces will dominate within the party. Its programme talks of democratic socialism. The logic of a desire to control one's socio-economic development suggests that a French Quebec nation must control its economy as well as its government. That threat of nationalization, while not very explicit, hangs heavy in the air. Whether it is fair or not, Quebec, like any economy dependent on private capital but proposing socialistically-oriented economic reforms, is caught in the short-term bind between the perversity of market forces and a lack of state resources or structures to take up the economic slack.

Nor can anyone absolutely predict the reactions of English Canadians. Will they, as the prime minister hopes, be calm and understanding? Will they have the desire and will to negotiate a new federal bargain with Quebec? Will the English-speaking technical and financial personnel in Montreal stick with Quebec? Will the other provincial leaders support constitutional change? Or will the backlash of recent months continue to grow, leading to more short-sighted cries of "let them go" and threats of strife? Taken to their "nth" degree such negative reactions could, over a period of time, lead to civil strife or the movement of the various Canadian regions towards the United States, and the consequent complete isolation of Quebec.

No one knows. If you do not know you cannot predict, you cannot plan. Planning is the basis of investment. Investors will tend, as they say, to "sit on their hands" or look elsewhere, mortgage money is less available. The normal result is that replacement and building slows down, unemployment grows, tax revenues decrease and governments cannot fulfil their programmes. Individual and group interests are harmed. All this, of course, has to be blamed on someone. The betting is it will be blamed by Quebec on Ottawa and the English. The important thing to notice, however, is that the cycle develops even without being fueled by intentional ethnic antagonism.

At the political level one can expect, at a minimum, the Parti Québécois will make heavy, strident demands on Ottawa and in federal-provincial conferences. However, it should not be forgotten the PQ leadership has two mandates: one from the electorate to govern well within the constitution; and the other from the party to proceed to independence. So, at a maximum, we can expect the new Quebec government both to seek to create confrontation within the federation and to take unilateral, "irreversible" steps within Quebec. The PQ will also be using its control of Quebec institutions and its better access to the media to turn the loyalties of Quebeckers away from Canada.

Ottawa, which in the very short run only has to react to Parti Québécois initiatives, will eventually be faced with a number of dilemmas. The federal government will be damned if it continues to fully develop its programmes in Quebec, and damned if it does not. Trudeau's leadership will be contested by the Conservatives who taste power and do not want it to slip through their fingers on a "unity" issue. He may be condemned by hard-line anglophones for negotiating Canada away and by francophone nationalists for being a traitor. Others will reprove him if he is too inflexible. Some are already claiming that Trudeau has lost his political base and the trust of the population.

A political situation of such instability is ripe for exploitation by foreign interests which may have ideological, ethnic or economic goals.

Meantime, Ottawa and Quebec will have continually fewer people who can move easily back and forth between them keeping open the lines of communication. Lack of information in the two camps, added to strained relations, will breed distrust and more difficult negotiations. Mutual recrimination, gamesmanship and tactics for short-term advantage will replace serious discussion and compromise. Each side will be trying to win the allegiance of the uncommited at any cost. Within the competing groups deviations from the party line will be tolerated less and less (as in the conscription crises of the last two world wars).

Distrust and resentment will spread to individuals. French and English, federalists and independentists, living and working side by side across the country will start to look at each other and ask "Which way is he going to jump?" More and more people will make the mistake (as is already happening) of considering Quebec and English Canada as single, monolithic groups—"them". There will be a greater tendency to support hawks rather than doves. Easy contacts will be a thing of the past; certain topics will become *verboten;* anger will explode easily.

The really fundamental difficulty with René Lévesque and his Parti Québécois is that it sets up the desires and ambitions of an ethnic, linguistic majority as the supreme political value. Unfortunately, this is a sword which cuts in many directions. No matter how democratic he is—or how "rational" and "serene" he would like everyone to be—the principle of the ethnic majority runs counter to the federal principle and can inspire ethnocentric reactions in others.

The episodes in this description of the "spiral of instability and antagonism" may be likely but need not take place, at least not in their most virulent form. The immediate task of federalists and Péquistes alike is to make sure that by taking preventative action it does not happen. Sometimes having one's eyes opened and knowing the worst possibility can help one to prevent it. One can work to make it a self-defeating hypothesis.

## The Long Term: Challenge and Opportunity

To return to the analogy used above, a strong shock to a system may kill, but it may also serve to bring the system to its senses. It is possible the election of the Parti Québécois will have this effect on Canada. If Canadians perceive the PQ victory not as a threat but as a challenge, there is reason for optimism. If a population recognizes there are fundamental problems to be solved, then it can proceed to a serious rethinking of its institutions and attitudes. From time to time, this is a healthy exercise for a society.

There is reason to believe this is the course that will be followed. First, the PQ win was greeted by general calm and openness on all sides. Second, calm does not seem to indicate apathy. More stimulating, exciting conversations about Canada's problems and potential are being held by all sorts of people than were heard in decades past. Third, the English-speaking population seems to be awakening to the forces underlying the reality of Canada. They know the PQ is serious. Fourth, there is increasing evidence that French Canadians voted more for good government than for independence. It is also possible that the sheer euphoria of the PQ victory and the chance of a referendum on their political future will prove of some satisfaction to Quebec's non-separatist nationalists. Fifth, Ottawa has backed off its original, harsh, moralizing tone and is indicating a willingness for co-operation and dialogue. Sixth, all Canadians are confronted by a real, not a theoretical, challenge. The cards are on the table. While it might be hoped ideally that a people could handle potential problems before they arise, it is unlikely. How could Ottawa or the Quebec or non-Quebec people have rallied to simply the possibility that the Parti Québécois might sometime, somehow take power?

But the Parti Québécois has become the government of Québec, and Lévesque the prime minister. As Trudeau said, Canadians cannot postpone the issue. The challenge, the crisis is immediate. Despite the Parti Québécois's election, however, there is a second major reason to believe that a form of federalism may still be the solution for Canada. The senior Parti Québécois leadership, while determined, seems moderate, open and firmly democratic. In addition, the election itself has created a difficult impasse for the PQ. Knowing (after the 1973 election) they could not win on the independence issue, they campaigned on a good government platform and the population expects them to govern within this framework. Separatist initiatives, while possible, may backfire. And yet, a lack of significant national and socio-economic achievements can also bring the party under fire. Nor should the PQ be considered as a monolithic, unbeatable force. Its members are considerably divided over ideological orientations as well as specific issues and tactics. Combined with the party's inexperience, it would not be unreasonable to expect a degree of factionalism and instability within the PQ as the tensions of governing and of negotiation with Ottawa increase. The possibility of both serious negotiations between the PQ and Ottawa and of electing another government in Quebec are thus apparent.

On the other hand, the federalists have no cause to underestimate their own strength. Canadians have traditionally been a mature "common-sense" electorate. They can be counted on to consider the issues, given the chance. Many families, friendships, and interests now straddle the "two solitudes" of French and English communities. Economic ties are strong and much of the Quebec media has traditionally been federalist. More fundamentally, in contrast to many other countries of mixed ethnicity, there is a legacy of relatively little outright hate, fear or distrust. While there are rednecks, the forces of mutual respect and tolerance are strong. In the background, there is in most Canadians that undefined, deep, abiding respect for Canada's achievements and potential which has held the country together in the past.

It is likely, however, that this optimism is ill-placed if Canadians and their leaders do not undertake a fundamental assessment of their situation and potential options. Short-term tactics and political expediency will not heal the breach. New economic and political structures must be imagined. Canada may be able to learn from the experience of other countries that have weathered similar problems. The crux of the problem is to reverse the erosion of French-Canadian allegiance in Canada. This would appear to require a strong attitude of acceptance from English-speaking Canadians.

It will also require political and economic structures that can guarantee the cultural and social development of francophones both as a collectivity and as individuals. Ottawa, so far, seems to have ignored the argument that collective and individual aspirations are intimately linked. It is not very helpful for a French Canadian to be able to speak French in Ottawa if he feels his culture is being assimilated or subordinated in the country. What is required is not only bilingualism in the federal government but constitutional safeguards, more aid to francophone communities outside Quebec and the strong predominance of French within Quebec. Heaven knows this will be difficult to sell to English-speaking Canadians but it is the basis of federation. And many French Canadians realize that great strides have already been made in these directions in the past decade.

It is possible that through the forthcoming debate and struggle French and English will find a new respect for their identity within Canada.

## What Can Be Done

Without attempting, at this time, to detail the policies necessary to maintain federalism in Canada (many of which follow logically from the analysis above) we may summarize here the main conditions which are fundamental to the success of such policies. They include a reinforcement of the "federal will", maintaining stability, creating a strong, federally oriented party in Quebec, a positive English-Canadian attitude, a willingness to negotiate in Ottawa and some imaginative constitutional thinking.

1. As pettiness may soon become the order of the day, exceptional efforts must be made to remind Canadians they live in one of the most fortunate countries in the history of the world. On a combined score of peace, stability, liberty, wealth, resources, social development, tolerance and potential, a few other countries might equal Canada but none surpass it. Reforms and changes should reinforce these conditions, not place them in danger. If Canadians have this basic belief, all else is possible.

2. An immediate and continuing priority is to maintain stability and reasonableness and keep open the lines of communication. Instability, no matter what its nature or source, can be used to entice a population into believing that "external forces" are plotting against them. One of the most difficult tasks of businessmen and the federal government may be in deciding to maintain their investments and their programme development in the face of possible separation.

3. The first major political condition would be a credible federalist alternative in Quebec. While the reactions of Canadians outside Quebec

will be of equal importance in preserving federalism, the struggle for the hearts and minds of Quebeckers will take place within Quebec. Federalists will have to direct their political activity toward the support of that party which is Canada-oriented but which has many of the popular attractions of the Parti Québécois. That is, it should be open, participant, protective of the French culture and economically reformist. Certainly Anglo-Quebeckers would have to demonstrate a capacity to work within such a party and within the majority culture of Quebec. Ironically, a renovated Liberal party may be the most likely candidate if it could incarnate a new reality, project a new image and launch a new leader. This is a large order and some may feel the Union National, the Democratic Alliance, and NDP sponsored party or even a new party may offer more hope. The question is, do any of them have the base and potential for rapid action of the Liberals? Only such a strong federalist party, offering the perspective of a new Quebec government dedicated to working out its problems within the Canadian framework is likely to reassure those who must finance economic development in the short-run.

4. Outside Quebec, there are a number of conditions. Ottawa would have to show a willingness to negotiate a "Quebec solution" and in this the federal government would need to be seconded by the other provinces. They could, for instance, apply the principle of zero budgeting to politics by justifying to each other the distribution of each of the power and financial resources that have so long been taken for granted in our federal system. Does, for example, the federal government have to have exclusive jurisdiction over inter-provincial communications? Could it not be shared? Does the federal government need all its financial resources which it claimed for economic development after the war but which it now returns to the provinces in fits and starts? Could they devise a flexible federal constitution which would allow governmental powers and financial resources to become more or less centralized or decentralized as befits the needs of the times?

Canadian federalists presumably will have their hands full in overcoming apathy and petty ethnic sentiments. Certainly, as a minimum, Ottawa will have to get off its hill and go out and talk to the population. New federal, pan-Canadian projects would help to direct attention to the benefits and potential of Canada for all citizens. Most important of all, English-speaking Canadians will have to get over the belief that all problems in a multi-ethnic society can be submitted to the "will of the majority". There are significant instances in which the will of an ethnic minority must be respected if federalism is to work. As mentioned above, this idea cuts in several directions. Vigorous attempts must also be made to convince the PQ that the French culture can be protected in Canada and that ethnic majoritarianism need not be the dominating factor in Quebec politics. In other words, an ethnic group does not have to be independent to flourish.

5. There will be two troublesome tendencies to be overcome. The first is the tendency to categorize everyone as "the French" or "the English", "us" or "them" without taking time to realize that the real differences are political (federalist-separatist) and not ethnic. Secondly, governments will tend to concentrate on federal-provincial, French-English, Quebec-Ottawa problems to the exclusion of social and economic development and reforms. This can only lead to stagnation, bad government and the defeat of federalism.

6. To a great extent the "Quebec" or "francophone" issue in Canada is related to the more general questions of language rights, education, and federal-provincial powers which have troubled the country throughout its history. More people in government, universities, economic institutions and research institutes should apply themselves to finding solutions for the really difficult problems which underlie the current conflict. Should education in provinces be divided on linguistic lines? If so, how is it best done? Can a "special status" be devised for Quebec? How much centralized political power is necessary to obtain the benefits of a unified economic system? Does the federal government need all its powers? Does it need to hold them exclusively? How can a flexible constitution be devised to cope with shifts in conditions? The best step for Mr. Trudeau at this time would be to set up a constitutional advisory council. Such a body might act as a foil for any centralist, Ottawa bias he may get from his own bureaucrats. It will also allow him to test many of his own long-held ideas.

It would be difficult and perhaps foolhardy to go beyond general recommendations at this time. The important thing is to understand the types of conditions and actions which will be helpful in preserving Canadian federalism. There is in fact some reason to believe that the main objective of the present leadership of the Parti Québécois is to force Ottawa and the rest of Canada to negotiate seriously and that the threat of outright separation is a means to that goal. More hysterical cries of alarm and demands for extreme action are premature. For the moment calm, serious analysis of our situation and the options for the future is what is required. This is mainly because we are in a very fluid situation. No one, not even the Parti Québécois or the federal government, knows exactly what demands are going to be made and how far these demands will go. Nor does one know what will be the reaction of the Quebec population or that of the rest of Canada. Preparation for presenting a strong federalist argument to the Quebec people and government is the priority goal.

The task will be arduous. But given Canada's current good fortune and high potential, other paths would seem less felicitous. Imagining both the dangers and the possibilities of the future should inspire Canadians to meet their challenge with optimism in the full knowledge that their problems are miniscule in comparison with those of most other countries.

# The City of Intellect Found Wanting

## Rosemary Sullivan

Earle Birney once called Canada a land dead set in adolescence. How, he implied, is the country to be forced into maturity? Quebec anticipated us in its recognition that we must be *"maître chez nous"* to achieve self-respect. How are we to descend from our attic into rightful mastery of our own house? Only crisis creates maturity. Now we will have to articulate our collective values if we are to find a reason to continue to exist as a country. This means painful reassessment of all our cultural goals and the institutions which embody them.

As a member of the Canadian university, I turn my attention to that institution. Where, I ask myself, are the English-Canadian universities in the current debate? Ours is a fragile culture in need of self-definition, and the past ten years have been a period of intensive national articulation, with the central issue the survival of an independant Canada. Have the universities in this period proven definers and directors of our cultural goals?

Take, for example, the place of the French university in recent Quebec history. The definition of core political values occurred first in the universities. The political science department of the Université de Laval in the 1950s was the forum for the definition of ideological principles now shaping the movement for self-determination. When we look to the English universities, we see only that they mirror our general cultural confusion. What are the deepest issues of strife in the universities now? The *Canadianization* of the Canadian university, and the inability of the current generation of young Canadian scholars, probably the best trained and with the greatest potential, to find jobs in the university. Both issues have been with us for a long time, and with what Hugh MacLennan has called our enormous casualness, our habit of never waking up to situations until they become desperate, little has been done about them.

In 1976, the Symons Commission, established to study the state of teaching and research in studies relating to Canada, released its report, *To Know Ourselves.* The report concludes that Canadian studies have been deplorably neglected. Universities offer courses in anthropology, sociology, history, literature, political science, history, etc., without adequately covering the Canadian dimensions of the discipline. Furthermore, too many humanities and social science courses are referenced to foreign cultures. Symons remarks that no other country evidences a comparable neglect of national cultural studies. This problem is beginning to be remedied by a new proliferation in Canadian content courses. However, past neglect has meant that several generations of Canadian students have graduated ignorant of their cultural heritage, and important areas of cultural study have been totally disregarded.

But a further distressing issue is discussed in the report. It also is an old issue. In 1968, in a book called *The Struggle for Canadian Universities,* Robin Mathews and James Steele pointed out the alarming rate at which Canadian faculty were ceasing to be in the majority at Canadian universities and that if the trend continued, it would be a programme for national suicide. The trend continued unchecked. During the expansion of the universities in the late sixties, the hiring of foreign academics led to a situation in which Canadian faculty often found themselves in the minority in many departments in Canadian universities. The current period of economic inflation has made the situation potentially tragic. At a time when there are excellent young Canadians to fill university positions and to redress the imbalance, there are no positions. Some of the finest young graduates, now in their late twenties, are floating from sessional appointment to sessional appointment. Most, if they cannot come up with jobs, will leave the universities for alternative careers. A Canadian hiring policy has never been implemented, although comparable policies exist in other countries. Even then such a policy would be too late, since there will be virtually no hiring in the next decade.

What does the dilemma in the universities tell us about ourselves? We are a nation who have condemned ourselves to perpetually beginning again. Our national disease is not paranoia about survival; it is cultural amnesia. With a colonial self-effacement, we have refused to acknowledge and protect our heritage, and each generation has had to start as if from nothing. We are content to be perpetual watchers, observers from "the far side of the street". We hedge on action, on passionate commitment. We congratulate ourselves on our tolerance, and objectivity, our capacity for compromise, and have mistaken for objectivity a deplorable casualness about the most important issues. Unless we determine to preserve what is a fragile culture, we will find we live in a "kingdom of absence".

# The Vanishing Nation

## Mel Hurtig

Since the so-called "New Nationalism" began during Centennial year ten years ago, foreign ownership in Canada has grown by the greatest amount of any decade in our history.

Since the Committee For An Independent Canada was formed seven years ago, the annual growth of foreign ownership has broken all previous records, each and every single year.

The recent annual increases in foreign ownership have, by comparison, dwarfed the enormous increases of the 1950s, and the 1960s.

During the period of so-called "New Nationalism", non-Canadians have been steadily buying up areas of the Canadian economy never before even mentioned by concerned Canadians. New areas such as the wholesale industry, the retail industry, the forest products industry, the food processing industry, grain companies, huge segments of the service sector, rural land and developed urban real estate.

In the period of the so-called "New Nationalism" the foreign control of Canadian industry has grown by an amount greater than during the first hundred years of Confederation.

In the nine years since Pierre Elliott Trudeau became prime minister, more than 80 per cent of the billions of dollars foreigners have used to buy up our country has been money raised in Canada.

Since the formation of the CRTC the many millions of Canadians watching American television has increased dramatically all across Canada, both in absolute numbers, and as a percentage.

Since the proclamation of the Foreign Investment Review Act,

103

FIRA has approved 86 per cent of all takeover applications decided upon, and 93 per cent of all new business applications.

And now we learn that FIRA, at the direction of the federal cabinet, is to become even more of a vehicle to foster even more the takeover of our country by foreign corporations. FIRA is to pimp the country.

How very typical of Pierre Trudeau, John Turner and Mitchell Sharp. Instruments of public policy ostensibly designed to further the national interest, introduced to Canadians as a means of protecting our national integrity, but instead actually fostering rapidly increasing foreign ownership, influence and control.

How typical of the failings of a prime minister who has never really understood Canada, so confused by Quebec "nationalism" that he's never been able to understand you can't possibly have a country if you allow foreigners to own and control so much of it.

How typical Bill C-58! Hesitant, stumbling, slipshod legislation, while at the same time an agency of the government fosters the national proliferation of all the American television physically possible, to as much of the country as possible—and while at the same time the government forces the CBC to operate with inadequate funding.

How typical, too, the so-called "Canadian" business community—whatever that means—endlessly complaining throughout 1976 about the "lack of investor confidence" in Canada while foreign investors last year were pouring an all-time-record astronomical $9 billion in long-term, very expensive, debt capital into Canada.

The "Canadian" Chamber of Commerce, the "Canadian" petroleum association, the Canadian-American Committee, the Conference Board of Canada, the C.D. Howe Institute, and even the Economic Council of Canada. . . . How can one possibly adequately describe them? "Sell off the country quicker." "Ship out our resources." "Welcome foreign investment on any terms." "Free trade." "Continentalism." Apparently it's not enough that non-Canadians already control more than 60 per cent of our manufacturing and mining, and more than 80 per cent of our oil and gas—some of our current generation of business leaders want to sell off the rest, for their own profit, as quickly as they possibly can. Forget about the generation of their own children! Never mind the generation of their grandchildren.

And these businessmen are in good company. Our prosperous oligopolistic Canadian banks want to help, too. And so do the trust companies and the insurance companies.

With zero imported foreign direct investment in Canada last year, foreign ownership grew by at least $10 billion and probably much more.

Sell the country off as quickly as possible.

Never mind the future generations of Canadians.

Never mind our history.

Never mind our possibilities for the future.

Sell to New York and Hong Kong. And London and Germany and Swiss bank accounts and foreign blind trusts controlled by God-knows-who.

And never mind the detailed studies that clearly show foreign investment—both the good kinds and the bad kinds combined—brings virtually zero net benefit to Canada.

Never mind the resulting bankrupting current account deficits ($14 billion in three years by the end of December 1977, and the insane crippling high interest rates that must follow. Never mind the burgeoning unnecessary parent-to-subsidiary imports that a branch-plant economy must somehow try to pay for.

Sell off the land so that young Canadians can't afford to buy farms.

Raise the interest rates so that young Canadians can't afford to buy homes.

And pass off with indifference the certain prospect of the highest long-term unemployment rates since the Depression. . . . Hundreds and hundreds of thousands of Canadians, approaching a million Canadian men and women, who desperately want work but can't find it.

It's been said that a nation is a group of people who have done great things together in the past and who hope to do great things together in the future. Since Pierre Trudeau promised us a "just society" not only have we not done great things, not only is there now no prospect for great things in the future, but instead the nation is in danger of falling apart.

The national spirit is being smothered.

There is no national economic strategy.

There is no national industrial policy.

There is no national energy policy.

Parliament is downgraded and instead we are asked to accept ten often very provincial premiers meeting secretly with the prime minister to reshape the country.

Provincial premiers so politically parochial that even 110 years after Confederation they are unable to agree to Canadians controlling their own constitution.

Provincial premiers smiling for Canadian press photos at 24 Sussex and then returning to their provincial capitals to rant and rage against Ottawa, to demand further massive decentralization in a country already—by far—the most decentralized industrial democracy in the world . . . a country that even now may be so decentralized that it may already be ungovernable.

Provincial premiers who wouldn't dream of giving more power to their own municipalities.

The basic characteristic of Canada now, Canada 1977, is the most remarkable, appalling absence of national leadership. Whatever the opposite of vision, we have it.

Myopia.

Greed.

Selfishness.

I am not, I am not, talking about the people of Canada. I am talking about many of our politicians and much of our business élite. We have their heritage: the real possibility of the disintegration of our country. Quebec, western alienation, excessive regionalism, separatist groups in B.C. and Alberta, petty provincial politicians clamoring for more attention and power while Ottawa fiddles away the nation with debates on capital punishment and gun control and televising of the Commons . . . as the country goes down the drain.

Sky-shops and Candu payoffs and judges affairs and enemies lists and dredging scandals and Polysar payoffs and senior ministers lying to parliament and excessive secrecy and oil company fishing trips and foreign companies financing federal and provincial politicians and the Lockheed fiasco . . . while the nation falls apart. The evidence is there.

In the national interest Pierre Trudeau should be removed from office as quickly as possible. There's only one small problem. John Turner or a Joe Clark Conservative government, from all the evidence available, and there's lots of it, will make the current Liberal government look like raving nationalists by comparison. Go back and look at their records, their public comments. When I hear or read Joe Clark on Quebec, on decentralization or on foreign ownership, or try to imagine the energy policies of a Peter Bawden or a Harvie Andre, I find it difficult to imagine the nation even surviving four years of a Progressive Conservative government.

And the NDP? The federal NDP with their so-called International Unions. The NDP has not a hope of being elected as the Government of Canada. Look at their polls at a time when Canadians are fed up with Pierre Trudeau and at best unimpressed by an elusive Joe Clark.

Millions and millions of Canadians who believe in, who want, a strong united Canada effectively have no vote. What an outrageous thing to say!

I believe it is true.

The Liberals are disorganized, exhausted, inept, falling apart.

The heir apparent is a fervid continentalist.

The Tories seem indistinguishable, perhaps worse.

The NDP are emasculated and unelectable . . . at this crucial time in the history of our country.

An irony, one of the greatest ironies of all, has to do with the CIC (Committee for An Independent Canada) and what we've been trying to do for the past seven years. Every month I travel across the country. A couple of weeks ago to Victoria, next Monday New Brunswick, Thursday in Yellowknife, next week in Regina.

Let me tell you.

There is a strong national spirit across our country.

Most Canadians, an overwhelming majority, want Canada to stay together.

Most Québécois want Quebec to stay in Canada.

Most Albertans laugh at the greedy, wealthy oilmen separatists. Almost the only time anyone in Alberta pays the slightest attention to them is when some Toronto or Ottawa journalist makes a one-day flying visit and writes a column about them.

Most western Canadians are Canadians first. Without question!

Most Maritimers love their country.

All across Canada, especially among the young, the immigrants, the first-generation Canadians, and the women of Canada, there is a strong feeling for our country, a strong feeling of goodwill, fellowship and confidence in the potential of Canada. A strong desire to continue together as a nation we can be proud of. Not chauvinism. Not anti-Americanism. Not isolationism or xenophobia. Not flag waving or even nationalism.

Not nationalism, but instead a growing resentment towards the anti-Canadians in our own country. But mostly, an understanding that at the very least we can and must be in control of our own home. We must control our own destinies as much as may be possible. And an understanding that we cannot continue to let foreigners take over our industry, our land and our resources, while our own politicians, through default and ineptitude, break up our nation.

If there was a stronger national spirit across Canada there would be less need for Quebec nationalism.

If there was a stronger national spirit across Canada there would be fewer western separatists.

But who among us could have voted for Robert Bourassa and his élitist, secretive, inept and corrupt government? Who among us, as Québécois, could have accepted the terrible unemployment in that province? Who among us could accept people who wouldn't even speak our own language owning and running much of our most important business?

What a contrast! The ecstatic, joyous faces of vigorous young men and women of Quebec on the night of November 15 compared with the pale, overweight chamber of commerce group applauding the prime minister at the Chateau Frontenac. The tragedy of Pierre Trudeau—and it is a real tragedy for all of us—can be seen in these two audiences. The tragedy of the man who was to keep us together, as peoples and as a nation, is his tolerance of and excessive reliance upon the remote, cold, élitist and inept Robert Bourassas, Marc Lalondes and Michael Pitfields —the technocrats and bloodless mandarins; it is his weakness and dependency on men so out-of-touch with the human realities of Canadian life.

The tragedy of Pierre Trudeau is the very real possible disintegration of the nation he was supposed to keep together.

Let me tell you about the future.

The Liberal government and Mr. Clark's Conservative Party are both enthusiastically prepared to allow the official entry of foreign banks into Canada and the construction of the Arctic Gas MacKenzie Valley Pipeline. They may deny it, but as they do so they mislead the nation. I think these may well be the very last straws—disasters so compounding our current economic difficulties that future autonomy will be unattainable.

Both the current government and Mr. Clark, should he be elected, with myopic political expediency will likely offer Quebec—and ultimately, as a result by necessity, the other provinces—so much in jurisdictional concessions that Canada ultimately becomes an ungovernable, balkanized, fractionalized group of political entities beyond national government, entities competing on bended knee to be easy prey to the foreign multinational corporations.

The outflow of interest payments, dividends and service charges will surely accelerate to crisis levels. Our imports, mostly by foreign subsidiaries, and in oil, will escalate well beyond our ability to pay. Canada will face a major balance of payments crisis and our standard of living will drop sharply. There will be many more unemployed, more and higher imported inflation, and higher taxes. The economy will stagnate, our productivity will continue substantially below capacity, more and more post-secondary graduates will be unable to find jobs.

The "New Nationalism" can hardly be described as a success. Paradoxically (and what a paradox it is!) we have been successful with most Canadians. The foreign oil companies are no longer believed. Foreign ownership is increasingly unpopular. The economic costs of foreign "investment" are better understood. The difference between foreign investment and foreign ownership and foreign control—three very different things—are at least somewhat better understood. Many Canadians are more conscious of our history, our problems, our possibilities and the dangers to our survival. On foreign ownership the polls tell us over 70 per cent of all Canadians are with us.

Yes, we've been successful with the people, in every region. But, in the most real and important sense, we've failed. And failed badly. The politicians and the business community have continued and even accelerated the takeover of our country.

Perhaps the greatest irony of all is that the policies to build and unite and strengthen our country are not difficult, complicated, radical nor revolutionary, but simple common sense policies followed by most other nations desirous of protecting their own national integrity and of fostering the best interests of their citizens.

I'm not going to try to spell out a comprehensive list of detailed policies. But here are some of the things we could do in Canada—the kinds of things I believe most Canadians want and would enthusiastically support.

We could reform government and have truly open government, accessible to all.

We could reform parliament so that members of parliament from every province and every region could play, and would be expected to play, a much more important role in the national decision-making process.

We could produce better election financing legislation and really meaningful conflict-of-interest and disclosure laws.

We could get rid of corrupt patronage practices and reform the manner in which judges are appointed.

We could reform the tax system and make it truly equitable and progressive so that poor and lower and middle income Canadians are no longer forced to pay excessive rates of combined direct and indirect taxation.

And we could reform the Department of Revenue to prevent a continuation of the billions-of-dollars-a-year tax ripoffs by foreign multinational corporations in Canada, ripoffs that mean substantially higher taxes for all Canadians.

We could reform government agencies such as the National Energy Board so that much fairer decision-making processes are established.

We could make it possible for many, many more women to seek office, at all levels of government.

We could take steps to halt further increases in foreign ownership: tax changes; expansion of the key-sector approach; a proper foreign ownership control board; restrictions on Canadian financial institutions financing foreign expansion and operations; non-employee public interest directors on the boards of all large foreign companies in Canada; an end to federal and provincial government loans and grants to foreign companies; a Canadian dollar pegged at a real value of between 85 and 90 cents; a strong urgent effort to double industrial and scientific research and development; the elimination of all forms of extra-territoriality; federal, provincial and municipal government purchasing from Canadian sources wherever logical; at least temporary foreign exchange-controls; the rationalization of Canadian industry; a sane national energy policy; a long-term macro-economic industrial strategy.

But first, any important steps to recover the Canadian economy must be undertaken only after the implementation of policies designed to produce as close as possible to full employment. This must be the first logical and possible step.

Canadian ownership in itself is no end objective. But greater domestic control of the economy can bring enormous financial and lifestyle benefits if combined with a truly just, progressive tax system based much more directly on real net earnings and ability to pay, allowing all Canadians to share in the benefits. The greatest benefit of all would be greater freedom. Greater freedom of choice for all Canadians to decide what kind of Canada we want in the future.

We cannot do all of these things overnight. But we could begin tomorrow morning.

And we could also see that some of those remarkably forgetful people who plan the curriculums in our public schools and post-secondary institutions are reminded about which country they and their students live in, and that Canadians expect our high school and university graduates to know something about our country's history and culture and contemporary problems when they leave school. What a radical thought!

I am dismayed when I consider government policies relating to culture that are essentially prohibitive in nature. They are unnecessary and unpopular and often unproductive. There are better, more effective ways of doing things, in television and in book publishing, for example.

Tonight I have not been talking about nationalism. Perhaps the biggest failure of every one of us is that we have allowed our opponents in this country to label us repeatedly as "nationalists".

I am not a nationalist.

I have always been an internationalist.

I believe in a world community of nations and I want Canada to play an important role in that community.

I am, though, against the anti-Canadians.

I detest them, be they our own politicians, the Calgary "freeze in the dark" bigots, be they Imperial Oil, Exxon or René Lévesque, or the anti-French-Canadian rednecks, or the anti-central Canada western separatists, or the Bay Street executives and real estate companies and developers who pimp our country.

I have painted a bleak scenario and briefly sketched some alternative policies. One of my fellow speakers has told me he does not believe

Canada is going to survive the current Bank Act amendments. Another friend, an internationally respected Canadian economist, recently told me he believes we have perhaps ten years left—at the most—if the Arctic gas pipeline is approved. For my own part I am now much more pessimistic about the future of our country than I have ever been before. Only one thing, and that alone, will make it possible for the important necessary changes to occur. That one single thing is our political process.

Perhaps if there is a remarkable change in one of the three existing political parties, and I mean a truly remarkable change, there may be hope for Canada. For such a change to occur many thousands of Canadians not now involved in federal politics will have to decide very soon that they really care about the future of our country and decide to alter radically at least one of the existing parties.

There are only two other alternatives.

One is the formation of a new, broadly-based, democratic political party, dedicated to a united Canada, committed to open and honest government, committed to full-employment policies, committed to reduced foreign control—a more responsive, truly participatory party of reform and a party dedicated to the future of one united Canada.

The other alternative you have heard all too much of in recent weeks. The other alternative is the break-up and end of Canada—a separate Quebec with possible violent repercussions, a balkanized remnant, even higher unemployment, drastically reduced standards of living, increasing foreign domination—the end of a nation . . . the end of a dream . . . the end of Canada.

# Two-Headed Poems

## Margaret Atwood


I

Well, we felt
we were almost getting somewhere
though how that place would differ
from where we've always been, we
couldn't tell you

and then this happened,
this joke or major quake, a rift
in the earth, now everything
in the place is falling south
into the dark pit left by Cincinnatti
after it crumbled.

This rubble is the future,
pieces of bureaucrats, used
bumper stickers, public names
returnable as bottles.
Our fragments made us.

What will hapen to the children,
not to mention the words
we've been stockpiling for ten years now,
defining them, freezing them, storing
them in the cellar.
Anyone asked us who we were, we said
just look down there.

So much for the family business.
It was too small anyway
to be, as they say, viable.

But we weren't expecting this,
the death of shoes, fingers
dissolving from our hands,
atrophy of the tongue,
the empty mirror,
the sudden change
from ice to thin air.


II


Those south of us are lavish
with their syllables. They scatter, we
hoard. Birds
eat their words, we eat
each other's, words, hearts, what's
the difference. In hock

up to our eyebrows, we're still
polite, god knows, to the tourists.
We make tea properly and hold the knife
the right way.

Sneering is good for you
when someone else has cornered
the tree market.

Who was it told us
so indelibly,
those who take risks
have accidents?

III

We think of you as one
big happy family, sitting around
an old pine table, trading
in-jokes, hospitable to strangers
who come from far enough away.

As for us, we're the neighbours,
we're the folks whose taste
in fences and pink iron lawn flamingoes
you don't admire.

(All neighbours are barbarians,
that goes without saying,
though you too have a trashcan.)

We make too much noise,
you know nothing about us,
you would like us to move away.

Come to our backyard, we say,
friendly and envious,
but you don't come.

Instead you quarrel
among yourselves, discussing
geneologies and the mortgage,
while the smoke from our tireless barbecues
blackens the roses.

IV

The investigator is here,
proclaiming his own necessity.
He has come to clean your heart.

Is it pure white,
or is there blood in it?

Stop this heart!
Cut this word from this mouth.
Cut this mouth.

> (Expurgation: purge.
> to purge is to clean,
> also to kill.)

For so much time, our history
was written in bones only.

Our flag has been silence,
which was mistaken for no flag,
which was mistaken for peace.


V

Is this what we wanted,
this politics, our hearts
flattened and strung out
from the backs of helicopters?

We thought we were talking
about a certain light
through the window of an empty room,
a light beyond the wet black trunks
of trees in this leafless forest
just before spring,
a certain loss.

We wanted to describe the snow,
the snow here, at the corner
of the house and orchard
in a language so precise
and secret it was not even
a code, it was snow,
there could be no translation.

To save this language
we needed echoes,
we needed to push back
the other words, the coarse ones
spreading themselves everywhere
like thighs or starlings.

No forests of discarded
crusts and torn underwear for us.
We needed guards.

Our hearts are flags now,
they wave at the end of each
machine we can stick them on.
Anyone can understand them.

They inspire pride,
they inspire slogans and tunes
you can dance to, they are redder than ever.

VI

Despite us
there is only one universe, the sun

burns itself slowly out no matter
what you say, is that
so?      The man
up to his neck in whitehot desert
sand disagrees.

> Close your eyes now, see:
> red sun, black sun, ordinary
> sun, sunshine, sun-
> king, sunlight soap, the sun
> is an egg, a lemon, a pale eye,
> a lion, sun
> on the beach, ice on the sun.

Language, like the mouths
that hold and release
it, is wet & living, each

word is wrinkled
with age, swollen
with other words, with blood, smoothed by the numberless
flesh tongues that have passed across it

Your language hangs around your neck,
a noose, a heavy necklace;
each word is empire,
each word is vampire and mother.

As for the sun, there are as many
suns as there are words for sun;

false or true?

VII

Our leader
is a man of water
with a tinfoil skin.

He has two voices,
therefore two heads, four eyes,
two sets of genitals, eight
arms and legs and forty
toes and fingers.
Our leader is a spider,

he traps words.
They shrivel in his mouth,
he leaves the skins.

Most leaders speak
for themselves, then
for the people.
Who does our leader speak for?
How can you use two languages
and mean what you say in both?

No wonder our leader scuttles
sideways, melts in hot weather,
corrodes in the sea, reflects
light like a mirror,
splits our faces, our wishes,
is bitter.

Our leader is a monster
sewn from dead soldiers,
a siamese twin.

Why should we complain?
He is ours and us,
we made him.

VIII

You can't live here without breathing
someone else's air,
air that has been used to shape
these hidden words that are not yours.

This word was shut
in the mouth of a small man
choked off by the rope and gold/
red drumroll

This word was deported

This word was gutteral,
buried wrapped in a leather throat
wrapped in a wolfskin

This word lies
at the bottom of a lake
with a coral bead and a kettle

This word was scrawny,
denied itself from year
to year, ate potatoes,
got drunk when possible

This word died of bad water.

Nothing stays under
for ever, everyone
wants to fly, whose language
is this anyway?

You want the air
but not the words that come with it:
breathe at your peril.

These words are yours,
though you never said them,
you never heard them, history
breeds death but if you kill
it you kill yourself.

What is a traitor?

IX

This is the secret: these hearts
we held out to you, these party
hearts (our hands
sticky with adjectives
and vague love, our smiles
expanding like balloons)

these candy hearts we sent you
in the mail, a whole
bouquet of hearts, large as a country,
these hearts, like yours,
hold snipers.

A tiny sniper, one in each heart,
curled like a maggot, pallid
homunculus, pinhead, glass-eyed fanatic,
waiting to be given life.

Soon the snipers will bloom
in the summer trees, they will eat
their needle holes through your windows

(Smoke and broken leaves, up close
what a mess, wet red glass
in the zinnia border,
Don't let it come to this, we said
before it did.)

Meanwhile, we refuse
to believe the secrets of our hearts,
these hearts of neat velvet,
moral as fortune cookies.

Our hearts are virtuous, they swell
like stomachs at a wedding,
plump with goodwill.

In the evenings the news seeps in
from foreign countries,
those places with unsafe water.
We listen to the war, the wars,
any old war.

X

Surely in your language
no one can sing, he said, one hand
in the small-change pocket.

That is a language for ordering
the slaughter and gutting of hogs, for
counting stacks of cans. Groceries
are all you are good for. Leave
the soul to us. Eat shit.

In these cages, barred crates,
feet nailed to the floor, soft
funnel down the throat,
we are forced with nouns, nouns,
till our tongues are sullen and rubbery.
We see this language always
and merely as a disease
of the mouth. Also
as the hospital that will cure us,
distasteful but necessary.

These words slow us, stumble
in us, numb us, who
can say even Open
the door, without these diffident
smiles, apologies?

Our dreams though
are of freedom, a hunger
for verbs, a song
which rises liquid and effortless,
our double, gliding beside us
over all these rivers, borders,
over ice or clouds.

Our other dream: to be mute.

Dreams are not bargains,
they settle nothing.

This is not a debate
but a duet
with two deaf singers.

# Canada: The One and the Many

W.L. Morton

Canada, in its history and at any moment of its existence, is an infinite variation on the theme of the one and the many. Canada, at any one moment, possesses an undoubted oneness, at any same moment a wilderness of regions, provinces, valleys, outports, peninsulas, villages, towns, districts, the Beauce, the Okanagan, the Bruce, the Yukon. Yet the one cannot be without the many, nor the many without the one. Canada cannot just be unitary; at Confederation the attempt was made and was thwarted. Neither can any part, the west, Quebec, Ontario, or the Maritimes exist alone; it would not be physically possible.

Why this is so any plain reading of geography and history reveals.

But look at the map of Canada, of all Canada. Pore over it, its extent, its indentations of far-reaching seas, its zones of the temperate and the arctic, its stretch of longitude from sea to sea, of latitude from the American border to the archipelago of the High Arctic. It is as vast as it is varied, one of the largest countries in the world, easily a world absorbed in preoccupation with its own distances. Space rules Canada; Canadians for relief must have resort to smaller things, parishes, villages, mere provinces, anything with order, form and visible boundaries.

If spatially vast, in population Canada is small, one person to every 150 square miles. The few Canadian peas rattle in their enormous pod. Why indeed should few people in so much space think of themselves as a country at all?

The answer is that they desperately need one another.

How this came about is as clear as crystal from examination, however desultory, of Canadian history. Canadian history, Canadian economic life, grew out of the fur trade. The traffic in furs was a traffic in luxuries, subject to fashion, whim and caprice. The taking of fur depended on the patient skill of the hunter and trapper in outwitting sly, alert, ever watchful creatures whose lives were linked moments of peril, the quick and fugitive marten, the remote fisher, the fearful deer, the slinking weasel. Only the plodding beaver with his dams and lodges gave a mass and stable character to the trade. Yet even there, so great was the demand for beaver pelt, that the "beaver frontier" ran like fire across the continent between 1603 and 1793. All Canada was taken in a few great commercial breaths, so fragile was natural life, so skilled the Indian trapper, so insatiable the European market. That wide-spreading, fragile, and retreating character was the essence of the Canadian economy in the days of the fur trade; it still characterizes much of our modern and highly technological economy. As the trader depended on the trapper, and the trapper on the trader, and as they spread, paddle stroke by paddle stroke, snowshoe stride by snowshoe stride, across the Canada that was to be, they spelled out the fact that a fragile economy must be extensive if it is to survive at all, and in the extension of this spider-web of wealth everyone depends on everyone else.

If that was so in the days of the fur trade, however, was it so thereafter? The answer is, of course, the inevitable yes and no. History repeats itself only inarticulately; sequence in history is faltering and ambiguous.

What is noteworthy is that the fur trade depended on two things—the trapper on the trapline and the trader in the trading post. And behind the trading post was the metropolis—London, or Rouen, or Amsterdam, as the case might be. Thus the fur trade was a fragile spider's web, to repeat a useful metaphor, of canoe routes, pitching tracks and traplines threading the country, but all knotting with local posts stretching to larger trading centres, Fort Chipewyan and Montreal, Cumberland House and York Factory. The larger fur posts tended to become the future cities of Canada—Quebec, Montreal, Fort Garry, Edmonton. York Factory did not, and Toronto owes little but its site to fur trading origins.

Thus the fur trade stretched and the economy of posts spread delicate fibres and strong nodal points over Canada. Yet this was always as a whole; it could not exist in parts, but shrivelled as does a strong spider's web in a few dismal strands. The fur trade, the grand trade, always made for monopoly. Here was the prototype of the Canadian economy and nation, the delicate teasing forth from much territory a sum of concentrated wealth, beaver, marten, mink—or whatever might be found for a market.

Can this prototype, however, be used for all the changes in the Canadian economy since 1821? Certainly not in any microscopic study. Local and provincial history at once became the history of township, parish and schools, interesting and important enough in themselves, but not cognizant of the Canadian whole. The wheat-grower in southern Ontario, the apple-grower in Nova Scotia, the grocer on a street-corner in Toronto, could be a sturdy yeoman of a solid citizen, well enough. But he was probably not taking in any sense of the whole. He reacted to the nodal, not to the dispersed, character of Canadian life. Here was the tension of the one and the many, the tension that kept the economic web taut.

It is true that while the lowlands of the St. Lawrence and the pockets of good land in the St. John Valley and the Ottawa were filling with farms and towns, Canada did seem, even perhaps became, only another American frontier society, replacing the wilderness in all possible speed with cultivated fields and elm-shaded streets. Rich, rewarding and bucolic it was indeed, and the wheat exports gave it a wealth that disguised its dependence on overseas markets. Yet this society too was collecting a cash crop from scattered fields, ever farther as fertility failed, for a distant market. All this, the continuation of the wide exploitation of fragile resources, was continued in the timber trade. The demands of the Napoleonic wars, the British lumber market after 1815, the growth of the Canadian and Maritimes merchant marine, made it profitable to fell the pine, the tamarack and the birch of the North American forest for export as lumber, or as ships. The rough and disciplined life of the lumber camp, the steady felling of mile on mile of timber, was soon a far cry from the fur trade. Yet essentially it was the same, the ever stretching out after a vanishing frontier for a resource supplied by nature for an export market. Behind both the wheat and timber frontier wealth accumulated, more massive than in the fur trade; banks sprang up to finance the lumber camps and the spring drive down the river and to make hay off a proletariat of lumberjacks. The economy did mature; society prospered; classes formed; but it still was an economy of reach and dispersion. It was still an economy in which the farm fed and harvested, the city supplied and forwarded and trees fell, that men might prosper. The interdependence, the web of dependence, remained.

Nor did it vanish when the timber age yielded to the railway. The railway—the Grand Trunk, that noble failure apart—served the timber camps and the market towns. It was nodal, not dispersed, until after Confederation. Then with the reaching out to Halifax and Vancouver, the railway became also the agent of a transcontinental economy, bringing together the scattered resources of a demi-continent, binding the regions, threading together the localities, creating a national diadem sea to sea. The spider's threads had become threads of steel, but threads they remained. Once more, as at the climax of the fur trade, a continental economy enabled the empty spaces and the fruitful pockets, the last and largest—the prairies—to be gleaned of grain.

So great a growth brought great change with it, of course. One was the growth of credit. As the country grew, the credit system grew with it until the Bank of Montreal, or the Bank of Commerce, or both, sat smugly on every main street in the country. They fed credit into the widening economic web, and drew back their profits along the concentric threads. For banking, like the country, was at once nodal and dispersed, squeezing out loans, drawing in interest. The second change was the rise of industry, manufacturing in growing factories locomotives for the railways, machinery for the farms, textiles and boots for the workers. It too was at once nodal and dispersed, nodal as to site in central Canada, dispersed as to markets sheltered behind the tariff.

This was the Canada that thrived until 1914, when the world which it sheltered with its lumber and fed with its wheat broke in two in a war that was disastrous for Canada. Disastrous because that war raised the question of the right of a majority to coerce a minority, a distinctive minority with its own way of life, its own expectations and its own sense of obligation, and unwilling to have its young men conscripted for military service. The web of assent, positive, or passive, which had grown up with the economic web, a web made in English and French partnership, was rent, never to be fully repaired. The economic and the political were in some measure, and for the first time, to be separate in Canada. Nevertheless, and for a full generation, marked not only by war and depression, Canada went on expanding its basic economy and its corresponding state. It evolved a state craft in the process, one not recognized nor admired sufficiently, for it was the sophisticated elaboration of that economy and that state. First was the principle of the "offset", the offset of the power of the nodal over the fragility of the dispersed, of Ontario and Quebec, of Montreal and Toronto, over the Maritimes and the western provinces. The Crow's Nest Pass Rates of 1899 are the earliest and still the best example of offset. To make the burden of the tariff tolerable on the prairies, the freight rates on grain moving for export were set. To the east, the Maritimes were given subsidies on their freight rates—simple and clumsy, the offset kept the threads of dispersion from snapping under the heavy pull of the centre.

Another was the federal payment, or transfer, conditional or unconditional, even in matters under the jurisdiction of the provinces. The principle of "debt allowance" dated from Confederation—that is, the greater credit of the Dominion based on its unlimited taxing power was used to bolster the credit of the provinces. Crude and simple in the application, the principle of using central credit to support the provinces could be made complex and subtle. In the Great Depression only the credit of Canada kept the weaker provinces solvent, a thought worth remembering when there is so much loose talk of separation of the federal union. In the aftermath that credit was once more used to take burdens off the provinces, as in assuming the costs of unemployment insurance. But it was also used in a wider, more positive form, the equalization payments. When a province was for want of revenue unable to give its people services of the standard of the national average, the federal government would pay a grant sufficient to enable it to reach the standard of the national average.

This was plain, practical and quietly revolutionary. Think once more of the vast spread of Canadian territory, of the thinness of its resources, the paucity of good soil, the everlasting wilderness which is by far the greater part of the country, the barren heights of the Rocky Mountains, and the glacier scoured rocks and muskeg of the Pre-Cambrian Shield. It is for communities in such regions, the have-not regions, that the have regions, the great cities, the nodal parts of Canada, are being taxed to help. This is the web of interdependence raised to a national policy. This was the work of the last generation, and it ought not lightly be destroyed by any separation.

I return to my beginning. I believe that Canada came together by the operation of facts, reinforced of course by sentiment, in a way which required the union of the whole country. Canada could not be Canada and be significantly less than it is; it would collapse like a spider web before the swing of a cane. It follows that proposals of separation are not only folly but most harmful folly, and that talk of separation by anyone, in Quebec or in the west, is not only folly but a denial of 300 years of history, of the very nature of Canada in its whole and in its parts.

# Counting the Cost

## Abraham Rotstein

English Canada approaches the coming negotiations with Quebec beset by a number of handicaps. Its own sense of self is thin and is essentially geographical. The territorial integrity of the country is the predominant image, the Dominion-from-sea-to-sea. But such a one-dimensional self-image—the territorial imperative—can only perceive Quebec's separation as a mortal blow and as an unthinkable possibility. The response (to the extent it is positive), is likely to be channelled into an orgy of goodwill. There seems to be a rising tide of "Quebec we love you!" This talent for liberal sentimentality is endearing (remember Biafra?), but it is too late today to rely on passionate waves of goodwill. It is the chief sign of our weakness for where does it take us in regard to the hard issues of the restructuring of power? In Quebec this will be dismissed as simply another self-centred way to preserve the *status quo*.

There is a virtual monopoly at the moment on the Canada-Quebec dialogue. Only one main channel exists—the Trudeau-Lévesque channel, crackling and highly charged. It is probably in the medium-term interest of both these parties to escalate the political temperature. Trudeau has to win his next election, and Lévesque has to prepare his constituency for his grand referendum. Everyone else is mum. Where are the corresponding conversations, between groups of academics, between Learned Societies, between public-interest groups, between the churches, the trade unions, the chambers of commerce, the professional associations, the media, the editorial writers? A paralyzed reticence stalks the land. Are some issues too sensitive or too important to be brought out into the open? Meanwhile, a mesmerized fascination keeps our ear glued to the Trudeau and company/Lévesque and company tournament. The hidden agenda of old scores to be settled, election points to be gained, pulls the issue into an unpredictable maelstrom.

There seems to be an implicit agreement among the mainstream in English Canada to avoid thinking the unthinkable. Perhaps in this way, the problem will recede. Nobody has done any contingency planning (except the army). How would a Bank of Canada operate with two political entities sharing a common currency as the Parti Québécois has proposed? What thinking has the Department of Finance done on the question of a viable co-ordination of monetary and fiscal policy, on a common foreign exchange rate for the dollar, on the possibility of regional interest rates? What has Industry, Trade and Commerce done to explore the question of a customs union, tariff changes, a common foreign investment policy? And has External Affairs begun to think about a reorganized foreign service, joint diplomatic representation, Quebec's role at the United Nations?

I suspect the answer is a uniform NO in Ottawa and throughout the country. No doubt some will object to self-fulfilling contingency plans, but far better to explore, now, our concrete options than to face the future clothed in all the nakedness of free-floating goodwill. (How quickly the latter can turn into its opposite. . . . )

The central issue at this late date is: How much separation? Quebec independentists have not spelled out their plans in detail and have not thought through, I suspect, the political and economic constraints that set the limits to their aspirations. They would wish to settle in the end for the symbolic victory that might legitimately be called "independence" or "sovereignty". But the international monetary system is profoundly unstable, and this is not the time for a new currency. Unemployment in Quebec is a deep-seated structural phenomenon, and will ultimately require immense resources for economic redevelopment and industrial growth. The creation of its own defence establishment would be an expensive burden for Quebec with a low priority. The substantive questions therefore are *how much* separation, and how would various schemes work? What, concretely, are the options? and what have English Canadians to propose in their interest in such a dialogue?

If we continue to play dog-in-the-manger and refuse to think about the unthinkable, Quebec does indeed have another option to which it may be forced. That option is to tie in with the American dollar and create an even closer link with the New York money market. With it will come a new important desk in the U.S. State Department. The possibilities for the American policy-makers in playing off English Canada and Quebec on every issue from pipelines to resources, to foreign investment policy, are too mind-boggling to contemplate. It is the ultimate scenario in divided-we-fall.

# The North American Triangle

## Mel Watkins

It should by now be a commonplace that Canada faces both an internal threat and an external threat to its existence. While English Canadians continue to underestimate the extent of the latter, after November 15 few can any longer shut their eyes to the former. But we seem to find it impossible to hold both in our minds at the same time, much less to admit of any interrelationship.

The internal threat, in its most dramatic form—the spectre of the separation of Quebec—is now at the centre stage of our politics. But the discussion is characterized by a deafening silence on the fact of our dependence on the United States, a matter which is equally true whether we are one nation or two.[1] This must be seen as a part of a general phenomenon noted by Daniel Drache that whenever this country faces a crisis that is not self-evidently related to our dependency, the national question drops out of sight.[2] (The other striking case in point is the economic crisis of inflation, unemployment, controls, and labour's response thereto. The CLC calls for first priority to job creation, but fails to mention moving the economy away from its present truncated status to a more independent variety capable of supporting more employment.)

[1]This is not a new phenomenon; for a brilliant exception see Kari Levitt, "Toward Decolonization in Canada and Quebec", *The Canadian Forum*, March 1972.

[2]Comments by Drache to the Seminar on Perspectives for Development—Latin America/Canada, Toronto, October 1976.

True to form, the U.S. connection hardly figures in the thousands of words that followed the dramatic PQ victory. We were told what was happening in the New York capital market to Canadian and particularly Quebec securities. We were warned by the pundits, Canadian and American, that all other issues, including tensions in the Canadian-American relationship, would now be put on the back burner by the Canadian government. We saw Mr. Turner make encouraging sounds about accommodating Quebec, but simultaneously call for the dismantling of the Foreign Investment Review Agency the better to create jobs and lessen economic discontent. In general, the prospect is for the erosion of the small gains made around the national question in the past decade.

None of this gets to the basic point of Canada's, and Quebec's, colonial status vis-à-vis the United States. It is of the essence of colonialism that it permeates all aspects of life. To discuss English Canada-Quebec relations without explicit attention to the continental connection is to shut one eye and necessarily to settle for very partial insights. And deficient analysis leads to deficient political response.

Historically, the Canadian experience cannot be understood except in the context of the North Atlantic Triangle. Our present crisis must be placed in a different but equally fundamental context, that of the North American Triangle. Since 1945, there has been a quantum leap in American economic domination of Canada. Canada is clearly America's most important dependency, while within Canada, Quebec is subject to American domination directly and indirectly through English Canada.

Belatedly and modestly, there has been a Canadian nationalist response to this penetration. It is, of course, severely constrained by the anti-nationalist position of the Canadian corporate élite, but it is also constrained in some part by the balkanization of the federal structure that is inherent in Americanization. The latter phenomenon is evident in all of the provinces; Quebec is not immune to the tendency to see the United States as a counterweight to the federal authority.

The result of all this has been that independentism vis-à-vis the U.S. exists in English Canada but is weak, and hence tends to drop away in the face of other problems. But the same forces have had, as we know, very different consequences in Quebec. Independentism, as separatism directed against English Canada, has flourished. On the one hand, for cultural and linguistic reasons with deep historic roots, Quebec nationalism necessarily sees English Canada as the "enemy". On the other hand, English-Canadian domination of the Quebec economy is both real in its own right and acts as a medium for American domination; hence American domination per se tends to be masked.

Quebec properly determines what is on its own political agenda, but in the process it also determines what is on the English-Canadian agenda. English Canada gets locked into a one-dimensional perception of Quebec versus English Canada, or Lévesque versus Trudeau. The cry goes up in English Canada for national unity, *not* for national independence.

To put the matter differently, there is (as has been observed by the American political scientist Robert Gilpin[3]) an important sense in which the debate in Quebec between those Québécois who favour federalism and those who favour separatism is between two different approaches to American investment. In effect, the federalists see the American relationship as being more beneficial for Quebec when Quebec is part of a broader political structure, while the separatists see greater benefits from working out a direct relationship with the U.S. not mediated through Ottawa or English Canada.[4]

There is unquestionably a logic to the separatist position. Who needs Ottawa and Toronto? And there is a potent hidden dimension. Ontario now has a disproportionate share of the American branch plants. An independent Quebec might get its fair share of the branch plants and the jobs that flow therefrom in the short-term. Ontario would be disadvantaged, and the issue is once again deflected into internal conflict.

This is to suggest that an independent Quebec might be even more of a neocolony of the U.S. than is Canada itself, while driving English Canada into trying to protect its monopoly on the American relationship.

Within Quebec there are those who understand that the U.S. is the real enemy, but of what use is English Canada to them as a counter-

[3]Robert Gilpin, "American Direct Investment and Canada's Two Nationalisms" in Richard A. Preston, ed., *The Influence of the United States on Canada* (1972).

[4]Three years ago, Jacques Parizeau rejected the suggestion that foreign capital would flee an independent Quebec in the following revealing way: "It is time people realized that the biggest enemy of Coca-Cola is not the Parti Québécois. It is Pepsi-Cola. The biggest adversary of General Electric is not the Parti Québécois. It is Westinghouse. The principal adversary of Sun Life is not the Parti Québécois. It is the Prudential." *The Toronto Star*, October 10, 1973.

weight against the United States? We must be honest about the past, while insisting on the *possibility* of a different future.

For there do exist within English Canada those who are nationalists, who want greater independence from the U.S. It must be admitted, however, that within that tendency there are some who show little sympathy for the aspirations of the Québécois. But the others, and perhaps the predominant group, recognize the *right* of Quebec to self-determination but fervently desire a new confederal arrangement between English Canada and Quebec which would permit of a common political strategy to ensure the survival of both nations independent of the United States.

The existence of such a grouping was evident at the time of the October 1970 crisis in the editorial pages of *The Canadian Forum* and in the (unrelated) activities of the Waffle. There was an English-Canadian nationalist response that transcended partisan politics and the ideological debate of capitalism versus socialism. That phenomenon attests to the fact that there is an interest within English Canada able to empathize with Quebec's independentist aspirations but also insisting on the right of English Canada to define, or more accurately redefine, its own agenda.

All of the federal parties have methodically suppressed nationalist sentiment within their ranks—from the removal of Diefenbaker by the Conservatives to the humiliation of Gordon by the Liberals to the expulsion of the Waffle by the NDP. Just as clearly, all of the parties have adopted intransigent positions towards Quebec. The legacy of Mr. Trudeau is ten lost years.

English-Canadian nationalists have no alternative but to regroup around these two interrelated threats to Canada's survival. While in no way underestimating the difficulties, we must take as an article of faith the possibility of working out wholly new confederal arrangements. One cannot do more than sketch out what their nature might be. On the one hand, there must be a dramatic degree of devolution of authority to Quebec appropriate to the growth of Quebec nationhood and, though to a much lesser degree that constitutes a difference in kind, to the other regions in recognition of the valid grievances of the west and the Atlantic Provinces against Ontario. We must transcend what Stanley Ryerson has called the two "evasions": "the simultaneous acceptance of cultural duality and refusal of political duality" and the "denial in practice of the binational fact in the name of provincialization".[5] On the other hand, there must be held for a central authority, the instruments needed to deal with the U.S.

(At the same time, it should be borne in mind that the aboriginal people, particularly in the north, are also demanding a new deal within Confederation. There is evidence of considerable support for these demands among southern Canadians. The issue of Quebec versus English-speaking Canada must not be allowed to push this into the background. Rather, new confederal arrangements must permit an accommodation that would redress the great historic damage done to the aboriginal people by both English Canadians and Québécois.)[6]

It is to be hoped that we can begin at least to see the possibilities. That should be sufficient for English Canadians to sense what might be done—if only we can transcend our now impoverished politics growing out of our colonized situation. It is idle to pretend that we know what Quebec would do in the face of new possibilities, but in the final analysis, the issue is not that but what we as English Canadians owe ourselves. Should Quebec separate, which is certainly a distinct possibility, we will be that much better prepared to stand as a nation in our own right.

There are moments in history when great change is possible. To challenge the state-structure as Quebec is doing, albeit in the name of nationalism, is to create such a moment. English Canada could use that moment to permit the federal state to deny, even openly repress, the legitimate aspirations of the Québécois—a Canadian version of the "Chilean solution". Or it could use that moment to attempt a dramatic restructuring of the state, not only with respect to Quebec but also with respect to the provinces proper, and, of critical importance, with respect to the long-neglected burden of defense against American domination. That choice lies with English Canadians.[7]

[5]Ryerson, "Quebec: Concepts of Class and Nation" in Gary Teeple, ed., *Capitalism and the National Question in Canada* (1972).

[6]Peter Russell argues that the Dené nation could, and ought to, be accommodated within Confederation even under the terms and spirit of the present BNA Act; see *The Canadian Forum*, November 1976.

[7]Some may say that this essay begs the fundamental question of whether English Canada exists. Undeniably, Quebec is a nation in a sense in which English Canada is not. But I agree with Stanley Ryerson: "There *is* some humus of an historic identity from which some things have sprouted, and a certain residual tough-rootedness remains. Why else would the American take-over encounter resistance, however sporadic and thinly scattered?" *op. cit.* Indeed, this is a minimal position; for an impressive presentation of a stronger position, see Herschel Hardin, *A Nation Unaware: The Canadian Economic Culture* (1974).

*Postscript*

The two themes of this commentary—which was written in the immediate aftermath of November 15—are the reality of the United States and the need for an English-Canadian nationalist response. The attempts by both Lévesque and Trudeau to curry American favour in their visits to the U.S. are striking manifestations of the former. Predictably, media discussion has been in terms of "Who won?", thereby masking the bitter fact that the behaviour of both demeaned us. Lévesque stressed the American interest in Quebec's James Bay project, though the latter is an incredible sell-out to the United States. Trudeau matched him by promising Carter that Canada would make a decision on a northern pipeline to move Alaskan gas across Canada—English Canada's James Bay project—in conformity with the American time-table, in return for which Carter spoke out in favour of Trudeau rather than Lévesque. Who would have thought that a contemporary version of the Panama Canal was an instrument for creating national unity!

The nationalist response from within English Canada has been two-fold. A number of the most prominant nationalists—Walter Gordon, Mel Hurtig, Peter Newman, Jack McClelland—have not only proven unable to empathize with Québécois nationalism, but have demonstrated a distinct lack of confidence in English Canada, in its viability as a nation, and the possibility of its surviving Quebec's independence. Faced with the reality of both the internal threat and the external threat, they have in effect denied any interrelationship—either in explaining the present situation or in pointing to a possible solution—and have thereby ended up, whatever their intentions, in the Trudeau "national unity" continentalist camp.

On the other hand, some of the nationalists, including this writer (with others who are not necessarily nationalists) have created the Committee for a New Constitution, arguing simultaneously that Quebec has the right to self-determination and that English Canada exists as a nation, thereby holding out the possibility that the two nations could find a common task in their survival on this continent independent of the United States. But it would, of course, be idle to pretend that this response is sufficient to the spectres that haunt us.

# The Quebec Problem

## Walter Gordon

I believe that most English-speaking Canadians understand and sympathize with the concern of Quebeckers, of all French Canadians, about safeguarding and preserving their language and their culture. French-speaking Canadians feel threatened, surrounded as they are by 250 million English-speaking North Americans. If the situation were reversed, we English-speaking Canadians would feel the same way they do.

I say this with some assurance because in an economic sense many of us worry about the dominating influence that foreigners, mostly American corporations, have on the Canadian economy and less directly on Canadian cultural and political affairs. If it were *our* language that was threatened, we would be disturbed indeed.

Some people seem to believe that Canada could survive if Quebec should separate. I am not one of them. If Quebec were to become a separate, independent country, English-speaking Canada would be divided into two unequal parts, with the Atlantic Provinces at one end, Ontario and the western provinces at the other. These two parts would be separated by a new, foreign, and conceivably unfriendly country in between. I do not believe such an arrangement would last indefinitely. More likely, some parts of the newly truncated English-speaking Canada would join the United States or negotiate special arrangements with that country. It would be the end of Canada as we know it.

Let us hope this will not happen; that some acceptable resolution of the problem will be found. It has been suggested that a parliamentary committee should be set up to consider changes in the constitution—

presumably including, of first importance, changes that would give Quebeckers firm assurances about the preservation of their language and their culture and a greater degree of control over their own affairs. This committee should hold hearings across Canada and welcome suggestions from all responsible associations and individuals.

While I believe that the federal authorities must retain full control in the fields of defence, foreign policy, relations with other countries, finance and economic policy, transportation, etc., I can see no reason why Quebec, subject to minority rights and interests, should not have complete control over cultural matters and education; over health and welfare and other social security matters (with the exception of unemployment insurance); and a veto over immigration from abroad (although not from other provinces). There may be other fields that should be allocated specifically to Quebec including responsibility for communications. And if Quebeckers would prefer to operate under a presidential rather than a parliamentary form of government within their own province and subject to the primary authority and responsibility of the federal government in the fields referred to previously, this also should be discussed openly and with sympathetic consideration.

At the time of the last census on July 1, 1976, only a little over 20 per cent of the total Canadian population of twenty-three million was represented by Canadians of French origin in the Province of Quebec. And, of course, a great many of these, still a large majority according to the opinion polls, are not separatists. But even supposing one-half or even three-quarters of all those of French origin in Quebec should vote in the proposed referendum in favour of separation, what would this mean? It would mean that 10 or 15 per cent of our total population had voted in a referendum to take an action that could mean the splitting up and eventually the end of Canada. What then?

René Lévesque, the premier of Quebec, has said that after Quebec has separated—which under the Canadian constitution would be illegal—he and his associates would sit down with the authorities in the English-speaking parts of the country and work out suitable economic arrangements with what remains of Canada. The Honourable William Davis, premier of Ontario, and the premiers of the four western provinces have said they would not negotiate with Quebec under such conditions. The federal government would have no right to acknowledge or accept the secession of Quebec or any other province. Therefore, they would have no right to negotiate with a Quebec that claimed to have separated from Canada. This being the case, the federal authorities should state unequivocally that they will not play René Lévesque's game; that they could not do so even if they wished.

If, despite these warnings, Quebec should decide to separate, Quebeckers should not expect English-speaking Canadians or the federal authorities to turn the other cheek. Quebeckers should know that in those circumstances they would be on their own; there would be no accommodation to be made with what remained of Canada.

Having said this, let me stress that in the affairs of civilized people, I am convinced much more can be accomplished by compromise in a spirit of goodwill than by threats and confrontation. Therefore, I would urge Lévesque and his associates not to put English-speaking Canadians in a position where negotiation becomes impossible. In the present climate of opinion, English-speaking Canadians would be more than ready to go along with much of what Quebec is seeking short of the dismembering of our country. But the time for a discussion of such matters is before, not after, Quebec holds its referendum.

I would hope also that arrangements for such discussion could take place before too many people in positions of responsibility make more provocative or naive remarks such as the suggestion of the unilateral extension of Quebec's borders into Labrador or the closing of the St. Lawrence waterway. The former could inspire a request by Newfoundland to the United States for help; the latter would mean serious damage to the economies of Ontario and the three Prairie Provinces as well as the United States. It is foolish to propose the closing of the St. Lawrence, for example, without thinking about the inevitable consequences of such action.

While the question of the future of Quebec will not be settled on the basis of material considerations, the economic consequences of separation should be clearly calculated and explained—in simple language. It would be unfortunate if Quebeckers were asked to vote in a referendum without knowing what the economic costs of separation might mean to them, without knowing what was going to happen to such Ottawa-initiated programmes as unemployment insurance, family allowances, old age pensions, hospital insurance, medicare, the Canada assistance programme, etc. The economic cards should be laid face upwards on the table.

Pierre Trudeau is an articulate, intelligent man who should know

Quebec as well or better than anyone else in parliament. However, at times he gives the impression of preferring confrontation to compromise and, sometimes, of preferring the process of discussion (the university seminar approach) to decisive action. The present critical situation calls for a conciliatory attitude on the part of all our public men coupled with some positive decisions. With this in mind, I believe it would be helpful if Mr. Trudeau were to strengthen his government by inviting two or three respected outsiders to join him in the task of holding our country together. If he were to set his sights high enough, Mr. Trudeau should be able to put together one of the strongest governments in Canadian history to deal with our country's greatest crisis. That in itself should be half the battle.

Present feelings of disquiet and uncertainty, which are contributing directly to the present economic malaise throughout Canada, including the record high level of unemployment, may be expected to continue until the Quebec crisis is resolved. With this in mind, I would urge the federal authorities to recover the initiative in this matter and to do so quickly.

# René Lévesque
## and the Sovereign State of Atlantica

### Silver Donald Cameron

Save Confederation. Just sign here.

It's Denis Smith, editor of *The Canadian Forum,* on the phone from Toronto. A group calling itself The Committee for a New Constitution will shortly issue a statement declaring that "English-speaking Canada exists as a viable national community. We have faith in its will to survive as an independent nation regardless of the choice that the people of Quebec may make about their future." It goes on to make various sensible proposals: a constitutional commission, a constituent assembly, a new constitution.

Would I, Smith asks, care to endorse this?

No, I reply, gazing out over the wind-whipped Atlantic waters, the wet brown fields of a Cape Breton April. I like the committee's open and exploratory tone, and I'd like to see those mechanisms tried. But I'm sick to death of being the token Maritimer whose endorsement gives a bogus "national" patina to such ventures, I think the unity of English Canada is an Ontario fantasy, and I'm Goddamned if I'll help manipulate the Atlantic Provinces during the death of Confederation as they have been manipulated throughout its lifetime.

Look here, Denis, I continue, you have twenty-eight people signing your statement: twenty-four are from Ontario. That's the way this country works: Ontarians cook up schemes, and the rest of us are conned, cajoled or bullied into going along. If we don't, we're pitied for our petty, provincial loyalties.

You want me to make a statement? Try this: if we can work out a just and equitable Confederation, I'm all for it. But if we can't, and Quebec pulls out, I'm prepared to contemplate independence for the Atlantic Provinces as well.

Your statement could have allowed for that, Denis, if you'd let us provincials play a part in formulating it. But Ontarians don't do that: they assume we'll simply buy their mythology along with their manufactures.

Well, says Smith apologetically, there wasn't time.

There never is.

An ironic footnote: one of the Ontarians who signed the statement is my brother.

*1843. Liverpool, England is home port to 150 ships of more than 500 tons. Of these, all but thirteen come from Canada's east coast— seventy-nine from New Brunswick alone. In Boston and London, the drawing-rooms are chuckling over the wicked satire of the Nova Scotian writer, Thomas Haliburton. In Halifax, Joseph Howe is demanding democratic self-government within Nova Scotia.*

*"We ask for nothing more than British subjects are entitled to," cries Howe, "but we shall be contented with nothing less." In 1848 he will succeed, setting a pattern for the entire British empire.*

*"A literary and philosophical society in Toronto in the 1840's," notes a Maritime historian drily, "lasted no more than a year."*

I live in an Acadian village.

What about the Acadians? A significant minority throughout our region, a powerful minority in New Brunswick: are they merely the Quebec diaspora?

Hardly.

The Acadians have no special love for the Québécois, or *canayens,* though they recognize that Quebec pressure in Ottawa has often worked to their benefit. "When I started in business, my father told me, Watch out for the *canayens,*" remarks Fernand Nadeau, a businessman, a former New Brunswick cabinet minister, a former mayor of Edmundston. "If you're going to be screwed, you'll be screwed by a *canayen.*"

Gerald Forgeron, a Nova Scotia contractor, opines that if Quebec separates our best bet would be to join the United States. Michel Blanchard, a young radical in Caraquet, New Brunswick, has lived in Quebec **and could** do so **again**, but he felt like a refugee there, he didn't belong.

That's why he fights for Acadian rights: he belongs to French New Brunswick.

To the Québécois, the Acadians are half-assimilated hicks who speak with a funny accent: Gallic Newfoundlanders. "To the Acadians," smiles a Radio-Canada producer from Montreal, "we are what the Upper Canadians are for you. I don't t'ink they like us very much."

The producer is in Cape Breton preparing to do a film for French TV. In 1977 Radio-Canada has lots of money available for films telling the *canayens* about the glories of the other nine provinces.

*1860. The shipping of the Atlantic colonies, the sale of vessels from their shipyards, has made each of the little colonies a commercial power in its own right. Nova Scotia and Newfoundland are among the most active trading nations on earth. One-fifth of Britain's imports come from New Brunswick.*

*In 1858, memoranda were sent east from the Province of Canada, that sprawling, disunited, landlocked colony up the St. Lawrence: the Canadians proposed discussions of a possible confederation of the British North American colonies. Most Maritimers considered the idea absurd. The seaside provinces were prosperous, peaceful and cosmopolitan; about a third of their trade involved the United States, and less than 5 per cent involved Canada. The Canadians squabbled among themselves, raised rebellions, burned parliament buildings. The Canadians were men of large ambitions and small means. What on earth could they offer the Atlantic colonies?*

"Cuntario," snorted the sawyer. "Cuntarians. They're worse than the fuckin' Yanks." We sat in the autumn sunlight, sharing a beer while the sawmill lay silent, the air sharp with the smell of sawn spruce and ripe hay, the truck already loaded with lumber. The sawmill is one of those little one-man affairs powered by an unmuffled engine from a dead truck, tucked away at the end of a dirt road. Around it stand the ruins of a farm, the house caving in, the untended apple trees bowing low with masses of little apples, a forlorn symbol of our lost self-sufficiency.

Cape Breton is a vast forest, cut these days chiefly for the Swedish-owned pulp mill at Port Hawkesbury, some of its wood exported as peeled logs to mills in Europe. For generations, Cape Bretoners have built their houses by felling their own trees, hauling them to miniature mills such as this one, paying to have them sawn, and building the houses themselves, with whatever help their friends and family can provide.

Now the county is adopting the National Building Code, which means all building lumber will have to be "stamped"—kiln-dried and inspected. Cape Breton has no facilities for preparing such lumber: it is trucked to Cape Breton from Montreal.

The National Building Code is a colonial instrument, used by our Upper Canadian masters. So is the National Housing Act: in 1967, a study showed that 34 per cent to 38 per cent of new Canadian homes were financed through NHA, but only 7 per cent of new homes in Cape Breton. To get an NHA mortgage, you required an income of more than $6,000—and in 1967 that eliminated about three Cape Breton families out of four.

The little sawmill is the last dying kick of what was once a great lumber industry. Its days are clearly numbered.

Bring in a regulation in Ottawa. Destroy a man's little livelihood. Boost the price of Cape Breton housing. Then complain about the lack of Maritime enterprise, the apparently endless welfare payments to the East Coast, the intractability of regional disparity. And blame the Maritimers for the poverty you organized.

*1864. "The Lower Provinces have all the elements of social, commercial and political prosperity and greatness without respect to Canada," declares the Saint John Globe. But times are changing. Railways and steamships are gaining ground. The Americans are ending their civil war and muttering about ending the lucrative free trade under the Reciprocity Treaty. Indeed, the victorious North is making threatening noises about annexation, and the Irish fanatics, the Fenians, are preparing to raid the North American territories of the hated British Crown. An Intercolonial Railway from Halifax to Canada via the Gulf of St. Lawrence begins to look like a military necessity, and the British are increasingly reluctant to pay for colonial defences.*

*Almost absent-mindedly, the Maritimes decide to hold a conference at Charlottetown to consider the possibilities of Maritime union. In Canada, Reform leader George Brown proposes to John A. Macdonald and his Conservative co-leader George Etienne Cartier a coalition government to push for a confederation of all the British provinces. The*

*Canadians ask to participate at Charlottetown—and there, aided by excellent food, copious drinks, sparkling oratory from the engaging Thomas D'Arcy McGee, "they carried the Lower Province delegates a little off their feet", as a Fredericton journal remarked. An October conference at Quebec firms up the proposals. Confederation is on its way.*

Regional disparity is not a problem: it's a policy. Regional disparity is the whole point of Confederation.

Subsidies to the *Atlantic Provinces* are out in the open: equalization payments, regional economic expansion grants and so forth. The much greater federal advantages to Ontario (and, to a lesser extent, Quebec) are concealed. Who paid the enormous capital cost of the St. Lawrence Seaway, covers its perennial operating losses, keeps it open all winter long with icebreakers, to the detriment of Saint John and Halifax? The Government of Canada. And who benefits? Ontario. Who does the tariff serve? Ontario. Who pays for the lavish life of the Ontario town of Ottawa? All the people of Canada.

Ontario Hydro imports coal from Pennsylvania at the same time that coal mines are being shut down in Nova Scotia and New Brunswick. Not only that, it's paid a subsidy to do so. Does the Cape Breton coal miner, by the same token, get a subsidy for buying a car from Sweden rather than Ontario? Don't be foolish.

We can't compete, they say, because we're remote. From what? We're half an inch from New England, a short sail from Europe, New York, the Caribbean. We're only remote if the centre of the universe is in Ontario.

The Arabs raise oil prices, and suddenly it's an economic imperative for Alberta to follow suit. Virtually all the electricity in Nova Scotia and absolutely all of it in Prince Edward Island is produced by oil-fired generators. Taken as a whole, Canada is self-sufficient, for the moment, in oil. But Canada is *not* taken as a whole. The Maritimes get a bit of "transitional" assistance, and then an explosive rise in power rates: Nova Scotia's are now by far the highest in Canada. People with electrically heated homes face bi-monthly bills of $400, $500, $600. They have to move out: and their houses are unsalable. An upholsterer near my home, an employer of two people, prepares to move out west: he can't pay the power bills out of what he can earn.

FOR SALE OR RENT—1973 Paramount mobile home, 12x68, partly furnished, skirting, oil tank, TV antennas, located in east Havre Boucher on 6 acres of land. Phone——. Reason for selling moving to Alberta.

*(Scotia Sun, Port Hawkesbury, N.S., April 13, 1977)*

Is this one country, or is it not?

*1865. The Confederation movement is well underway. It has vast support in Canada—but in New Brunswick, this spring, a general election defeats* every single delegate to the Quebec conference who held a seat in the House. *The government of S.L. Tilley is replaced by a violently anti-Confederation government headed by Albert Smith. One new MLA describes Canada as "a bankrupt wanting to assume the debts of a rich man".*

*"Forty-eight thousand men," exults Fredericton's Billy Needham, "have said we don't want Confederation, and that should be the end of it."*

Late in 1976, Premier Alex Campbell of Prince Edward Island thought the Council of Maritime Premiers should initiate a study of Maritime options in the event of Quebec's separation. Hatfield of New Brunswick and Regan of Nova Scotia declined: Quebec separation was simply unthinkable, and thinking about it would somehow increase its likelihood. So we blunder on through the darkness, assuring one another we can see.

Politicians have always loved Confederation, which gives them a larger stage on which to play their odd roles. Its demise, they chorus, would be disastrous for the Atlantic Provinces. Campbell says "it would take us fifty years to get back to just where we are right now". Tory MP Elmer Mackay considers it "criminal". Robert Stanfield says "it's important for the people down here to understand that they could be very badly hurt".

Allan J. MacEachen, who represents my own area, invites his constituents "to think about . . . the fundamental question: 'Do I want Quebec to remain within Confederation?' " Apparently he believes that warm thoughts in Inverness will somehow change opinions in Chicoutimi. He continues: "A clear distinction must be made between what the people of the Province of Quebec want and what the Parti Québécois is saying they want. The Parti Québécois was elected to provide good government, not to negotiate independence." Alas, the same argument could be turned more forcefully against MacEachen's own gang on the question of, say, wage and price controls: Lévesque, at least, never campaigned *against* independence. Father Andy Hogan, the NDP member for neighbouring Cape Breton-East Richmond, is far more incisive, pointing out that none of the provincial parties in Quebec, "including the provincial Liberals, favoured the kind of inflexible federalism traditionally expounded by Mr. Trudeau".

And yet Hogan himself falls into the same trap of assuming that well-meaning actions taken elsewhere are likely to affect a decision which will obviously be made *in Quebec*: he concludes with a lame call for more French in Nova Scotia schools.

Hogan is no fool, but he's trapped inside the federalist assumptions. Listen to that delightful man, the Quebec novelist Roch Carrier, saddened as long ago as 1971 by "that inevitable war between the French and the English". Why was it inevitable?

"You don't accept that somebody takes what's yours," Carrier explained. "I think that for an English Canadian Quebec is his property, because it's part of his country; and nobody wants to lose what belongs to him. It's not possible to imagine Quebec leaving smoothly."

He sounds chillingly correct. Listen to Elmer Mackay: "I just can't see how we can *allow* one-third of our country to secede."

*Our* country. You don't accept that somebody takes what's yours.

*1866. A bad Fenian scare, the end of Reciprocity, heavy pressure from England (where the Canadians have powerfully lobbied the Colonial Office) and a highly irregular use of the royal prerogative to dismiss Smith's anti-Confederation government. Reluctantly, New Brunswickers are becoming persuaded that Confederation is the best of a series of unpalatable alternatives. New elections, in which tens of thousands of Canadian dollars flow east, and in June a solid majority for Tilley and Confederation, the Acadian counties remaining firmly opposed.*

*Joseph Howe tours western Nova Scotia and reports he "could not find five hundred confederates" in eight counties. But the Tupper government was elected in 1863, before Confederation was even an issue; it does not need to go to the people again before the fall of 1867. Indeed, it doesn't dare.*

Consider Irene's teeth. Better yet, consider her gums, since she has no teeth to speak of.

Irene is a pretty, good-humoured thirty-year-old who has lived on welfare since her husband deserted her and her five children four years ago. One Saturday night five friends dropped in.

"Going to the dance, Irene?"

"Now how in the hell can I go to the dance? I got no teet'."

"Use mine," said George, pulling out his plate.

"Use mine," said Bernice, doing the same.

"Here's mine," said Freddy.

Five of them, none over thirty, and all with false teeth. The nearest dentists are thirty miles away, and they are taking no new patients; they're booked up for more than a year. Regular check-ups? You're joking. Add in poor food, no money, no public transportation. Irene's teeth never had a chance.

Finally they abscessed. Her jaw bellied out, she gnawed on painkillers, and on an emergency basis the dentist pulled all her uppers. He proposed to pull the lowers as well. But she had to appeal for a special allowance to get false teeth. The welfare committee in Arichat decided that she didn't actually *need* teeth; she only needed to deal with the abscess. False teeth, said the committee, are only "cosmetic".

Before Confederation, Arichat was a prosperous shipbuilding town, centre of an international trade, the seat of a college and a Catholic cathedral. In 1873, Arichat boasted 143 sailing ships and a steamer. Today it's little more than a couple of food and hardware stores, a consolidated high school and a poignantly oversized church.

Regional disparity is a community so straitened it has to quibble about paying for a deserted mother's teeth.

Regional disparity is the obscene spectacle of the federal government spending $3.5 million to send celebrities around the country to celebrate Canada Day, or Dominion Day, or whatever they call it now. Commercials on TV, Bobby Hull and Anne Murray selling Confederation like patent medicine, free wieners on Parliament Hill.

Nice to have the wieners, no doubt. Nicer still to have teeth.

*May 22, 1867. Tupper still has not submitted the Confederation plan to the Assembly. Joseph Howe speaks in Dartmouth:*
*A year ago Nova Scotia presented the aspect of a self-governed*

*community, loyal to a man, attached to their institutions, cheer-*
*ful, prosperous and contented . . . . Now all this has been*
*changed. We have been entrapped into a revolution . . . . The*
*Canadians are to appoint our Governors, Judges and Senators.*
*They are to "tax us by any and every mode" and spend the*
*money. They are to regulate our trade, control our Post Offices,*
*command the militia, fix the salaries, do what they like with our*
*shipping and navigation, with our seacoast and river fisheries,*
*regulate the currency and the rate of interest, and seize upon our*
*Savings Banks . . . .*

"I'm very glad you called," gushes the federal bureaucrat over the
phone from Halifax. "Our department has funded several welfare rights
groups in the past, and I'd like you to invite me to come down and tell
you how to tailor your programme to fit our national priorities, and
make you eligible for funding."

*Your* national priorities, buddy? Who is this group supposed to
serve: the poor people who organized it, or the Master Planners of
Ottawa?

Nevertheless, they wrote to invite him. Six months later he hadn't
replied.

*June, 1867. An obituary in the Saint John* Freeman:
*Died—at her late residence in the City of Fredericton, on the 20th*
*day of May last, from the effects of an accident which she re-*
*ceived in April, 1866, and which she bore with a patient resigna-*
*tion to the will of Providence, the Province of New Brunswick, in*
*the 83rd year of her age.*
*July 1, 1867. The first day of the new nation's existence. Newfound-*
*land and P.E.I. are having no part of it. A front-page obituary in the*
*Halifax* Morning Chronicle, *edged in black:*
*Died—Last Night at 12 o'clock, the Free and Enlightened Province*
*of Nova Scotia.*
*September 18, 1867. Tupper at last faces his infuriated electors, in*
*simultaneous provincial and federal elections. Of thirty-eight provincial*
*victors, thirty-six are committed to the immediate repeal of Confed-*
*eration. Of nineteen federal members, the only supporter of Confedera-*
*tion even to win a seat is Tupper himself.*

Consider the views of E.F. Schumacher, in *Small is Beautiful: A*
*Study of Economics As If People Mattered.* Large countries, he says,

don't work: most large countries are terribly poor, and those that are rich are perpetually riven by gross disparities and social strains.

Some people ask, "What happens when a country, composed of one rich province and several poor ones, falls apart because the rich province secedes?" The rich will continue to be rich and the poor will continue to be poor. "But if, before secession, the rich province had subsidized the poor, what happens then?" Well then, of course, the subsidy might stop. But the rich rarely subsidize the poor; more often they exploit them. They may not do so directly so much as through the terms of trade. They may obscure the situation a little by a certain redistribution of tax revenue or small-scale charity, but the last thing they want to do is secede from the poor.

The normal case is quite different, namely that the poor provinces wish to separate from the rich, and that the rich want to hold on because they know that exploitation of the poor within one's own frontiers is infinitely easier than exploitation of the poor beyond them.

After the Quebec election, Canada was swept (I hear) by a wave of unity movements, One Canada organizations, and similar effusions. Oddly enough, the Atlantic Provinces—whom all official voices claimed had most to lose from Quebec's separation—have shown no such patriotic panic. The popular agitation is an *Ontario* agitation, and to a lesser extent a western agitation. The economic muscle of Canada is in Ontario, and to a lesser extent in the west.

The last thing the rich want to do is secede from the poor.

*1868. Two yeras earlier, Joseph Howe carried a petition to London with 31,000 signatures—from a province of 400,000 people—begging that Confederation be delayed until after an election. He failed. In 1868, now an MP in the federal House himself, and bearing a commission from the intransigently separatist government in Halifax, he tries again.*

*"Nova Scotia," writes John A. Macdonald, "has declared, so far as she can, against Confederation; but she will be powerless to harm, although that pestilent fellow, Howe, may endeavour to give us some trouble in England."*

*Again Howe fails—and the next year Macdonald offers some financial adjustments to Nova Scotia. Howe considers all the alternatives*

*including armed insurrection, and concludes that further resistance
would be futile. He accepts the improved terms, and a seat in the
federal cabinet for himself.*

*1886. Premier W.S. Fielding fights a Nova Scotia election on the
platform of Maritime separation, and Maritime independence. He wins
handsomely. Again the federal government comes up with more money,
and takes Fielding into the federal cabinet. Saint John is still the
fourth-largest wooden ship-owning port in the world, but the Maritimes
have already become what they remain to this day: colonies of Upper
Canada, captive Third-World countries in a federation they never had
reason to love.*

*Third World? A Cape Breton doctor's survey revealed that by all the
usual indicators the level of public health in my home county is comparable with that of Kenya.*

*1887. Newfoundland again rejects Confederation.*

The Maritime public, as opposed to the politicians, seems distinctly
cheerful about the prospect of Canada's disintegration. Lévesque's case,
people whisper, is the same as ours, and his solution is the proper one.
"The separation of Quebec," declares a Nova Scotia harbour pilot,
"may be the best damn thing that ever happened to us." A Cape Breton
historian, Terrence MacLean, agrees: "November 15, 1976, may well
turn out to be a more significant date in our history than July 1,
1867."

The Halifax *Chronicle-Herald* runs speculative pieces about an independent Nova Scotia, and publishes huge ads throughout the region
explaining Tupper's chicanery and the illegality of Nova Scotia's forced
entry into Canada. New Democratic MLA Paul MacEwan publishes a
book, *Confederation and the Maritimes* (Lancelot Press, 1976), con-
cluding that "very soon after Quebec independence, we in the Maritimes would have to follow suit". Nor does he seem reluctant: "In the
next few years, Maritimers are going to be giving Confederation its one
last chance. There is no great sentiment within these provinces to leave
Canada; but *there will be* if Canada does not end its systematic
injustice."

MacEwan points out that Canada's trade arrangements, notably the
tariff, mean that Maritimers must *sell* in the international market, as we
have always done, but cannot *buy* there. The tariff protects Upper

Canadian manufactures, not Maritime raw materials. Of Canadian jobs dependent on the protective tariff, 49 per cent are in Ontario, 37 per cent in Quebec, and only 14 per cent in all the other provinces together. And MacEwan warns Quebec, rightly, that the vision of economic association between an independent Quebec and the rest of Canada is probably pie-in-the-sky; the Maritimes, at least, "would have no desire whatever to participate in any such set-up".

*1895. Newfoundland again rejects Confederation.*

*1911. In London, one Beckles Willson publishes a book:* Nova Scotia: The Province That Has Been Passed By.

*1936.* Maclean's *publishes an article: "Will the Maritimes Secede?" by S. Leonard Tilley. A joke, or an irony? Samuel Leonard Tilley led New Brunswick into Confederation in the first place.*

*1938. Addressing the Canadian Club of Toronto, Nova Scotia's perennial premier Angus L. Macdonald reminds his audience of the arguments of the anti-Confederates, their claims that the union would wreck Nova Scotia's economy, and admits he finds them "well-founded". In economic terms, "it would have been distinctly to Nova Scotia's advantage to remain out of Confederation".*

I have a mother in Vancouver, relations strewn across the Prairies, two brothers in Ontario, children in New Brunswick. Yes, I'd prefer a united Canada. But not at *any* price—and the price the Maritimes have paid in political, economic and human terms has been outrageous.

May, 1977. I am speaking at the college in Sydney, I am interviewed by the Cape Breton *Post.* What did you say? ask my tablemates at lunch—young, bright people who are building one of the most innovative and interesting colleges in Canada.

I said I had told the *Post* reporter that Quebec's separation might be a sovereign opportunity for us. That the four Atlantic Provinces might make a nation comparable to Norway or Denmark. That if the Scandinavians can use similar resources to make cars, furniture, films, sailboats and surgical instruments for the markets of the world, so can the people of Atlantica. That if China, for generations the sick man of Asia, can pull itself together so that a mere twenty-five years after a crippling civil war it can export work shirts and teacups to Cape Breton, we can do it too.

That Canada, in short, is an encumbrance, and that René Lévesque has done us all a favour by declaring that this corrupt, lopsided Confederation is finished. Things unthinkable a year ago can be thought about today.

Had we all been thinking these things in solitude? Suddenly the table was crackling with plans, prospects and opportunities. Visions began to crystallize, farmland coming back into production, sawmills and woodworking plants springing up, the triangular trade with Europe and the Caribbean flourishing, films, publishing, boatbuilding, the liberation of Maritime vitality. Like a lightning rod, the very thought of independence seemed to concentrate energies which had been dissipated in a century of stagnation.

What was happening to us? I wondered, and then I saw it: the graphic demonstration of Confederation's failure. For these young people were electrified by the mere idea of *a country of their own*, a country where their humanity would be respected and their labours needed, a country which they might develop for the glory of their gods, and for the flowering of their people.

If Confederation had succeeded, they might have felt that way about Canada.

# Hangin' 'Er Tough

## Alden Nowlan

Since last November 15 I've felt like a little boy who overhears his parents talking divorce. I suspect that the reaction of many of my compatriots to the Parti Québécois victory and its repercussions has been equally childlike. The grass is green, the sky is blue, one belongs to a certain country. When I was eight years old and listening to a radio broadcast of *Superman* the one thing that frightened me about the destruction of the planet Krypton was its sky turning red. When that voice shouted, "Look! The sky is red!" I could feel the butterflies trying to get out through my belly button. Could Earthlings live on a planet with a red sky, I wonder, or would we put on blue eyeglasses for fear of being driven mad?

Not that we'll go crazy if Canada disintegrates. But we'll every last one of us become at least a little more neurotic than before. Canadians of my generation are probably already a bit more neurotic than they'd otherwise be, from having ceased to be shareholders in the British Empire. Although our historians seem to be strangely unaware of this, we never thought of ourselves as colonials. Almost until the Empire collapsed, the overseas Britons were in their own eyes the true Britons. Take Lord Beaverbrook, Bennet and Bonar Law. Take Rudyard Kipling. For that matter, take the late Lord Thomson. We looked up to England but down on the English. Emotionally, Canadians were citizens of the most powerful country in the world.

It's surprising that no one has researched and published a study of how the Canadian psyche was affected by the loss of what we had always looked upon as Our Empire. Deep within each of us who was born in the 1930s or earlier there must be a feeling faintly akin to that experienced by the German Austrians who lived through 1918. It's not easy to go from being members of the highest caste in an Empire on which the sun never sets to being nationals of a country which, on a population map, closely resembles Chile.

In any event, television probably would have dispelled the illusion. As far as our ancestors were concerned, Queen Victoria spoke with a sensible Canadian accent. They'd not have said that, if anyone had been silly enough to ask them. But it's how they thought. Not even the most schizophrenic monarchist in Victoria or Fredericton could refuse to believe that Queen Elizabeth II is an Englishwoman.

Here in the Maritimes there's very little talk about the future of Confederation. In the first place, Maritimers don't usually talk about the things that trouble them. They tend to believe that the less one talks about a problem the more likely it is to go away. Don't laugh. It often works. It's possible and, perhaps, even probable that the crises in Northern Ireland, the Middle East and elsewhere would by now have been resolved if everybody had simply shut up about them. When English-speaking Canadians impatiently growl, "Let Quebec go," what they sometimes mean is, "For God's sake, let's all of us call a halt to this ceaseless nattering."

Yesterday, however, I talked with a man who said his brother had recently emigrated to the United States because, as a young man beginning his career and the father of small children, he was unwilling to endure years of uncertainty as to his country's continued survival. The fear is aggravated where I live by the likelihood that a break-up of Canada would almost inevitably bring about a break-up of New Brunswick. At present, there's very little separatist feeling among the Acadians, who comprise 35 per cent of the province's population. But it's a reasonable assumption that if Canada fell apart they'd sooner or later turn to Quebec.

Maritimers don't move to New England as casually as they used to do. There was a time when everybody in Nova Scotia and almost everybody in Prince Edward Island and New Brunswick had a sister or a brother in Boston. Now it's more likely to be a great aunt or a great uncle. The Maritime baseball fans who were once the most loyal supporters of the Red Sox have switched their allegiance to the Expos, for the most part. Twenty years ago, many Haligonians and Saint Johnners thought nothing of driving to Boston for the weekend. Nowadays, the Saint Johnners fly to Toronto, instead, and the Haligonians stay home.

The Maritime attitude toward Confederation has always been ambivalent. Nobody loves Canada—and nobody hates Canada—more than we do. And nobody but us knows or cares about the price we've paid for being Canadian.

A month ago or more I watched a very silly programme on CBC television. An assortment of allegedly representative Canadians had been assembled to discuss the future of their country. The gimmick was that they were all of them bilingual (which, ironically, showed that none of them was truly representative). They were to natter for a while in English on the English network and then natter some more in French on the French network. My only clear recollection of this absurd undertaking is of Patrick Watson, the co-host, continually admonishing the speakers, in effect, to cut that boring historical crap and get with it. In this age of television, he seemed to be saying, nothing that happened more than fifteen seconds ago is of the slightest consequence.

We may choose to remain ignorant of history. But we can't choose to ignore history. It's there, as surely as the rock that Johnson kicked to refute Berkeley.

A Toronto nationalist was dumbfounded when, at a cocktail party in Fredericton, a New Brunswick-born university professor told him he was delighted that the Yanks were taking over Upper Canadian industries "because now you SOBs are getting a taste of the medicine you gave us". (When Maritimers talk like that it's with no more but also with no less conviction than that of a Highland Scot berating the English for Culloden and the Clearances.)

U.S. investment in Canada has, at least, created branch plants. When Upper Canadian companies bought Maritime factories it was generally to shut them down. The market was then supplied with goods shipped in from Ontario.

This process was so widespread and so bitterly resented (especially by the men who lost their jobs as a result) that it has become a part of Maritime folklore. Old-timers talk about it the way old-timers in the southern United States used to talk about the Carpetbaggers.

Perhaps I ought to pause here to explain that the term "Upper

Canadian" survives in the Maritimes not because of a regional penchant for archaic figures of speech but, mostly, because it's convenient. If we abandoned it, we'd have to devise a substitute, because we're east of the East.

The Québécois believe, fallaciously, that there is only one English-speaking Canada. Many influential and articulate inhabitants of Ontario believe the same thing, with much less excuse. *The Canadian Forum*'s Committee for a New Constitution would create a constituent assembly, the membership of which would be divided equally between French Canada and English Canada, as if nothing had changed since the Act of Union of 1841. In fact, the Atlantic Provinces differ from Ontario at least as much as Scotland differs from England. And if there were a mythology to give it credibility, separatism might be more vigorous in the Maritimes and Newfoundland than in Quebec.

If, for instance, our most pugnacious foe of Confederation, Joseph Howe, had carried out his threat to fight on the Tantramar Marshes and had died there at the head of his troops . . . but instead he capitulated and joined Sir John A. Macdonald's cabinet, ending up as lieutenant-governor of Nova Scotia.

You can't base an independence movement on the fact that this is the only place in North America where there's widespread use of "bloody" as a universal adjective and taverns are as often as not referred to as "pubs". Nor can you create a nationality merely because a people drink tea for breakfast, pour molasses on their buckwheat pancakes and continue to eat salt codfish, although there's no longer any practical reason why it should be salted and it has come to cost not a great deal less than steak.

We've acquired a distinct ethnic image, but it's not the kind you can build on. A friend of mine applied for a job as a labourer in Toronto. "I know you Maritimers," the boss said to him. "All you care about is cheap rum, country music and one another's women." The typical Maritime reaction to such an anecdote is ambivalent. There's resentment, but there's also an odd kind of pride. In his heart, the most respectable Maritimer or Newfoundlander likes to think of himself as a bit of a roaring boy.

Yet the people of the Atlantic Provinces are probably the most resolutely Canadian of Canadians. This isn't as paradoxical as it may sound. We look to Canada in almost the same way as the last tattered shreds of the Empire look to Britain. Like the Falkland Islanders and the inhabitants of Gibraltar, we fear that any conceivable change in our status would leave us worse off than we already are.

Everybody here—barber, cabbie, senator—points to Bangla Desh as an example of what happens to a country that's geographically bisected. Economically and culturally, the comparison is absurd. But maps are highly potent symbols. Colour Quebec blue and the other provinces pink and you'll have set up a barrier more effective than a line of customs houses.

As for entering a common market with an independent Quebec, the suggestion is likely to evoke a sardonic laugh. Ever since Sir John A. Macdonald's National Policy cut us off from our natural suppliers in New England we've been subsidizing Upper Canadian industries. Why in God's name should we make the same kind of sacrifice on behalf of a foreign country?

Only the region's artists, its poets and writers, who are more numerous and more successful than at any time since Bliss Carmen and Sir Charles G.D. Roberts were in their heyday, might look with a measure of hope to the setting up of a sovereign successor state, a Dominion of Acadia or a North Atlantic Republic. And they'd have grave doubts, suspecting with some justification that the leadership of the new state, cut off from outside intellectual influences, would be as unenlightened as that of the Republic of Ireland between the First and Second World Wars, and in much the same way.

Everyone else, except Newfoundland Premier Frank Moores who has mentioned, perhaps only half-seriously, the possibility of economic union with Norway, seems to assume that the orphaned provinces would join the United States.

However, I've yet to hear anyone express any enthusiasm for the idea. It's generally accepted in the same spirit as children who have been deprived of their natural parents accept the fact that they'll have to enter a foster home.

Besides, why would the Yanks want us? They've got problems enough already, without taking in four poverty-stricken second cousins, twice removed. And, judging from statistics, fourteen of the fifty states are in worse shape, economically, than we are.

The dominant mood of Atlantic Canada is one of quiet desperation, which is far from being synonymous with mute despair. Denis Ryan of

Ryan's Fancy, an Irish-born, Newfoundland-based trio of folksingers, says that in his experience there's nowhere else in North America where the people are as vibrantly alive as in Atlantic Canada.

I doubt that anyone in the Maritimes or Newfoundland lies awake nights worrying about the future of Confederation. As Samuel Johnson said, a man who is unsure of his dinner or trembling at a creditor is not much given to abstract speculation. If you ask a native of these provinces how he's doing he may reply that he's hangin' 'er tough. To hang 'er tough isn't to sink into the lethargy of self-pity; rather, it's to think, things are bad and are likely to get worse confounded soon, but there's bloody little we can do about it and, so what the hell, we might as well dance.

None of the region's political leaders, an unimaginative lot, is as representative of its people as is Stompin' Tom Connors who has said that his life's ambition is to "sing Canada to the world". It's significant that Connors, who says that he'll start singing Yank songs when the Yanks start singing his songs, was born in Nova Scotia and grew up in New Brunswick and Prince Edward Island.

The Canadian Identity is alive and well and living in the wet canteen of the Royal Canadian Legion branch in Whitney Pier, Cape Breton.

If I've sounded pessimistic in this piece it's because I assume it will be read mostly by university-educated, middle-class residents of southern Ontario, the people Maritimers have in mind when they use "Upper Canadian" in a somewhat depreciatory sense. The average Toronto waitress knows more about her country than the average Toronto journalist, and may very well have seen more of it. Certainly, she's likely to have seen more of the Maritimes because if she isn't an immigrant the chances are she came from here. The largest ethnic minorities in Toronto are the Portuguese, the Italians and the Maritimers, a friend once said to me, and the Maritimers are the hardest to assimilate.

The great Canadian tragedy may be that the centres of power are situated so far inland. We might never have found ourselves in our present predicament if the nation's capital were Montreal. In a sense, English Canada is in the position the United States would be in if its political capital were Kalamazoo and its cultural-intellectual capital were Buffalo.

# The Overwhelming Question

## Reshard Gool

If Quebec goes—manages to leave our present degrading form of Confederation—should the Maritimes follow?

From what port does the insistent question sail? Where does this constantly shifting cargo of pain and fear, of intense bitterness, originate? Someone must have known the answer as long ago as 1867 because, although Charlottetown was the birthplace of Confederation, Prince Edward Island would not join until 1873, six years later; the terms were unfavourable.

The terms are still unfavourable. What Pierre Vallières describes in *White Niggers of America*—the destruction and demoralizing of his people in Ville Jacques-Cartier—is what has been happening to us ever since we joined Confederation. If anything, the Maritimes are worse off. Every new scheme tailored and parachuted out of Ottawa by DREE, every new CBC programme hatched in Toronto, is another nail in the Maritime coffin. Call it U.S. and Upper Canadian monopoly capitalism working against the smaller and more remote regions. Use the statistics of Left or Right. What this means, practically, is that Charlottetown buckles under the highest food prices in the country and the lowest wages. For me this means that a family two corners away eats meat once a month, sends its children to school without food, and cannot afford decent winter heating. Quebec workers may fetch low wages, but at least they have unions. Here in the Maritimes, as recently as 1970, the Cape Breton fishermen struck to establish their right to unionize, and lost.

162

In terms of broadcasting and the arts the region has been totally colonized. CBC radio in Charlottetown is little more than a relay station for outside programming, everything geared to the ever-so-smart, ever-so-trite current affairs model of *As It Happens*. A year ago, CBC Halifax did a programme on the work of a local artist, Hilda Woolnough, which was not even broadcast locally. If the Québécois are North America's white niggers, what term will serve to describe the more destitute and spiritually besieged Maritimers?

How can I give other Canadians, embalmed as so many are in self-congratulation, disinterest and ignorance, any idea of what it really means to live in the Maritimes?

Consider, for example, the Hypro case. The Hypro plant was set up by Comeau Seafoods, the P.E.I. Department of Industry, and DREE. It was located in the port town of Souris, King's County—a western outpost of the island. Hypro combined two quite shrewd ideas, and its path was strewn with the best intentions. It's purpose was to link two traditional industries: shipbuilding and fishing. For years the Georgetown yards had lain idle; now they would ring with the staccato of rivetters, the crash of the boilermakers. The Souris plant would process the catch from the two new trawlers, to create fishmeal.

Four million dollars later (one million for the plant, two for the trawlers, and about one for consulting, operating costs, etc.), after speeches, festivities, launching, the plant closed down and the trawlers, *Lady Janice* and *Lady Maria*, lay rusting in Georgetown harbour, great expectations scuttled along with public funds.

For the plant to operate economically, it needed 40,000 tons of fish annually. Only about 19,000 tons were processed in 1971. In 1972, when the plant closed, Comeau Seafoods was found not to have paid taxes to Souris for three years. The whiz-kids of IEI, a local think-tank, had predicted the plant would create twenty new jobs; when it closed, the plant employed only eight workers.

Of course experts blamed the low herring catch of 1971 on unusual rainfall conditions. On the government level, the Hypro case showed how out of touch with each other certain government departments were, not just at the federal/provincial level. The aim of the local Department of Fisheries was to encourage, and indeed spawn, a new industry. However, federal fisheries, under the direction of Jack Davis, favoured the big B.C. fishing interests which had fished-out B.C. waters and were now determined to rape the Maritimes. What brave little P.E.I. was trying to do was muscle in to a foreign-dominated industry, thereby contradicting the general thrust of the federal fisheries policy and also placing an unnecessary burden on the agencies I have mentioned, agencies committed to coping at different levels with communities rooted in traditional ways of life.

Even the two trawlers, each worth more than a million dollars, were doomed to rust because they had been built to specifications which made it impossible to convert them except at prohibitive expense. But let me not go on about this case, which is one of many that has eaten away at the fabric of life here and sent our young people "down the road".

Against this scenario of incompetence and bungling must be seen the almost heroic efforts of local politicians and civil servants to create a more dynamic province. When the Shaw government was defeated a few years ago, the new premier Alex Campbell could not even raise a levy in Ottawa: provincial credibility was at an all-time low. In the sixties farms were going out of business at the rate of one a week. Campbell is an astute and dedicated politician. There are others, too, like John Eldon Green, who almost singlehandedly reorganized our local Department of Welfare, or Andrew Wells who heads our Institute of Man and Resources, a breakthrough organization for the island.

These people must struggle not only against very real social and economic realities, but against inherited preconceptions, frameworks, institutions and procedures that cripple intelligent and decisive action. They must watch while Confederation Centre for the Arts, a multi-million dollar federal white elephant, spends its one-and-a-half million dollar budget to host foreign art and drama, with token respects paid to the regional dead (Robert Harris's paintings and the perennial *Anne of Green Gables*) while young, alive and dynamic local artists go ignored, or find their way strewn with bureaucratic obstacles.

And we are asked to *shake hands with Canada*, like good colonials! Shake hands with Ontario is more to the point. But we are learning that when you shake hands you become vulnerable: you can't reach for your gun, or your slide-rule, or your calculator. Instead of this rhetoric and buncombe we need honesty and understanding. There can be no equality of regions, races, nations without each having achieved a modicum of pride and self-respect. This will not come from fragmenting, separating; nor will it come from eliminating differences, from centralization or standardization.

What we suffer from most in Canada is ignorance, ignorance of ourselves and ignorance of our respective regions and cultures. And it's a vicious circle: the ignorance breeds insecurity; the insecurity breeds grandiose schemes, which are doomed to failure; and the failure, finally, breeds doubt and lack of faith in oneself, as well as distrust of others, perhaps also violence. One of our finest prose writers, Marian Engel, was warned recently by someone in the Canada Council not to be surprised if no one in francophone Quebec had ever heard of her when she went there in connection with her work. Maritime writers and artists and publishers often express the same concern over their lack of a fair reception in Toronto. Can anything good come out of Prince Edward Island? or Cape Breton? or the Maritimes generally? How can such a situation exist in a country committed, at least in spirit, to the encouragement of, and rejoicing in, diversity?

There are two books I want to recommend at this moment, both on the brink of publication, in Ontario of all wondrous places, that push this debate further. One is Silver Donald Cameron's *The Education of Everett Richardson*, a beautiful, funny, loving book about the Cape Breton fishermen's strike, a necessity for anyone who loves this country and its regions. The other is Rein Peterson's *Small Business: Building a Balanced Economy.* What is urgent about these books is their emphasis on the particular, the specific, rather than on the general, the abstract (read here General Motors or Canada-in-general). Peterson argues the role small business has played in the national theatre; it is a book that restores my faith in our collective future, that gives the lie to wild and grandiose schemes like Hypro or Glace Bay or Rayonier or Gulf Garden Foods. Small schools, small businesses, small provinces have value, can operate successfully, whereas overcentralization and uniformity tend to cripple, to destroy the uniqueness, the dynamism of a people, or peoples.

Here on the island we know that "small is beautiful", or can be. But we also know that small-mindedness is not, whether federal or regional. So we wait, as we did in 1867, but this time saddened and made doubly wise by experience, to answer the perpetual, the overwhelming, question.

# Civil War and Other Alternatives

## Harold Horwood

If Quebec ever leaves the Canadian union, it will probably be after fighting a war of independence. New nations are born in blood. Established nations do not dismember themselves voluntarily, and Canada isn't likely to be an exception. In discussing Quebec separatism, Canadians treat the subject of violence as taboo. It is high time they learned to be less squeamish, and began considering at what point they may be ordered by their various governments to begin killing one another.

There are two crucial questions: If Quebec passes its Act of Secession, what happens after that? And how much, if any, Canadian territory are we prepared to concede to a new nation in the unlikely event that we allow one to emerge in our midst? The pious hope that these questions can be settled by negotiation is naive.

When Nova Scotia elected a separatist government and proceeded to announce its "withdrawal" from Confederation it discovered to its dismay that it could withdraw only after the federal parliament had passed an Act of Separation, and after the whole process has been ratified in London. In the end, Nova Scotia settled for cash. The constitutional position has not changed, except that nowadays London would merely rubber-stamp whatever decision was made in Ottawa. Canadian provinces still cannot leave the union without the consent of the rest of the country. Referenda have nothing to do with the issue. Before Quebec can peacably leave the Canadian union, a majority of the members of parliament in Ottawa must be persuaded to vote for a bill authorizing Quebec's separation. If you can imagine that happening, then you can imagine the issue being settled without the use of force.

The only alternative method of secession is for Quebec to set up a revolutionary government and declare its independence, hoping that other nations, including Canada, will eventually establish normal relations with it. The chance that this could be done without a guerilla war intervening seems to me even more remote than the chance that parliament could be persuaded to vote to dismember Canada. On the contrary, the government in Ottawa has shown itself, time and again, to be almost trigger-happy in its readiness to send in the troops.

But even if you can imagine parliament voting for Quebec's separation, you can hardly imagine it agreeing to Quebec's territorial claims. How much of Canada will go with Quebec? A third of the Arctic? Eastern Ontario? Northern New Brunswick? Labrador? And what about the agreement of the other provinces concerned?

I deeply regret all this. It's a pity the issues are not simple, and easy to resolve, as they would be if Prince Edward Island, for example, voted for separatism. I'm a pacifist and idealist who would like to see every ethnic group, whatever its size, permitted to experiment with "freedom", if that's what it wants. But I'm not soft in the head, either. And if Canada decides, as is almost certain, that the interests of "unity" are more important than the aspirations of 20 per cent of its population, then there's little hope we can negotiate ourselves out of an impasse. Decentralizing the country into a sort of North American common market won't do it. It would not satisfy Quebec, and it would alienate the Atlantic Provinces.

People living in imperial Toronto look at Canada from the point of view of Romans viewing their empire. How it hangs together doesn't really matter to them so long as it continues to be their captive trading area and source of cheap labour. So they are prepared to make all kinds of compromises with lesser centres of power such as Quebec City and Edmonton, forgetting, or never realizing, that Canada looks attractive from St. John's, Halifax, Charlottetown or Fredericton only because it is centralized and provides services that these small capitals could never find the money to provide for themselves. In a decentralized Canada such colonial parts of the empire as the Atlantic Provinces would become much poorer, much more exploited, much more depressed than they are now. The unfair trading relationship that already exists with the centres of power would continue, while the subsidies that partially offset this exploitation would dry up.

"Unity" must be based on some kind of economic fair play. If there is any way to satisfy Quebec while preserving economic fair play, then we certainly ought to try, but balkanizing the country isn't the way to do it.

If Quebec cannot be persuaded, then the whole question of the Act of Separation, or alternately keeping Quebec by force, must be faced. When we consider an independent Quebec, what chunk of land are we talking about? Do we mean the present geographical area of the Province of Quebec? If so, why? Quebec separatists think of their nation as including eastern Ontario and northern New Brunswick, where most of the people speak French. They also claim the Arctic on the "sector" principle, not because the people there speak French (none of them do) but for some other reason. They claim most of Labrador, not because the people there speak French, or are of French descent (few of them are) but because a handful of French-speaking fur traders operated there in the nineteenth century.

Historic Quebec was not much bigger than the present province of New Brunswick. It consisted of an oblong block of land on the banks of the River and Gulf of St. Lawrence from the Ottawa River to the Gaspé Peninsula, and north to Lake St. John. It did not include any part of Labrador, Anticosti or the Magdalen Islands (all of which were part of the Colony of Newfoundland) or any part of the Arctic or sub-Arctic. These areas were added to Quebec for administrative reasons by Britain or by Canada at various periods during which Quebec was a British colony or a Canadian province. The last and largest addition was made by Canada as recently as 1912 when a huge area of Canada's northern territory was placed under Quebec administration. This was done without consulting the people who live in the territory (who still speak only native languages and English, no French). In three-quarters of the territory now called "Quebec", French is not only a foreign language, but a foreign language that nobody understands. During the James Bay negotiations, which Quebec City insisted on conducting in French in order to make matters more difficult for the natives, they had the greatest difficulty in finding two translators who could translate between French and Inuit. The Inuit Brotherhood prepared its case in Inuit and English, and then hired a translator to translate from the English into the French. This whole vast area was attached to Quebec precisely because Quebec was a province of Canada and for no other reason. Canada would be insane to permit Quebec to take this territory and treat it as a colony against the wishes of the people who live in it and own it, not to mention the rest of the nation. If it comes to alienating territory it would be much better to alienate eastern Ontario and northern New Brunswick.

I do not think the people of James Bay and Ungava should be treated as non-persons in this issue. They have spent the last two generations learning to deal with Ottawa, becoming fluent in English, sending their young people to English-speaking schools and universities, and thus creating a corps of negotiators who can deal on something approaching equal terms with their government. Quebec has never taken any part in this process. If the Indians and Inuit were to vote on the question of belonging to Quebec or to Canada, the vote in favour of Canada would be unanimous.

There is a strong argument for creating a new Arctic province to include Labrador, Ungava, the former and present Northwest Territories, and the Yukon. The area has numerous common interests and a recent sense of nationhood. Making it a new province would be a step toward granting justice to Canada's native peoples. Passing them over to a French-speaking Balkan state in the midst of an English-speaking continent would be a monstrous injustice viciously compounding the injustices that they have already suffered at our hands. If Quebec has the right to opt out of Canada, then surely the Inuit and Indians have the right to opt out of Quebec.

Such issues will not lie down, and will have to be considered in the terms of separation between Quebec and Canada if terms of separation are ever considered at all. It's likely that they won't be. A confrontation involving force is, unfortunately, much more probable.

Confrontation can happen all too easily. The present federal government is not so pacifist that it would be willing to back off and allow Quebec to take over the vast properties that it owns in that province. What about airfields and military bases, to mention only some of the most obvious? Let's not mince words. Policing these places means, quite simply, that the federal government is willing to shoot trespassers. Let's exercise a shred of imagination. If Quebec, failing to get from Canada the agreement that it wants, makes the slightest move to take over the real centres of power within its own borders, the paratroopers will be there within hours, and English Canadians will be waving flags and beating drums and howling for blood, as they have done in similar situations before.

Avoiding such a confrontation will not be easy. We must do everything we can to make the people of Quebec feel welcome in Canada, equals of other Canadians. There is nothing we can do about the fact that French Canadians are a minority in this country, and a minute minority in North America, but we can stop treating them as inferiors and getting mad about their language sensibilities. English is not God's language, and English culture is not the ultimate expression of the human spirit. English Canadians have done themselves a great deal of harm, in the past, by their racism and language-snobbery, and if they don't want to find themselves fighting a civil war, they'd better get over these vices in a hurry.

Though I'm pessimistic about what's likely to happen in Quebec (and have been consistently pessimistic ever since the day parliament lost its head and sent in the troops last time) I have some grounds for hope, too. I believe, for instance, that Pierre Trudeau, for all his obvious faults, can still beat René Lévesque in any election campaign. If Quebec separatists are determined upon independence within the next quarter century or so, then the assassination of Trudeau should be their first priority. English Canadians tend to forget that he is Québécois too, and that his popularity in his own province is immense.

The money in Quebec—French as well as English—favours coming to a settlement after squeezing everything possible out of Ottawa. If Quebec leaves Canada, wealthy French Canadians have a lot to lose, and by no means all of them put nationalist sentiment ahead of dollars. We live in a world where most things are for sale, and Quebec independence may not be an exception. Nova Scotia settled for cash. Quebec may settle for cash, too, and if separatism loses this time it is likely to remain underground for at least two or three generations.

Lastly, I think the popularity of ethnic nationalism throughout the world is already beginning to ebb. It has been at flood for about thirty years, creating as much misery as happiness, as many conspicuous failures as conspicuous successes. It served a useful purpose in breaking up the great colonial empires, British, French, Dutch, Belgian and Portugese, and in halting the empire-building of the Americans, but its usefulness is now about over. If, by the end of this century, ethnic nationalism is no longer a respectable political stance, then Quebec separatism will lose most of its steam. Holding Canada together through the next twenty years, bridging this period, is our problem. I hope we can do it without a great deal of bloodshed.

# The First Obligation

## Lionel Groulx

The first obligation that English and French Canadians owe to each other, and I would also say, the primary condition for a *bonne entente,* is frankness. Let us say it: the two races do not get along well because one of them wants legal equality all right, but on condition that it keeps for itself the lion's share. I know there is nothing new about this truth. I know also that it is a crude truth. But it is true. In the final analysis one category of Englishmen cannot forgive us for existing—and for claiming to exist with the same rights as themselves, the same liberty, the same dignity. There does exist a category of open-minded and generous Englishmen with whom we can get along. But there exists this other that cannot realize that everybody does not think and feel and react *à l'anglo-saxonne,* as if the human race inhabited an Anglo-Saxon universe.

In the minds of the Fathers of Confederation it was to be the legal expression of a free collaboration: collaboration between the races, collaboration between the provinces. They supposed that they had settled for ever, beyond dispute, the French fact, the question of races and languages. An article of the constitution proclaimed the legal and political equality of French and English. According to the statement of the most authorized leader of the English Canadians, there were no longer either conquerors or conquered in Canada, but only associates possessing equal rights in all domains.

These were the basic ideas that gave birth to Confederation; these were the masterly stipulations of the contract of 1867. But what has been the policy, in regard to the French fact, that has generally been followed in the English-Canadian provinces and in Ottawa? The direct opposite of what it should have been. In all the provinces the French minorities have been submitted to a rationing of their culture and to restrictions in the teaching of their religion. Canada does not deserve to be considered an example to the world for its liberal solution of the problem of nationalities and minority rights, so long as one nationality, ours, which is 30 per cent of the population, is not content to see served on the family table bones already picked over by the lion.

Let us beware of the illusion of bilingualism as a miracle worker of national union. English Canadians and French Canadians would need to talk more together only if their variances rested on misunderstanding. The Irish of Ireland eventually learned the language of their oppressors. Did they become reconciled thereby? In general, Irishmen and Englishmen speak the same language today. Do they get along any better? We ourselves have pushed bilingualism to the point of imprudence. We have scorned universal experience, forgetting that bilingualism generalized is usually the first phase of a nationality's pangs. We have been led into this imprudence in the name of economic liberation and national unity. However, bilingualism has not prevented us from becoming more than ever the servants of the minority in our province. I do not see our Anglo-Canadian compatriots taking us more closely to their hearts for having learned their language more than they have learned ours.

To come to an understanding with the English, said Jacques Bainville, it is hardly necessary to cough or spit like them. We can unite; we cannot and we never should become unified. In the name of common sense, let us stop dreaming of a marriage of love where only a marriage of reason is possible.

In Quebec let us be strong with all our strength. Let us take heed of the incomparable value of our geographic position. In 1867 Confederation could not have been made without us; we have remained indispensable to Confederation. We are the arch that links the east and the west. By the river we guard the great door to the sea; through our territory we give passage to the transcontinental railways on their way to the ports of the Atlantic and the Pacific. Quebec, the nearest Canadian territory to Europe, furnishes aerial transport with its most convenient bases and landing fields. There may be richer lands than ours; nevertheless, we possess some of the most opulent riches of Canada and of

America. We possess them in sufficient variety to build one of the best-balanced economies of the world. These riches should no longer be offered to the stranger for some handfuls of cents or dollars. Let us regain those we have lost by every means that we can learn from our economists, particularly by the co-operative system. We have considerable purchasing power. Following the example of the whole world, let us use it for our own benefit first. Would certain mercantile races insult or frown upon us if we ceased to make their fortune for them? We have labour; let us not lower the market for it. Let us exact a just return from those who live and grow rich at our expense. Let us not abandon our workers to leaders from beyond our borders or elsewhere who ask nothing better than to sell us a Trojan horse.

We have political power. We should keep it entirely for ourselves. We should tear it from the domination of financial powers, from the claws of Ottawa. Let us above all have a definite policy. We must play an important part in the federal capital. We should remember that for a state the first condition for a strong foreign policy is a strong internal policy. See where a policy empty of all French-Canadian national interest has led us. In Quebec, it has led us to become the tools of the minority; in Ottawa, of the majority.

If we remain French in essence and a people of faith, we can, for the good of Canada, be esteemed by those who do not stop at material greatness. We can also be a ferment of marvellous life for the whole continent, the dispenser of one of the greatest cultures of the world.

Through ignorance, passion, or the folly of party spirit, politicians of the old school have destroyed our great ideas, the great feelings that are basic to the idea of patriotism or of national brotherhood. These ideological vacancies in our spirits have deplorably increased our individuality as Frenchmen. Today, not only are we disunited, but so much has this anarchy become a part of our blood that the best among us seem unable to exorcise the devil of discord. Youth who have thrown to the nettles the old empty partisan shells, you of a generation more homogeneous because of a firmer national doctrine, you will have understood that in these evil days, the first duty of French Canadians is to establish a united front at home before trying to do it elsewhere. In this way you young people will serve far better than anyone else, better than the professional *bonne ententistes,* the cause of Canadian union. If disunion exists between the races, particularly because French Canadians are too divided to make themselves and justice respected, we conclude that it always will exist in Canada until there is national union among French Canadians.

Whatever may be said, we are a little people who have never had much happiness to spare. At last there may come an hour in our life, a day of wholesome retaliation, when it will be possible for us to say to ourselves as others do: "I have a land of my own; I have a soul of my own; I have a future of my own."

# Occupied Country

André Laurendeau

*Translated by Philip Stratford*

"... when a nation stands unanimous, and when it expresses this solidarity on a subject which everyone takes deeply to heart, and when all that is to no avail, why then, unless you are completely "gutless', you experience a feeling of revolt that you never get used to."

War and conscription stimulated their (Québécois) will to autonomy, and provincial autonomy means escaping from the control of Ottawa, hence from the majority, on vital issues. But they never envisaged a break with Ottawa. In this regard French Canadians continued to be conformists. They have always chosen to be on the side where the power lies.

During the war, many French Canadians in Quebec had the feeling that they were living in an occupied country. The English were the occupiers, they were the ones who dictated our conduct and prevented the national will from freely asserting itself. Our own politicians were *collaborateurs.* In comparison with Hitlerized Europe, it was a benign occupation. All we risked were our liberties, and here again the threat seldom became reality. But its very existence is enough to poison one's life. . . .

I sometimes have felt to the point of suffocation the bitter solitude of my own people in the world.

The real problem, the real anguish, comes from being a minority in North America, a tiny minority of one to forty in the middle of a mass civilization.

And if this minority should become a very small independent republic on the United States border, would it really have gained anything? It would possess new and important tools of autonomy; there would be an upsurge of national vigour; that is true. But as a state it would be much weaker, hence in much greater danger of falling under the influence of American colonization. It would have to hunt for allies elsewhere. And do we, a minority that is not backed up in America by an immense reservoir of human resources, really believe that we are capable of becoming another Cuba?

What remains for us to do is to use what we have—the provincial state of Quebec—but to really use it and not just go on shouting like children about everything we could do if only we lived under ideal conditions. What also remains for us is the task of patiently widening our powers and establishing the foundations of a new federalism.


You would be wrong to suppose that because I am not a separatist the prospect of such an evolution seems reprehensible to me. It is, on the contrary, natural and organic. Either English Canada will see the light in time, in which case it will begin to work with us towards a fundamental transformation of the central state, a development I have never ceased to hope for, or else it will continue to forget that we exist (except in Quebec), it will prevent, obstruct, or emasculate any real attempt to renew Canadian federalism, and it will remain indifferent, off-hand, distant, or scornful towards us. If it does, then one day, inevitably, we will take a stand and it will be the entire nation that will opt for another solution. It was a moderate in politics, Maxime Raymond, who, right in the middle of the war, told the English-Canadian majority: "We are perfectly willing to share the house, but it has to be a livable place for everyone." It is possible, after the experiment has gone on for years, that French Canadians may slowly become convinced that the house is not, in fact, habitable. Then, given the right international context, given *(and this is most important)* that independence has become a serious project and is not just an adventure, given that we have successfully laid the foundations of our own dwelling, why then the will to be completely free under our own roof will become irresistible.

My stand is that Confederation is better than separation, as long as it is made over. But in the domain of language rights (and this is far from being the only vital area; the sharing of powers between the central state and provincial states is undoubtedly even more important), what is implied in "making over Confederation"?

To me it seems that it consists in this: Canada proclaims itself a bilingual country, but it barely is one. It is therefore essential to make it truly bilingual. I am speaking, of course, of its political institutions and not of individual citizens. . . .

It's an urgent task. Events move quickly, and the concept of Canada is becoming more fragile by the hour. (March 1962)

Old "British" Canadians, at a time when the English ascendancy was still in force, never looked to us for aid in self-identification. They knew they were very different from Americans. Today's anglophone establishment, which coincides with its American counterpart, is anxious and leaderless, if not already assimilated. This is why they are feverishly trying either to get closer to us or, on the contrary, to find in the present state of affairs additional reasons for ignoring us completely, since in what concerns them we are neither competitors nor adversaries. It goes without saying that I am speaking here of thoughtful, contemporary English-speaking Canadians, and not of any of those groups that are historically or otherwise retarded.

This is doubtless the reason why it is so difficult for French Canadians to find points of communication with the other culture.

Of the two groups, we still remain less numerous and, more significant, less powerful. Yet despite all our contradictions we know better what we want. English-speaking Canada is the majority, firmly established, and still vigorous in its grasp of reality. But it is in its will to survive that its weakness is most apparent. Its real problem is not us but its own attitude towards the United States, and it so happens that our demands aggravate this problem. It finds itself questioning whether it is really worthwhile continuing to exist as English Canada. Or if it is possible, how much it will cost. And whether it is worth paying the price.

I am interpeting here dozens of conversations, hundreds of articles, countless political speeches, all of which betray this vast collective hesitation before which we are nothing but powerless witnesses.

It is possible to imagine that to protect itself against the troubles in Quebec, English Canada might forge a new sense of unity and learn to define itself once again. Then we would have *someone to talk to* and they could talk back, and the battle would be fierce. But that would be better, it seems to me, than messing around in the kind of swamp we are all bogged down in now. (July 1963)

Political decentralization is justifiable on several counts. It places the authorities closer to the people, and makes them better able to respond to the people's needs. It tends to forestall the arbitrariness of the single state and consequently protects the liberty of the individual citizen by more widely distributing responsibility.

That is probably the most valid justification for Confederation.

The facts are simple. Thanks to Confederation we have a state within which we are a majority and where we can take the political initiatives which best correspond to our own ideas and interests. Whenever the state of Quebec is diminished, to that extent we lose the possibility of autonomy. Quebec is the political reality to which our destiny as a people is tied.

It is an abuse of language to hear the centralizers called federalists. In fact they are destroying Confederation, which is a regime of balance between governing powers.

# An Ill-Fitting Imported Ideology Won't Suit Canada

## Roger Lemelin

Couldn't we say that the Canadian unity has mainly been maintained by European wars, whereas the peace years have made our rifts to fester? To all appearances, we have found it easier to fight foreign wars in the name of liberty and universal democracy than to assume the responsibilities of a long and just peacetime at home.

It is a strange paradox. Armed wars in Europe and the world have helped us stay together; today this unity is being threatened by these same countries' ideological conflicts. Social unrest, socialism in its many faces, upsurges of self-determination, political terrorism, counter-culture explosions, all these phenomena we are currently experiencing. Yet, at the bottom of our hearts, we have the nagging thought that these are neither heterogeneous nor essential.

If indeed we are colonized, we are colonized through the élites, by the sophisticated notions of countries which are showing their age and the age of their institutions, whereas we are still here a federation of young ethnic groups grappling with a yet untamed nature, scarcely dented natural resources, and a fantastic future opening for us. We are trying to design our own identity through other people's problems instead of striving to create one upon the knowledge of our own differences.

In his comments on the Burgos trial, the trial of a group of terrorists who were commandos of the Basque separatist movement against Spain, the French writer Jean-Paul Sartre says that the real Hiroshima explosion was that of the centralist states, with the ensuing revival of a multiplicity of minute states—a fascinating intellectual perception. But it does not stand up to reason, for it does not take into account a natural instinct for survival which does not feed solely on culture but relates foremost to economic survival, and to survival itself. It is, after all, the history of the world that little ethnic kingdoms merge into powerful nations, each one willing to relinquish a part of its absolute tribal powers in favour of an unavoidable centrifugal force. The tribal monarchs found rapidly enough that whatever little fringes of personal power they had relinquished were more than compensated for by the common front of defence of the group and the common benefits of stronger commercial ties.

Sartre endeavors to justify the existence of the Basque separatist movement and, stretching General de Gaulle's line of reasoning, goes as far as to wish that France itself would explode in as many little nations as there are ethnic definitions: Britanny, Occitany, Basque. . . .

And he goes still farther. In order to prove the worldwide acceptance of this notion, he uses the separatist movement of Quebec as an example. To a certain group of intellectuals, anarchy is a tempting mistress, but the people in general are best reassured by the notions of order and stability.

I have referred to Jean-Paul Sartre in order to stress that in trying to justify a very particular situation on this continent of our own, there is a danger in making use of examples which are born in an entirely different context. Too many of our intellectual idols of the present fall into this trap. They feed, they drool, on the Cuban revolution, on Algerian independence. They compare these situations with the situation in Quebec, they universalize generous social reforms which threaten to disrupt the delicate balance of our present economy.

In order to promote social democracy in Quebec and in Canada, we use Sweden, Germany, England and Austria as examples. All those high-risk transplants come at a high price, and none of them is going to make our secondary industries sprout spontaneously like so many mushrooms in the beautiful garden of the just society.

The true picture is different: it shows Canada and consequently Quebec as tied together by this Confederation pact, as moving inexorably along the path of the North American economic system; and any ideological or economic trip must take this inevitable fact into account.

And then, in spite of this fundamental reality, Quebec has elected a political party whose basic objective is to tear Quebec from Confederation and create its own sovereign social-democratic nation.

Panic grips Canada. Only yesterday we were dilettantes busy crocheting the National Comforter. Four months afterwards, panic strikes, and all those who believe in Canada bury their personal hatchets and rejoin forces in order to save it.

The only real bit of good news for the federalists since November 15 has been the incredible popularity rise in Quebec of the prime minister of Canada, following his speech in Washington. It is not only by the cold rhetoric of his speech that Mr. Trudeau has seduced Americans, Quebeckers and Canadians alike; it is by his heartfelt appeal to the generous, abstract values of mankind, the higher of these being liberty and tolerance, values without which any political society is in danger of running into social disorder and crypto-fascism.

The enthusiastic, positive reaction of the French Canadians to this appeal to higher values shows in which way lies the solution to our national unity problem, provided all Canadians agree to play fair.

The question now is not What does Quebec want? It is How does Quebec feel? How is it that when confronted with the most powerful reasonings of federalist proponents, the Péquistes become impatient, lose all reason and accuse them of being too rational?

After a few months in power, being now responsible for the complex and daily chore of managing Quebec, the Péquistes sometimes give the impression that they are chained to the iron ball of their uncompromising separatist ideal, an ideal which appears more and more difficult to define, for their strategy is being held in check by the acute economic problems which confront them. But it would be a great folly on the part of Mr. Lévesque's political opponents to try to exploit such an apparent confusion and to consider the Péquistes as loud-mouthed Sorcerer's Apprentices or dream-dealers. The heart of Quebeckers has reasons in which reason has no part.

But should the long-past frustrations of a proud people, its cultural nostalgia, its determination to stay French, be made the basic platform of a political party whose objective is independence, possible maybe in the short term, but fatally destructive, both culturally and economically, in a very near future? Even before the fact, the disastrous consequences of such a move are determined. Would the French Canadians really go so far as to risk embarking on such a suicidal adventure?

I come back to what I said earlier about Jean-Paul Sartre. It is an historical fact that revolutions have been bred and fed by the bourgeoisie. Mussolini had thus formulated his strategy to bring his party into power: "All I have to do is to breed a feeling of ultra-nationalism among the bourgeois classes, and give them an army, and that's it. The people will follow."

The Parti Québécois is mainly made up of a well-to-do, ultra-nationalist middle class of civil servants, university people, teachers and media people, led by a hard-core group of intellectuals bitten by the bug of such European ideological fantasies as self-determination, independence, Marxism, socialism—all indiscriminately feeding upon a frustratingly obsolescent spirit of vengeance.

Drawing to him all these forces and trying to keep them in balance, René Lévesque, a sincere democrat who is very close to Mr. Trudeau in his concept of a just society, fortunately is looked upon as a guaranty by the Quebec federalists who secretly respect him, for he expresses their own frustrations as Quebeckers wandering between their reason and their heart.

The Parti Québécois has yet to grow solid roots inside the majority working class. The non-partisan citizens who voted for the PQ first of all voted to elect an honest government, because they were led to believe that the former one was not honest. Any misgivings they may have had about the separation idea were smothered under the promise of a referendum. But only four months after coming to power, the Péquiste government talks of the independence of Quebec as if it were already consummated.

For how long will the masses let themselves be brainwashed by this strategy? For as long, in any case, as the panic-stricken federalist opponents will fall into this trap and, all senses lost, will keep campaigning for a revamping of the constitution, as if all the members of the family had to undergo an operation because one of the children has developed appendicitis.

What is much more urgent is that the anglophone section of Canada deeply modify its attitudes towards Quebec. Quebeckers are not without faults, and they do not accuse the anglophones of being responsible for all their ills, but they do not want to have to fight, day after day, for that measure of respect and justice which should naturally have been theirs since the first moment this country was founded.

Quebeckers are a nation whose culture is bubbling over along all the different paths of knowledge and the arts. In fact, they themselves have to choose whether they wish to re-enter Confederation, for in their minds many of them have already left Confederation.

Trust them. They know where their bread comes from, but they are not going to settle for just any kind of bread, nor have it served them in any fashion whatsoever. If, falling short of obtaining the just and equal treatment Canada owes them, the people choose the route of independence, and this route brings them economic disaster and internal disorder, please do not make the mistake of rejoicing, for this, the second defeat of the Plains of Abraham, could end in tragedy. Remember that on the night of November 15, 1976, a great many people in Quebec had tears of joy in their eyes, and many could not exactly tell why.

The real urgency is to give Canada, this abstract country, a high collective national passion, a set of accessible goals toward which, over and above language and racial or religious prejudices, our young people could strive, whether they are from Vancouver or Toronto or Quebec or Saint John.

Considering that the Parti Québécois has succeeded in generating such an impressive passion in Quebec behind a dead-end idea, wouldn't it be possible for the Canadian people to generate such a passion for something feasible which would be an inspiration for future generations?

# A Note to the Editor

## Gabrielle Roy

If I had the least hope that by my words I might be helpful to my
country, I certainly would be writing all day. In a sense, most of my
books have tried just that: bring more understanding between the two
sides of our country which I both love. Today I don't feel that it has
helped much. Still I would be willing to try again if I saw my way
clearly: what to say and how to say it, and if I had all the time I need.

# " . . . A Difficult Country, and Our Home"

## Joyce Marshall

I wonder how many English-speakers in Canada did what I did that night—turned off the television and stared around them, wondering whether this was still the same room and the same furniture, the same world. I turned my set back on again, of course, reminding myself that writers aren't allowed to shirk emotion, and made myself look at those rows and rows of ecstatic faces—the faces of my people for I too am a Quebecker—all singing and rejoicing at the thought of getting away from me. I had flu that night, had planned to stay up just long enough to "get the trend of the election". And the trend became a surge, keeping me trapped in front of my television till Lévesque's triumphant entry into that screaming auditorium. So the memory will always be linked for me with sweating, shivering spells. And pain and a sense of exclusion so terrible I was glad that no one, above all no outlander, no non-Quebecker, was there to try to share it with me.

I'd tried to be ready. Dread that the PQ might some day come to power was like a dying tooth in the back of the mouth—reasonably painless if you don't press on it but every now and then you bite down, deliberately, as a reminder of what may come. But it's no real preparation. The pain surprises. In those first days after *le quinze novembre* I said and thought some extraordinary things. I still say and think them half a year later. *They can't take my River away from me. The River is mine. The Eastern Townships too. They're mine. My parents are buried in Quebec*, I've actually found myself thinking though I've never much concerned myself with graves. *My grandparents. Six of my great grand-*

186

*parents. Two of my great great.* . . . I still can't think of this country
and its possible dismemberment in other than emotional terms. Nor, I
believe, should I try to pretend I can. Separatism, for those who desire
it, is an emotional matter. It can only be prevented if the rest of us
permit ourselves to be equally emotional. Leave economics to the
economists, the totting up of taxes against expenditures to the ac-
countants. Let those qualified to amend the BNA Act set about doing
so. Godspeed to their efforts. They're needed too. And surely no one
thinks of a statute passed by a British parliament as something writ on
stone. For me Canada is an emotion and a challenge I've only begun to
understand and Quebec, though I've lived elsewhere for more than half
my life, is still and simply my home. And I can't bear the thought that I
might some day, if I could bring myself to do it, have to go to my own
place as a foreigner, on sufferance. Even if we didn't have to show
passports at the border. And I'm not at all sure we wouldn't have to.
For if separation comes, it will be bitter. Cut the tension that is also our
link and connection and our quarrels, no longer family quarrels, will
keep us at one another's throats for a hundred years.

It was the land I thought of first, and then the Québécois people and
the challenge, for they entered my life in that order. This huge country
is mine, all of it is, even aspects and vistas I've never seen and may never
see. But to be truly loved, a landscape must be looked at freshly,
closely and yet carelessly, as only a child can look. It then becomes part
of our fabric, provides our criteria, our norms of proportion and scale.
I'm attached to nothing I have seen as I am to certain corners of the
Eastern Townships, so open and free, human in scale, the sort of landscape you could touch. Above all to the view from a hill that overlooks
a little lake. I wrote of it once, when it was closer to me in time,
recently searched for the passage, desperately, as if it were the picture
of one dead:

> It was the most beautiful place in the world, Ann was sure. The
> delicate modulated hills that folded into each other. Everywhere
> you looked you saw those warm merging curves of hill. . . . And
> in this light there was a scarf of shadow across the sweep of each
> hill.

That is still the place to which I compare all other places. Just as the
River, and to me there's only one, the St. Lawrence, is the river to

which I compare the Rhône, the Rhine and find them tepid streams. I have never felt the north-south pull I hear about. As a River-child, I'm conscious always of the watershed and of rivers and their tributaries drawing us to the sea.

I made the journey once from the Gulf upriver to Montreal. I'd been away for twenty-seven months, had lived in those most rational of societies, Denmark and Norway, learned that they weren't mine, that homogeneity bored me to death, I needed diversity, the rasp and unease of difference. Bombs had exploded in mailboxes during my absence and I was a little frightened. But it was early October and the one shoreline visible from the ship was misty gold. It seemed to me that you need take so little away—black Russian freighters ferrying wheat, the few settlements, spires—to see what our discoverers saw. My own ancestors too, driven by private necessities to cross the ocean in sailing ships. An English schoolmaster determined that his sons should own land, a young Norwegian couple, part of the great Scandinavian exodus that saw the population of Norway and Sweden cut by a half in twenty years, a Scottish soldier who had no money and no prospects but longed to live "in green fields"—and did so after his twenty years service was up. A generation earlier a Welshman of whom little is known except that he "had something to do with building wooden ships". All converged upon the city on the rock, which I saw lit up royally at night that homecoming October, and by so doing gave me life—and a home.

I once tried to explain to a young separatist, now a PQ backbencher, that I too felt bound to Quebec and that after those two years away my heart had leaped when I first saw that light characteristic green of the River water. He smiled for he was—still is, I'm sure—a courteous youth as he conceded that I did undoubtedly feel some lesser sort of tie. On another occasion, discussing seventeenth-century New France with a French Canadian, I used the words "our history".

"But that was still the French Régime," he said, clearly puzzled by my memory lapse.

"Yes," I said, "but my history just the same."

Both times I didn't try very hard to explain. Some queer kind of guilt came into this, I think—a sense that since they wanted, perhaps needed, to believe their attachment unique, I—in their minds at least "one of the conquerors"—ought to let them. I was wrong, I see now. I

should have argued my right to feel bound to the land and its history—
and to them, my not always willing brothers. As a child I loved early
Canadian history. I still love it. I've no idea which Danish king ruled
over Norway in 1608 or what life was like at that time for ordinary
people in north Wales. I don't particularly want or need to know. *My*
ancestors were with Champlain, founding that perilous little settlement
on the rock. Later my ancestors were defeated with Montcalm. I badly
wanted them to win. Montcalm's dying words, "Thank God I shall not
live to see the fall of Quebec" (alas, in English translation in my book)
broke my heart. Is this ridiculous? Lévesque, Laurin and the others
would undoubtedly think it was. But I do feel that the first white
settlers in Canada were my people. Which makes me guilty with them
of misdeeds to the native people but not of words written by Lord
Durham in 1838.

I am aware of all the injustices. I may even, as a little Anglo growing
up in Montreal, have added my bit to the resentment that culminated in
recent events. At four or five I used to join with friends to shout "Dirty
French peasoups" at children who shouted back "Cochons." But in
Quebec there was so much, I say it now in apology, to turn the children
into aliens, into enemies. Language first. I still recall my terror at
hearing people who looked as human as my own parents making what
seemed to me empty senseless sounds. And after I'd learned a little
French—some in school, some from street signs and cornflakes boxes—
there was religion and, along with religion, school. No one speaks any
more about the Catholic Church and all it did for so long, not only to
foster inward and backward looking but to give us stereotypes of one
another and so isolate the cultures. (It should be spoken of. Twenty
years is not very long in the life of a people—or of a human being.)
When I was growing up the two groups of children didn't even dress
alike. The little French-speaking girls looked solemn and dull to me in
their black long stockings and convent dresses. Furthermore they were
paraded about by nuns, who as all little Protestants knew were sinister
and acquisitive, longing only to draw us in. Apart from this I simply
ignored those little girls and, quite literally, I hadn't a single French-
speaking friend till after I'd left the province at twenty-two and begun
to return as a visitor. I missed a lot that way and I regret it. More than
that, I resent it. Because if we'd been able to know one another in time,
those little girls I found so quenched and strange, and their children,

might not have grown up to hate me as so many of them do.

It's the hatred that frightens me. Hate lies in every human heart, just waiting for an excuse. And how much easier—and more respectable—to join with others to hate a group than cope with lonely hatred of your sister-in-law. Hate is loose around us now, in all its meanest forms. In the cries of "Let the bastards go!" In much of Bill 1, the so-called Language Charter—its bitter ethnocentricity and sour school-masterish tone. I don't want to see the haters cut us away from one another, eliminating forever our chance to make something unique. I had my fill of homogeneous, linguistically monolithic societies in those two years in Denmark and Norway. Such countries are much easier to govern, thoroughly admirable but—and this is what brought me home—dull beyond belief.

Everything I've said is true—I am attached to the rocks and the River and certain corners of the Eastern Townships; they're as much part of me as my arms and legs—but what I really love, what I honestly feel I couldn't live without, is that other strand, the rub and bite of difference that keeps us alert and alive. My people of Quebec whom, to my sorrow, I came to know so late. Even those whose laughing singing faces filled me with such pain that night in November. Whether or not they hate me. They'll never quite be free of me, of course. Joined or sundered, we'll have to deal with one another more often and more intimately than with anyone else. Boundary lines will just make accommodation harder to reach. Diplomatic notes instead of federal-provincial conferences. Ultimata. Blackmail. One side bigger and richer, the other controlling the River.

But I don't believe the game and the country are lost yet. Nor do I feel that we can safely leave things to the politicians and businessmen. Or, for that matter, to the flow of events. Most of us ordinary human beings were in a state of shock after *le quinze novembre*. Among my own friends, I remember, we scarcely mentioned the matter for weeks. But we've had time to examine our thoughts and, now that we've examined or in some cases discovered them, we must speak. And we're shy, most of us, half shy, half guilty in the face of separatist and Quebec nationalist feelings that seem determined to shut us out. The Québécois find us cold and will think us all the colder if we answer their emotion only with talk of tariffs and balance sheets. They think of us as a monolith because they've been taught to see us so, and we've done little to show with what diverse voices we speak. Though I don't think we should overemphasize our differences. This book should make some of these apparent if nothing else. The Québécois will continue to insist, and they're quite right, that history has made them the most different. Why can't the rest of us accept this while those whose bent lies that way go about amending the constitution? Or tear it up. So we can make ourselves a new Canada and go on for a while with that.

I can't say what kind of a new Canada I'd like to see though I do know it must be looser. And if we try very hard, we may even manage to be more generous with one another. Otherwise I don't think we should try too hard to imagine what the future will be. Because we're never going to be finished or even settled long enough to sum ourselves up, as we're always so anxious to do. "Life . . . is a difficult country," wrote Edwin Muir, "and our home." So is Canada. I know that we'll continue to have crises even after we've struggled—or muddled—through the present one. There may always be an edginess, an element of the not-quite about us. And why not? Perhaps the best thing history has given us is the chance to shift, make new and partial adjustments, then shift and mesh again. Bickering and rasping as we go. We may finally come to acknowledge that this is what we've really wanted all along.

# Bringing 1867 Up To Date

## Eric Kierans

Let me begin with a paragraph from a recent article by Claude Castonguay in the *Globe and Mail* "Can Canada Survive?" series:

> What must be understood is that there is in Quebec a quite
> specific collectivity with an identity of its own, its own culture
> and its institutions, to which belong five million French-speaking
> citizens. This collectivity has, by its cohesion, its numbers and its
> state of development, all the attributes of a distinct society.
> Quebeckers want this society to remain dynamic and they want it
> to develop.

As a Quebecker I can only say "Amen" to every word in that statement
and then follow up with the question, "Where do we go from here?"

The first step might be to elevate the level of the debate. Expressions
used to describe Quebec or Quebec-Canada relations such as "two
scorpions in a bottle", "Quebec the kept woman of Confederation" and
"born losers" are ludicrous caricatures of reality, or downright false. As
a Quebecker I have never felt myself fitting any such description and I
do not expect that I ever will. The Canada that Premier Lévesque is
repudiating is strictly his own version and one which I too would
repudiate if it did in fact exist. But it does not.

Nor do I consider that using such expressions is anything but self-
defeating. After all, who wants to invest in a born loser? I know that is
not a nice remark to make either and would prefer to get rid of such
demeaning rhetoric and riposte.

There is a point to be made, however, and it is this. If we are to

192

carry on a dialogue about the future of this country, we cannot conjure up distorted images and unreal effigies to tear apart. Let us be sure of what it is that we are supporting or would destroy, and that it is not something else. And this goes for both sides. If Quebec today has "all the attributes of a distinct society" as Mr. Castonguay has written, that does say something for Canada. The survival of "one of the toughest and most exclusive nationalisms in the world" (Bernard Crick) gives both cultures something to look back upon with pleasure, pride and gratification—*that the federation of 1867 did enable a people, which desperately wanted to carry on their own culture and the language expressing that essence, to live creatively and in freedom to the point where they can now contemplate going it alone.* Bottles, scorpions, born losers, kept women, let-them-go, speak-white, etc., are, I repeat, ugly caricatures that have no place in a debate which must appeal only to enlightened public opinion, generosity of thought and good taste if we would be fair to ourselves and to our children. Ten years ago, I wrote that "Canada is one federal state, created by two peoples with different traditions, cultures and languages—two founding nations. The symbols of that state must be one constitution, one flag, one anthem, and one federal government. These are symbols that can unify, command respect and inspire allegiance!" That is still true.

Our problem is that such symbols *should* unify, command respect and inspire allegiance but obviously they no longer do so. In other words, while the facts of geography and history proclaim the fact of Quebec *in* Canada, some Quebeckers have never accepted the fact that they are a part *of* Canada. The advantages of making them feel so are obvious. The costs define the issue before us.

The modern emphasis on man, his autonomy and open future means that appeals to history, to shared experience as justification for the continuation of one Canada have little significance for many. Tradition, a static constitutionalism, legal interpretations of the clauses of Confederation provide singularly empty categories in an age and environment which value independence and the power to create new values and order in one's own lifetime.

The "Canada is dead" philosophy is shared both by the man who says that "we have been born losers" and by the man who screams "Let them go back to France." Both men discard our history, the cultural bonds that have been built up, the economic links, the geographical constraints and necessities imposed on a North American north, the common sharing of success and setback. Forward is the watchword. Never look backwards for then we might want to go home again and that is the only freedom that our secular mood will not allow.

The simple objective of the Parti Québécois is to create a new Canada which shall not be a nation, a country, a state but simply a federation of two or more independent states. Citizens of the nine English-speaking provinces could combine into a rump federal Canada if they so wished but the Parti Québécois's expectation is that the country would divide into regions, going their separate ways.

This would enable an independent Quebec to conclude trading arrangements separately with Ontario, the Atlantic Provinces (?), the Prairie Provinces (?) and British Columbia (?). In the highly improbable event that the negotiations were successful, *then Canada would re-emerge as a federation of these five independent states,* as a new governmental community supervising and carrying out the fiscal policies, monetary accords and customs arrangements determined by the constituent members. Such a central (?) body would clearly have no policy-making role or fiscal resources of its own, but a budget provided by the contributions of the federated partners à la United Nations, NATO, EEC, etc. *A federation of states is not a nation.*

This scenario is not as great a fantasy as one might claim at first sight. In fact it follows inexorably from the Quebec objective of complete independence. Promises of monetary union and common markets are a sop to pacify the doubtful, the hesitant and the uncertain in Quebec by suggesting that one can separate and still live together on the same old terms. Such statements are intended purely for Quebec consumption. Independence leads to independence and nowhere else. There is no halfway house or home in which the Canadian community survives after it is destroyed.

In fact some ministers are not interested at all in a common market with a Canadian rump and they make no bones about their desires for a complete break.

Hon. Rodrigue Tremblay's position as outlined in *Indépendance et Marché Commun Québec-Etats Unis* is that the withdrawal of Quebec from Canada and subsequent entry into a Quebec-United States common market would, far from weakening the Quebec economy and lowering the standard of living of its people, result in a clear economic gain. Such a common market would, says Mr. Tremblay, need the support of American financial institutions and the co-operation of the Federal Reserve Board of the United States in making known that it stood ready to support a Quebec dollar against speculation and other causes of monetary instability. The minister is very optimistic that the advantages of such a common market to the United States would ensure such support!

Now, I do not wish to cast doubt on the minister's reputation as an economist for he is held in high esteem by the profession. The above recommendation says more about the manner in which economic analysis is carried out than it says about the economist author. Axiomatic, formalistic analysis, leaving out institutions, endowments and man himself, can lead to conclusions that would make lesser men tremble. Quebec entrepreneurs, for example, were not asked what they thought of such a "matchup" nor was any account taken of the differences in labour productivity, levels of technological expertise, the huge differentials in capital availability and industrial location determined by the relative size of markets.

However, this reference to Hon. Rodrigue Tremblay's book is not put forward to tear down his analysis, but simply to make clear that talk about common markets, etc., is directed solely toward Quebec, to lead the people gently down the road to separatism by implying that there would continue to be close, if undefined, association with their own history. In fact, the Parti Québécois has every intention of making the separation final and complete. "Adieu, Canada, pour toujours."

The Second World War concentrated political and economic power in Ottawa. Provincial governments have had an extraordinarily difficult time in recovering the areas of jurisdiction and authority that were accorded to them by the constitution. In part, this was due to inertia and their own lack of initiative. In part, the reluctance of the federal government to give up the expansion of its responsibilities was reinforced by the intellectual foundations provided by Keynesian economics for the enhanced role assigned to governments in achieving national objectives of growth and full employment. Both politics and economics combined to reduce the role and responsibility of provincial governments in relative terms, hence the current frustration.

The justification of a separate state of Quebec, in economic terms, rests on its capacity to provide a greater flow of goods and services to the population than can be furnished under the existing federal system. How valid is this claim? What changes in the economic environment are intended for the private sector which we will assume provides 60 per cent of all goods and services and the public sector which supplies the remaining 40 per cent?

John Dewey *(The Public and Its Problems)* once described the main business of a parliamentary democracy as the making "of property interests secure". Premier Lévesque's speech to the Economic Club of New York last week made clear that he is no visionary seeking to revolutionize society. There is no question of freeing Quebec from the domination of foreign capital, English-speaking capitalists or commercial-industrial-financial ideologies. "In a nutshell, we are not against foreign investment as such and we have no intentions of picking fights with private enterprise." "Our program does not envisage any direct takeovers and we do not intend to launch any policy of nationalization." "We do not intend to tax [our people] any further" and "any increase in spending must be geared to the normal rise in tax revenues".

Premier Lévesque's policy is his policy and I am not suggesting that it should be any different. But if there is to be business-as-usual in the private sector, then separation accomplishes nothing positive or beneficial in the reorganization of industrial activity and, indeed, expands enormously the costs of risk and uncertainty by spreading fear and worry throughout the economy *to no purpose.*

The New York speech has, of course, caused problems for the premier by scattering confusion, doubt and disappointment among those supporters who had pinned their hopes for political and social reform on the new government. But this, as the premier told the Economic Club of New York, is no proletarian revolution. A more balanced social distribution of income is not a priority and even the guaranteed annual income promised to the people in the previous election has fallen by the wayside as the government prepares for the costs of separation.

One can make a good case for Premier Lougheed being a better social democrat than Premier Lévesque. Mr. Lévesque promised the bankers in New York not to interfere with Quebec's biggest monopoly, Bell Telephone, but Alberta has its own system. We are currently talking in Quebec of buying 51 per cent of one asbestos company where Alberta has bought 100 per cent of an airline. Even in its worst days Alberta managed to appropriate 16 per cent of the value of its petroleum resources and now, of course, much more. We are content with a 2- or 3-per cent royalty value in iron ore and other minerals. Social democracy seems to be a matter of definition or proclamation rather than substance.

Without claiming that there is not room for improvement, it can be said that the private sector has made enormous progress in recognizing and settling into a Quebec society in which the French language, culture and social life are the determinants of a new integration and unity. The respect for the majority language and culture which Premier Lévesque demands of new investment is being rapidly achieved at home. Pluralism and bilingualism will always be a fact of life in Quebec but this is imposed not so much by intransigent anglophones (who may however take advantage) as by the overwhelming presence of the English-speaking fact in North America. One cannot go much further in striving for homogeneity and unilingualism without running the risk of an exclusively French-speaking Quebec, a sect in an open world.

If we can expect little change in the structure of the private sector under the Parti Québécois, then the costs of separation—increasing risk and uncertainty, a decline in investment, growth and employment—will have been incurred to no purpose. If separation is still to be pursued, then it can only be because the independence of the Quebec government promises enormous benefits to the people of Quebec. Where these benefits are to come from, what they might be when the premier himself has said that the province has been living beyond its means, remains to be spelled out.

How radically can a government sector which provides approximately 40 per cent of all goods and services be changed? In effect, would the absorption of all government functions, both federal and provincial, by an independent Quebec bring an improvement in the standard of living of the people of Quebec? If yes, then independence should be considered. If the answer is no, then independence might still be considered but the costs of rupture with Canada in terms of the deterioration in the quality of life of the people of Quebec should be clearly spelled out and communicated to them so that they know what they are doing. Independence could be for always.

There are two fundamental economic reasons for entering into a federal system: the attainment of greater wealth, output and employment than would be possible to the members individually and the distribution of that wealth equitably so that a standard of services is available to all citizens. Out of the greater surplus that comes from unity and co-operation—and who will deny this?—all provinces will be better off and all citizens will share in the larger income than would be available if they acted on their own. But federalism need not be centralism.

The trend away from the centre in Canada is given impetus not only by cultural factors (the two founding nations) but also by economic forces (the five regions, distinct because widely separated), by political reality (the constitutional powers of the provinces in the area of social policy) and by the expanding supply of administrative talent (the increasing capacity of provincial élites to define and manage their own programmes). History may be full of examples of federal systems evolving into unitary states but the centrifugal forces listed above have already defeated this movement in Canada, a fact which must finally be recognized in Ottawa.

A nation can present only one international image at any given time and can settle its accounts with only one monetary unit. Two monetary units means two separate states and that is that. The essence of a federal government's exclusive authority (obviously the more consultation the better) is defined in control of monetary policy, fiscal policy, trade policy, external affairs, defense and, in Canada at least, transportation. In other words, a federal government sets the rules and policies that describe our international personality and assure a fair and equitable domestic environment for carrying on our separate economic and social objectives. Restraints and rules of conduct are imposed in everyone's larger interests.

It is hard to see where Quebec jurisdiction would change much that is fundamental in present economic planning or in our external policy. In fact, the foundations of Quebec economic policy are the same twin pillars that have supported Canadian growth since Confederation: the exploitation of resources and the encouragement of heavy capital investment with the aid of foreign capital inflows. There is no reason here to separate, and to risk recession and stagnation, when exactly the same means are being used to pursue the same economic objectives and international policies. If the Parti Québécois wishes to pursue a Quebec-U.S. common market, of course, the organization of a better society in Quebec would take place in Washington by American economic and foreign policy planners.

The real dissatisfaction and division in Canada between the Province of Quebec and the federal government has been the erosion of independent provincial fiscal authority by the attempt of Ottawa to create a largely unitary state with a central government possessing overwhelming authority in the social and fiscal policy-making sectors. Until recently, Quebec stood virtually alone in the battle against federal encroachment and this increased the sense of isolation and frustration in Quebec.

If a unitary state is unacceptable to all sectors of this country, provincial premiers should say so with the same vehemence that they oppose the balkanization of this nation into a federation of independent states.

Barbara Ward Jackson, a detached and objective observer, saw this quite clearly as far back as 1964 when she was a visiting professor of economics at Laval University. At that time, acknowledging that a unitary state could never work in Canada, she suggested to me that it was my primary responsibility, as an English-speaking minister in the Quebec government, to persuade one other provincial government of the importance of opting out of at least one federally imposed programme to support the basic principle of federalism. Not a single province did so even though for many, opting-out would have been justified on economic and social grounds of differing priorities as well as the overriding reason that programmes imposed without prior consultation are an affront to provincial fiscal authority and independence in a federal system. Upholding provincial rights by deed and act and not merely words was deemed to be giving aid and comfort to Quebeckers and separatists, inviting the epithets of treason and disloyalty from Ottawa mandarins.

When a federal government turns inward, when it seeks to expand by appropriating the jurisdiction of the provinces and assuming their responsibilities, it turns away from the purposes for which the confederation was created and negates the very principles of federalism. When it concentrates on the centralization of internal power and authority, forcing the development to a unitary state, a federal government neglects its primary responsibility, which is to establish a clear national identity and purpose, one acceptable to the whole community, from Newfoundland to British Columbia, and recognized as independent and important in the councils of the world.

The increasing centralization since the Second World War has ignored the basic reality that questions and policies relating to health, welfare and education can be better handled at the regional or provincial level than by a central authority laying down uniform policies for a nation that cannot possibly be compressed, unless by some horrible genetic interference with human personality itself, into a single mold and in which our wonderful diversity of habits, language and culture demands a wide variety of approaches to issues and qualitative differences in methods of operations. To carry out its responsibilities, a province has to have the required resources *before the fact, not after.* It is not decentralization to impose a programme and then to provide the resources to administer it. Even unitary states grant local units the power to operate if not to reason why.

A new federalism would take account of the increasing capacity of all provinces, not just Quebec, to manage their own affairs, to set policies, to provide better services and to attend more efficiently to the needs of their people. *What we need in Canada is not a special status for Quebec as much as a new status for all provinces.* The real strength of this Confederation will depend on the response of those provincial premiers (and governments) who will refuse to continue to be submissive bystanders and witnesses to decisions in which they no longer have an entrepreneurial input but are forced to accept, much like the passive rentiers and remittance men of a managerial society.

For a long time, centralism looked like a way out of the impasse caused by the mutual distrust (let me say this bluntly) that existed and still exists between our two cultures—a continuation of the shrieking debates of the 1850s and 1860s that helped bring on a hopeful solution in the Confederation of 1867! Until we learn to accept, if not glory in, the Canadian duality there will always be stresses and strains. This does not mean and never has meant a bilingual Calgary or Halifax. It does mean, which is in the slow process of achievement, a bilingual commitment at the federal level.

Legislation is necessary but it is not the message. The message is the expression of sentiments and beliefs which exist in the hearts of all Canadians. *People* give to the principle of two founding nations its real life and meaning and until there is mutual respect and regard in Canada there cannot be a true equality and unity.

What does the French-speaking Canadian want? Simply this: the assurance that we, the English-speaking majority, are not out to integrate him into our habits, values, language; an assurance, incidentally, that he would never get from the United States. To persuade him we need not only to point to history and how far the five million have come, but also to convince him that a Canada, democratic, plural and which reaffirms provincial rights, will function as a society in which all groups have the right to make themselves heard in the development of the directions in which the whole community evolves.

This recognition of an open society, putting people ahead of bureaucracy and treating man as an end, introduces risk and uncertainty into our political structures, invites change and demands faith in our potential for progress and improvement in the terms of our living together. In an era which rejects integration and centralization, this is our challenge.

# Our Nation's Reach Exceeds Its Grasp

## Bruce Hutchison

The first reflection of any old Canadian is that the journey of his lifetime has been a rough and tortuous ride over an unmapped terrain, even rougher and less mapped than the wilderness of the Rockies, but a thoroughly enjoyable and satisfactory ride for my generation.

Still, near the end of it, we know less about our real business and the problems of our time than our grandfathers knew about theirs when life was simpler and its problems more understandable . . . when Alberta was Indian territory and the ranchers, the long horns and the whisky traders marched north on the Whoop-Up Trail with no doubt about the future.

This, I suspect, is the most remarkable—and disappointing—lesson taught in the course of our experience: the fact, I mean, that all our efforts, all our achievements, all our cunning technological knowledge and all our brave assumptions have lagged far behind our necessities.

As never in the past, the reach exceeds the grasp, in Canada and everywhere; and let me quickly confess that in my own trade the gap between perfection and performance is especially wide, and no newspaperman worth his salt is satisfied with the media, as they are now called, when no happy medium has yet appeared.

So we have much to learn, and more to unlearn, as we hand on to another and possibly wiser generation this fortunate but sadly mismanaged transcontinental estate of Canada.

At least we have learned that, on the whole, as things go in a world not yet quite perfect, Canada has been a grand and literally unique success.

But among candid friends and fellow Canadians it would be dishonest to pretend that our immediate affairs are going well these days, since it is clear to all of us that they have been going badly.

For example, Canada, with all the opulent natural resources envied by the majority of mankind, has been running the largest trading deficit among the Western nations because its sky-high cost of production, its comparatively low rate of productivity or output per man-hour of work and its ceaseless industrial strife have blunted Canada's former cutting edge in a ruthlessly competitive world which, oddly enough, does not agree that it owes us a living on the scale demanded by Canadians as their inalienable right, almost a law of nature, an act of Providence.

To maintain that scale without fully earning it in the uncontrollable world market place we are borrowing more than any other Western nation from foreign lenders, piling up huge external debt for repayment in hard currencies of unknown value and thus gambling recklessly in foreign exchange.

To be sure, many other nations are doing the same thing on a lesser scale and some of them, notably the United States, are paying for imported oil by selling the most sophisticated weaponry to the oil exporters in the most sensitive and dangerous strategic areas where the instruments of war, even world war, are in the nervous hands of trigger-happy strong men. What a gamble that is!

It should be quickly added that a young country like ours needs all the capital it can find at home and abroad to develop its resources, expand its productive machinery and create jobs for its people—more capital than it can easily find anywhere, far more than it yet realizes; and at the moment—again incredibly—Canadians are investing in the business of other nations more money than foreigners are investing directly here. The tide that used to flow in our favour now ebbs against us, though it may be reversed as conditions improve and confidence is restored.

But no nation can safely continue for long to borrow money, as we are doing, in large volumes, merely to finance governmental budgetary deficits, to buy consumer goods, to pay its household expenses, its grocery bill. No nation can safely raise its costs and prices as we are doing, much faster than those of its primary market, the United States.

In sum, we have been wildly distorting a national economy which, with anything like sensible management, should be the richest, per capita, on earth.

Fortunately the rate of inflation—which is both a cause and symptom of our economic disease—has been falling, under a control system, and without that system the rate would have risen faster and might well have doubled by now. But a man submerged in five feet of water drowns just as surely as if the depth were ten feet.

Lacking a head for figures, I am unable to calculate precisely when our currency and fixed savings will lose all their value, but at their current rate of shrinkage they would be totally extinguished within another lifetime at most, probably sooner.

In our cranky national humour, any man who mentions these plain facts will be denounced as a pessimist—worse, as a capitalist—still worse, as a conservative; and any man who notes that our society is unjust—as it certainly is—will be called a Communist or, in ultimate denigration, a Liberal!

Nevertheless, the facts, however described, can mean only one thing. It is that Canada, on its present course, is headed toward the kind of crisis which afflicted many great nations of the past and threatens others today.

With that clear warning sign before us, and similar examples throughout history, we in Canada need not imitate them. We have the natural assets to avoid them, possibly the largest per capita assets in the world, and until recent years we enjoyed the world's second highest living standard in material terms, though several smaller nations like Sweden and Switzerland have now surpassed us, unbelievable as that may appear.

Besides material assets, we also have time to mend our ways, though not as much as we have usually supposed. It is already later than we think—later than our politicians in general have told us, if they know themselves.

While the temptation to name names and mention various public policies is nearly irresistible, I resist it with stern courage and observe only that we seem to be approaching some kind of political watershed from which the currents will run in directions unforeseeable to ends unknowable, currents leading on to fortune or binding us in shallows and miseries.

On such a full sea are we now afloat—if I may quote a non-political authority long deceased—but whether we shall take the current when it serves or lose our ventures—that remains to be seen.

Meanwhile, without any taint of partisanship, Canada must ask itself—and no one else—how it got trapped in its present dilemma, because, quoting Shakespeare again, the fault, dear Brutus, is not in our stars but in ourselves, and so, too, is the only chance of escape from our home-made follies.

Since politics are merely the surface reflection and operating mechanism of the public will in a free society, it is not to the politicians, however eminent, that we must go in searching for the origin—and the cure—of our troubles. No, we must go much deeper and examine our own minds—individually small but jointly decisive.

So examined, the Canadian mind, during my generation, can be seen retrospectively as moving through four distinct phases, and moving, most of the time, with a shrewd and quiet wisdom, not brilliantly, perhaps, not with the gusto and the pendulum swings of our next-door neighbour, but moving steadily and confidently to fashion a way of life that suited us, a special identity, as it is called, rather pompously, nowadays.

The first phase of hope and resolution was marked by Wilfrid Laurier's famous announcement that the twentieth century belonged to Canada, and while this was only a wild surmise, as we all knew, it gave us a goal to aim at—and our aim looked accurate as the west filled up and a cluster of little British colonies spread from Atlantic to Pacific and became a nation.

Then followed the years of war, business collapse, a second war and the victory of 1945 to which Canada has made its full contribution.

Throughout this half-century, the Canadian character was distinguished by a sure practicality, by thrift, hard work and skilled management, above all, by the instinctive knowledge that Canada, with its hard northern climate and lonely distances, was a difficult and very complex nation to govern, that the price of nationhood must always be high, not only in money but in patience, endurance and understanding.

The price was willingly paid and, in the payment, the nation developed the qualities needed to master its peculiar environment, economic, political and social.

These qualities could be summed up, for lack of a better definition, as responsible common sense, a most uncommon commodity.

But then, after the last world war, came the third phase—the phase of euphoria, of vastly exaggerated expectations, even some hints of arrogance, when much of the world was poor and devastated, when we could sell almost anything, at any price, and the century seemed indeed to belong to Canada.

In this phase, quite uncharacteristic of our past, like a basic change of personality, we overreached ourselves, lost our sense of proportion and undertook to do more, spend more and consume more than even our lavish resources could possibly afford.

Our governments, federal and provincial, expressed the general mood and flattered our ego in the contest for popularity, with the results now well known: budgets as a whole (Alberta excepted) in huge deficit, foreign and domestic debt ever increasing, an inflated currency used to disguise our unwillingness to pay for the services that we demand from the state while always denouncing our governments for spending too much and, probably worst of all, we have neglected the need for saving to finance capital investments and social facilities of all sorts in favour of immediate consumption.

Whether we are seeing not a change of our national personality but merely a passing mood or aberration soon to change again when we recover our original Canadian balance—these questions have yet to be answered in public policy and, more decisively, in private behaviour.

All of which offers a fascinating study for the psychologist or, still better, the psychiatrist.

Being neither, I shall attempt no answer. In any case, the economic problems do not seem to me the most vital problems now confronting us.

A nation, though it must eat, does not live by bread alone, by gross product, a stable currency or any mathematical formula. It lives by a contract, never written into law, by that give and take, that daily compromise and mutual forgiveness which is the invisible—and essential—cement holding any household or any society together.

If the cement leaches out, if the household cannot forgive, forget and agree, the family, and the society, disintegrate. Throughout the world we are now witnessing such disintegration, individual and collective, until the supreme question confronting free peoples everywhere is whether freedom itself, and the democratic apparatus supporting it, can survive the strains, internal and external, now endangering them.

Every nation feels its own special strains and Canada is not unique in this respect, but it has been unsurpassed, so far, in its ability to govern what has been from the beginning and will remain a dual state of two distinct communities, histories, languages and cultures. If it had lacked that peculiar talent, the nation would not have appeared in the first place or, if built, would have broken up long before now.

Our greatest Canadian achievement is not economic, is not to be measured by our material living standard, and is not likely to be understood by foreigners or new arrivals on our shores. Our greatest achievement is the partnership of two diverse human groups, a partnership never easy, always clumsy and prickly, but it has worked—and it must work or else we must confess that the whole experiment has failed, that we have betrayed the faith of our grandfathers who dreamed big, that we are unworthy of the estate which, through their toil and humble genius, they willed to us.

Yet in the fourth and most dangerous phase of our history, now beginning, we have actually begun to debate the dismemberment of the nation, as if it were a failure, as if the majority of mankind did not envy our success, as if, in fact, we had suddenly taken leave of our senses.

What, then, are we really debating?

We are debating a certain intangible for which the dictionary provides no exact word; but of course there are no words that adequately describe anything of final importance in human life, and so, lacking a better name, we call our Canadian intangible a nation. But we all know that it contains for us many things more precious than our laws, our governments or physical possessions—among those things a land as fair and a life as free as human creatures have ever enjoyed in any time or place.

Yet, incredible as it seems to all foreigners, some Canadians in Quebec, and a few elsewhere, are actually proposing to destroy all these assets, as if our endowment of half a continent, with all its treasures, tangible and intangible, were a bankrupt corporation, as if such a single, interdependent economic organism could be chopped into several pieces and still live happily ever afterwards.

In non-economic terms this proposition makes no sense either for an imaginary sovereign state of Quebec, washed, eroded and finally submerged by the cultural ocean of North America or for the two English-speaking segments of the Maritimes and the west which inevitably would subdivide themselves and then, rather sooner than later, would petition for entry into the great republic beside us—and on its terms.

Like most Canadians, I have long been a warm admirer of that republic and traveled widely among its friendly people, but I do not want my nation to become, piece by piece, its northern colonies. That, however, is what a few, a very few, Canadians have always wanted, and if a majority should ever want it the best and surest method of achieving their purpose is to begin by dissolving the national state of Canada. The rest will follow naturally—and rapidly. On a different level, we are debating a tangible economic proposition that makes no more sense than the intangibles of separatism. For what are the separatists really proposing?

They are proposing that a constitutional and commercial dam should be erected on the St. Lawrence, the central bloodstream of the economy blocked, the vital flow of goods obstructed and, incidentally, that Canada should lightly discard about a quarter of its total wealth which is produced in Quebec with no assurance that the Quebec republic would assume its share of the national debt.

But the separatists tell us, and may even believe themselves, that nothing of economic importance would be changed, that a common market, a common currency and a common business management would join and enrich the three fragments of the Maritimes, Quebec and the provinces west of the Ottawa River.

To any economist, business man or sensible citizen all this is a fantasy, a fraud, a non-starter, for we may be quite sure that in the bitterness and heartbreak of separation and in the regional conflict of interest between the three remaining fragments of Canada—no common market, no cosy business arrangement and no prospering transcontinental economy will emerge. Instead, each of the three segments, their joint organism disrupted, their single body transected, will all be impoverished, and even the affluent province of Alberta could not escape that impoverishment for long.

When we debate these propositions, tangible and intangible, any foreigner, coveting our good fortune, may well ask what, in God's name, has happened to national sanity—and we had better ask ourselves the same question. If John A. Macdonald and the Fathers of Confederation were here now to watch us, they would say that the notion of destroying their work was just plain madness; and so it is.

But I cannot believe that Canadians, apart from a tiny lunatic fringe, have yet gone crazy, and I cannot believe that the moment of truth now suddenly facing us is an accident or a calamity. If it forces us to reconsider and correct the mistakes of recent years, if it reminds us of our unequalled opportunities, if, in short, it impels us to return, as it were, to our beginnings and the instincts of adventure and calm daring that subdued the harsh northern flank of the continent and this bounteous land around us here today, why then the threat of destruction will do far more good than harm.

Precisely how the future is to be managed in constitution, government and the use of public revenues I do not know, but our grandfathers didn't know in their time, either. They just went about the day's work and, at the end of the day, saw that the work was good. We can do as well, once we put our minds to it.

Of course, the work is never finished and a federal system like ours never static. In human events every day is a new day and all societies must continually renew themselves or die of old age.

Canada is not dying. It is only suffering the withdrawal symptoms of a prolonged economic debauch, a fever of unrealistic expectations, the normal family disputes of its dual nature and the inevitable but temporary punishment for its blunders.

They will be repaired and, despite all the varied lunacies howling around us now, an old Canadian will judge that our nation's greatest days have yet to come, if Canada regains its native spirit.

But not otherwise.

# A Handful of Earth:
# To René Lévesque

Al Purdy


Proposal:
let us join Quebec
if Quebec won't join us
I don't mind in the least
being governed from Quebec City
by Canadiens instead of Canadians
in fact the fleur-de-lis and maple leaf
in my bilingual guts
bloom incestuous

Listen:
you can hear soft wind blowing
among tall fir trees on Vancouver Island
it is the same wind we knew
whispering along Côte des Neiges
on the island of Montreal
when we were lovers and had no money
Once flying in a little Cessna 180
above that great spine of mountains
where a continent attempts the sky
I wondered who owns this land
and knew that no one does
for we are tenants only

Go back a little:
to hip-roofed houses on the Isle d'Orléans
and scattered along the road to Chicoutimi
the remaining few log houses in Ontario
sod huts of sunlit prairie places
dissolved in rain long since
the stones we laid atop of one another
a few of which still stand
those origins
in which children were born
in which we loved and hated
in which we built a place to stand on
and now must tear it down?
—and here I ask all the oldest questions
of myself
the reasons for being alive
the way to spend this gift and thank the giver
but there is no way

I think of the small dapper man
chain-smoking at PQ headquarters
Lévesque
on Avenue Christophe Colombe in Montreal
where we drank coffee together six years past
I say to him now: my place is here
whether Côte des Neiges Avenue Christophe Colombe
Yonge Street Toronto Halifax or Vancouver
this place is where I stand
where all my mistakes were made
when I grew awkwardly and knew what I was
and that is Canadian or Canadien
it doesn't matter which to me

Sod huts break the prairie skyline
then melt in rain
the hip-roofed houses of New France as well
but French no longer
nor are we any longer English
—limestone houses

lean-tos and sheds our fathers built
in which our mothers died
before the forests tumbled down
ghost habitations
only this handful of earth
for a time at least
I have no other place to go

# Contributors and Credits

Margaret Atwood is the author of three novels including *Surfacing* and *Lady Oracle*, a thematic study of Canadian literature, *Survival*, and several volumes of poetry, the latest of which are *Selected Poems* and *You Are Happy*.

Silver Donald Cameron lives in D'Escousse, Nova Scotia. He is best known as a journalist and interviewer. His published works include *Conversations with Canadian Novelists* and *The Education of Everett Richardson*.

Louis Desrochers is an Edmonton lawyer who has been active in various groups including the French-Canadian Association of Alberta.

Reshard Gool lives in Charlottetown, where he teaches political science at the University of Prince Edward Island and runs Square Deal Publications. His first novel, *Price*, was recently published.

Walter Gordon, well-known nationalist and critic of Canada's dependence upon the United States, is a former federal member of parliament. His article originally appeared in *Maclean's* in abbreviated form.

Lionel Groulx, a philosopher-priest, a professor of history at the University of Montreal, a tireless analyst and exponent of French-Canadian nationalism, is best known for his *Histoire du Canada français depuis la découverte*. The excerpt included here is from *Pourquoi nous sommes divisés*, translated by G.O. Rothney and appearing in *French-Canadian Nationalism*, edited by Ramsay Cook (Macmillan, 1969).

Herschel Hardin lives in Vancouver, where he has worked as a playwright, a lecturer and public activist. His most important contribution to date is *A Nation Unaware: The Canadian Economic Culture,* from which his selection has been taken.

Harold Horwood is a Newfoundland writer who once represented Labrador as an MLA. His works include *White Eskimo, Tomorrow Will Be Sunday* and *Voices Underground.* He lives in Beachy Cove.

Mel Hurtig is an Edmonton publisher who has been active in politics and in the Committee for an Independent Canada. His article is the text of a speech delivered at The Strains of Confederation meeting in Toronto in February 1977.

Bruce Hutchison, one of Canada's best-known authors and journalists, is former editor-in-chief of the *Vancouver Sun* and author of *The Unknown Country* and *The Other Side of the Street.* Included here is the text of a speech given to the Canadian Club in Calgary and published in *The Albertan.*

Naim Kattan is a regular commentator on the state of the arts in Canada. He is also head of the Writing and Publication Division of the Canada Council. His latest publication is *Farewell, Babylon.*

Eric Kierans teaches in the Department of Economics at McGill University. He was a cabinet minister in the Lesage government and a contender for the federal leadership of the Liberal Party. His article is the text of a speech delivered to the Social Sciences in Canada symposium in Calgary in February 1977.

Robert Kroetsch grew up in Alberta and has written a substantial body of prose fiction about that province, including the trilogy *Words of My Roaring, The Studhorse Man* and *Gone Indian.*

Margaret Laurence is best known for her novels, *A Jest of God* (filmed as *Rachel, Rachel*), *The Stone Angel* and *The Diviners,* but she has also published short stories and a critical study of African writers.

André Laurendeau was French Canada's most beloved journalist. He became editor of *Le Devoir* and was a regular contributor to *Le Magazine Maclean.* His selected essays and his book, *The Conscription Crisis,* 1942, have been translated by Philip Stratford and published under the title, *Witness for Quebec,* from which the excerpts included here were taken.

Roger Lemelin, publisher and editor in chief of *La Presse,* is also the author of *Au pied de la pente douce, Les Plouffe* and *Pierre le magnifique.* His article appeared first in the *Globe and Mail.*

René Lévesque, former journalist and television personality, is now leader of the Parti Québécois and premier of Quebec. His article first appeared in the July 1976 issue of *Foreign Affairs.*

Joyce Marshall is a translator and writer of prose fiction. She is the author of *A Fine and Private Place.*

Ken Mitchell is a novelist and playwright who teaches at the University of Regina. His latest publications are *Everybody Gets Something Here, Horizon: Writings of the Canadian Prairies* and *Cruel Tears: A Country Opera.*

W.L. Morton, born and raised in Manitoba, was for years head of the Department of History at the University of Manitoba. His major works are *Manitoba: A History* and *The Canadian Identity.*

Alden Nowlan is the best-known contemporary writer of the Maritimes. His books of poetry and prose include *The Mysterious Naked Man, Miracle at Indian River* and *Various Persons Named Kevin O'Brien.* He lives in Fredericton.

Leonard Peterson is best known for his numerous contributions in the field of drama on CBC Radio and Television. His new play, *Etienne Brûlé,* will soon be published and produced on television.

Al Purdy lives in Ameliasburg, Ontario. He is the author of numerous books of poetry including *Cariboo Horses, North of Summer* and *Wild Grape Wine.*

Richard Rohmer, Q.C., is a Toronto lawyer and novelist. He is the author of *Ultimatum* and *Exxoneration.* His article first appeared in the *Globe and Mail.*

Abraham Rotstein teaches in the Department of Political Economy at the University of Toronto. Among his publications are *Beyond Industrial Growth* and *An Industrial Stategy for Canada.* He contributes regularly to periodicals such as *Foreign Affairs* and *The Canadian Forum,* where the article included in this book first appeared.

Gabrielle Roy is the best-known French-Canadian writer of her generation. She is the author of *The Tin Flute, The Road Past Altamount* and *Where Nests the Water Hen.*

Robin Skelton teaches in the Department of Creative Writing at the University of Victoria, where he edits *The Malahat Review.* He is a prolific poet, critic and editor, his latest book of poems being *Callsigns.*

Rosemary Sullivan teaches in the English department at Erindale College, University of Toronto. She has published a book on the poetry of Theodor Roethke and articles on Canadian literature.

John E. Trent teaches political science at the University of Ottawa and is secretary-general of the International Political Science Association. His article first appeared in *The Independencer.*

Mel Watkins teaches in the Department of Economics at the University of Toronto. He is a regular contributor to *The Canadian Forum,* where the article included in this book first appeared, and has recently published *Dené Nation: The Colony Within.*

Rudy Wiebe, who teaches at the University of Alberta, has edited anthologies and published several novels, of which the best known is *The Temptations of Big Bear.* Included here is an excerpt from his new novel, *The Scorched-Wood People.*

George Woodcock, founding editor of *Canadian Literature,* has written the classic study, *Anarchism: A History of Libertarian Ideas and Movements,* as well as books on travel, the Doukhobors, George Orwell and all aspects of life in Canada.